THE TRANSFORMATION
OF THE HUMMINGBIRD

Cultural Roots of a
Zinacantecan Mythical Poem

SYMBOL, MYTH, AND RITUAL SERIES
General Editor: Victor Turner

* Also available as a Cornell Paperback.

THE TRANSFORMATION
OF THE HUMMINGBIRD

Cultural Roots of
a Zinacantecan
Mythical Poem

EVA HUNT

Cornell University Press

ITHACA AND LONDON

Cornell University Press gratefully acknowledges a grant
from the Andrew W. Mellon Foundation that aided
in bringing this book to publication.

First published 1977 by Cornell University Press.
Published in the United Kingdom by Cornell University Press Ltd.,
2–4 Brook Street, London W1Y 1AA.

International Standard Book Number 0-8014-1022-3
Library of Congress Catalog Card Number 76-12909
Printed in the United States of America
*Librarians: Library of Congress cataloging information
appears on the last page of the book.*

FOR MY PARENTS,
who believe that growing
children need poetry as much
as they need good food.

Foreword

Recently both the research and theoretical concerns of many anthropologists have once again been directed toward the role of symbols—religious, mythic, aesthetic, political, and even economic—in social and cultural processes. Whether this revival is a belated response to developments in other disciplines (psychology, ethology, philosophy, linguistics, to name only a few), or whether it reflects a return to a central concern after a period of neglect, is difficult to say. In recent field studies, anthropologists have been collecting myths and rituals in the context of social action, and improvements in anthropological field technique have produced data that are richer and more refined than heretofore; these new data have probably challenged theoreticians to provide more adequate explanatory frames. Whatever may have been the causes, there is no denying a renewed curiosity about the nature of the connections between culture, cognition, and perception, as these connections are revealed in symbolic forms.

Although excellent individual monographs and articles in symbolic anthropology or comparative symbology have recently appeared, a common focus or forum that can be provided by a topically organized series of books has not been available. The present series is intended to fill this lacuna. It is designed to include not only field monographs and theoretical and comparative studies by anthropologists, but also work by scholars in other disciplines, both scientific and humanistic. The appearance of studies in such a forum encourages emulation, and emulation can produce fruitful new theories. It is therefore our hope that the series will serve as a house of many mansions, providing hospitality for the practitioners of any discipline that has a serious and creative concern with comparative symbology. Too often, disciplines are sealed off, in sterile pedantry, from significant intellectual influences. Nevertheless, our primary aim is to bring to public attention works on ritual and myth written by anthropologists, and our readers will find a variety of strictly anthropological approaches ranging from formal analyses of systems of symbols to empathetic accounts of divinatory and initiatory rituals.

Eva Hunt's "decoding" of the Zinacantecan text with which she begins her analysis has affinities with what Paul Ricoeur has called Freud's "semantic archaeology." For Hunt, as for Freud, symbols are embedded in real historical time, dependent on concrete historical events, even dates. I am speaking, of course, of "iconic" symbols, where there is a link of analogy or association between *signifiant* (*signans*, sensorily perceptible vehicle) and *signifié* (*signatum*, "meaning," denotation, connotation—often multiple), and not of "signs" (Sapir's "referential symbols"), such as are used in mathematics, semaphores, and logical systems, where the link is conventional or "arbitrary." Such "signs" have no necessary relationship to history, whereas the meanings carried to *symbol*-vehicles (whether verbal or nonverbal) are part of a historical and social context (though in non-literate societies the context may be hard to recover, even with the most sophisticated techniques, such as those used by Jan Vansina). In this book Hunt probes historical records to reach the strata on which the apparently disconnected symbol-vehicles scattered throughout her poem of reference are interconnected with one another in highly structured systems of *signifiants* and *signifiés*. But where archaeologists find dead worlds in scattered and eroded fragments of material culture, Hunt detects a living though occulted meaning in the "shards" of her song. Broken systems live on in their debris, in parts, formerly coordinated, which have now become scattered over many levels and domains of the contemporary culture. Nevertheless, they retain traces of their former connectedness—indeed, by the intuitive genius of poets, who still hear in modern words the resonance of archaic structures, the old time may be transiently reestablished in its systematicity by a pregnant metaphor or other trope. Formerly coherent cultures die hard. Indeed, they trouble the "preconscious" thinking of contemporary culture-bearers, with vague "memories" of relations among what now, on the surface, seem to be quite disparate phenomena and images.

Hunt has well shown how such apparent disparities as a *big* hummingbird—which is also "like a dove" or "as big as a hawk"—are not really such at all, if one conceptualizes the total culture of which these symbol-vehicles are elements as a space-time continuum. In this continuum things formerly connected become disconnected and vice versa.

But in the dialectic of connection and disconnection, Hunt shows that there is no blurring at what one may call the "syntactical" level of expressive culture. Lévi-Strauss has argued that "history erodes structure." Hunt has demonstrated that "deep structure" remains sharp and clear, has not been "decayed" or rendered smooth by the passage of history. What *have* decayed are the earlier "contents" or "substances" that have been articulated by structural rules in the various "pasts" of a culture's history. But the implicit syntax has not decayed—it merely works with continually new inputs of materials, the changing imagery of successive "modernities," the cumulating experience of the culture-bearers.

VICTOR TURNER

University of Chicago

Contents

Appendixes

Illustrations

Charts

Tables

Preface

Some books are born like Pallas Athene, fully grown and well-dressed, out of their authors' heads. Others seem to grow accidentally, haphazardly, after unexpected conceptions. This book belongs in the second category.

In the spring of 1973 I was invited to give a luncheon talk to graduate students in anthropology at Harvard. I planned to discuss some of the ways in which I used historical data to further the analysis of contemporary Indian mythology in Mexico. It occurred to me that since my own data had not yet been published, I should take an example from the literature that was likely to be familiar to graduate students. The mythical poem "The Hummingbird," from Zinacantan, seemed a good choice. It was short, and I hoped that since Evon Vogt taught at Harvard, the students would be acquainted with Vogt's published work, especially *Zinacantan*.

That talk was the first version of what is now this book. The students seemed interested. Professors Vogt and Nur Yalman, who were present, told me that I should write it up for publication. The following summer, when I was frantically working my own data into a book on Cuicatec religion, I fell into a classic trap. Writer's block attacked me in the middle of a chapter. To avoid the torture of moping around the house hating myself for the rest of the summer, I decided to try to write a short article on "The Hummingbird," from the small seed of the notes for my talk.

Apparently this little seed had the properties of Jack's beans, for my article grew into a giant, too long to be published in that form. What to do? I consulted my colleagues and friends. Unanimously, they advised: do not cut it down, expand it into a book.

Victor Turner offered the final argument. If I turned "The Hummingbird" into a book, he might be interested in including it in the Cornell series Symbol, Myth, and Ritual. I was not sure I could do it. I was also somewhat reluctant to publish a book in an area of ethnographic inquiry on which I had not done field work myself, while my own field data remained unpublished. During my graduate student days I had worked in the Chiapas highlands in a community not far from Zinacantan (Aguacatenango). However, my major research has been done among the Cuicatec people of Oaxaca, also in Mexico. Friendly advice convinced me that my worries were not relevant to scholarship, and I finally decided to return to the typewriter and make a brave attempt.

It is certainly no Pallas Athene. All I can hope is that it is decently clothed.

Many people in Mexico over the years have unknowingly contributed to the creation of this book. Professors Ricardo Pozas and Gonzalo Aguirre Beltrán, then of the National Indian Institute (INI), gave me my first opportunity to do field work in Chiapas, trusting the quality of my enthusiasm when I was an inexperienced undergraduate. For a summer I worked primarily with Oxchuc, Zinacantan, and Chamula informants, collecting "folktales." That was my first exposure to Mexican Indian society, and this book testifies to the significance it was to have for me.

Pedro Armillas, Wigberto Jimenez Moreno, and Arturo Monzon kindled my interest in prehispanic topics. From Jimenez Moreno I acquired an enduring interest in Mexican religion. Fernando Camara introduced me, in the classroom, to the complexity of contemporary Mexican Indian culture.

Javier Romero gave me my first "professional" job, as a National Museum anthropologist–research assistant, working in the Cuicatec region, with *Papa* Roberto Weitlaner. Over the years, the Directors of the National Institute of Anthropology and History of Mexico (INAH) have approved of my research and facilitated entry into the field as well as access to documentary materials.

Many other friends in Mexico City, Chiapas, Oaxaca, and elsewhere, school peers of the old days with whom I shared studying hours in our *palomilla* gatherings, taught me through their lives and shared thoughts about a country that I love committedly and try hard to understand in depth.

Kim Romney, Sol Tax, Duane Metzger, and Norman McQuown gave me a chance to study at the graduate level in the United States and to return to Mexico for field work. Robert McC. Adams, Fred Eggan, and Eric Wolf were major influences in my intellectual development. They kept alive my interest in history *together* with anthropology by convincing me of the importance of history for social anthropology and the value of the cultural approach to history.

Preliminary versions of my argument benefited from the commentaries of many colleagues and students. I am especially grateful to Evon and Catherine Vogt, who patiently discussed the Zinacantan evidence with me. Evon Vogt made available a draft manuscript of his new book on Zinacantan religion, *Tortillas for the Gods*. George Appell, going beyond the call of friendship, offered me a concise and elegant summary of the technical zoological literature on hummingbirds, and provided many more references than those I could use in my brief discussions. Without his help I probably could not have understood the complexities of hibernation, aestivation, and torpidity. My colleagues and students at Boston University were challenging and encouraging while I was writing the early drafts. Students and colleagues at Harvard University, Brandeis University, and Dartmouth College patiently sat while I unraveled versions of my arguments in lectures, and their questions enabled me to eliminate some of the weaknesses of the original draft.

Victoria Bricker read the first draft and gave me subtle, delicate, honest, and pertinent criticism. Robert Laughlin, who read a later draft, improved the spelling of Tzotzil words and provided me with some new data and the original Tzotzil of "The Hummingbird." Victor Turner, whose work I consider the model of which my own thinking is but a distorted mirror image, was the godfather of the hummingbird. Mixed metaphors aside, I will always be grateful for his confidence that my words deserved an attentive hearing. Edith Turner lovingly applied her talents to the difficult task of editing my very peculiar English. My husband, Robert Hunt, tried to make sure that I kept my word about anthropological canons of evidence.

I am grateful to Doris Heyden for providing the photographs from which Illustrations 10, 18, and 22 are reproduced.

The National Science Foundation has made possible much of my research over the years. Field work and the ethnohistorical research on the Cuicatec and prehispanic Mesoamerica were supported by National Science Foundation Grants Nos. GS–87 and GS–3000. Wenner-Gren Grant No. 3077 helped me to finance the typing and other costs of preparing this book for the publishers. All this help is gratefully acknowledged. I alone, however, am responsible for the final statement.

The text is divided into several sections. Chapters 1 and 2 present the problem to be researched, the methods and assumptions which bias my analysis and the frame for the analysis. Chapters 3 to 6 discuss, through the use of a series of illustrations and examples, the transformational levels of prehispanic religious symbolism, which I believe are relevant to an understanding of the symbolism of Zinacantan and other Mesoamerican Indian communities. Whenever drawing precise connections seemed possible and advisable, I have related the historical symbol units to the "survivals" of these symbols in the contexts of present-day Indian life. Although I do not claim that the symbols of the past have not been transformed, the parallelisms are presented to show the processes by which they have become redefined, have merged, or have been made arbitrary. Chapters 7 and 8 bring the symbols up to date, no longer as a set of unique or isolated units, but as part of a dynamic structure, a sacred armature that organizes, blends, and gives them their ultimate meaning in the present. Chapter 9 is an epilogue or postscript, which spells out various theoretical points implicit earlier in the book. Some of my incipient ideas about the nature of the evolutionary transformation of symbol systems emerge there; I hope to be able to discuss them further, in the future, in meaningful dialogues with my fellow anthropologists.

EVA HUNT

Newton, Massachusetts

THE TRANSFORMATION
OF THE HUMMINGBIRD

Cultural Roots of a
Zinacantecan Mythical Poem

CHAPTER 1

Introduction

> But the argument of most weight with me is this, that many of these fables by no means appear to have been invented by the persons who relate and divulge them. . . . But whoever attentive considers the thing, will find that these fables are delivered down and related by those writers, not as matters they first invented and proposed, but as things received and embraced in earlier ages.
>
> Sir Francis Bacon, *Essays*

The aim of this book is to demonstrate the value of using a documented historical approach, in combination with structural analysis, in the interpretation of mythical symbolism. Methodologically, what I have written follows from the works on myth and symbolism of Freud, Malinowski, Durkheim, Cassirer, Lévi-Strauss, and Turner, but these approaches are combined with analysis of data derived from proper historical sources selected by traditional historiographical methods. Ethnographically, the inquiry is illustrated by the analysis of "The Hummingbird," a mythical poem from Zinacantan.

Much has been published about Zinacantan, a contemporary *municipio* of Tzotzil-speaking Indians in the highlands of the Mexican state of Chiapas. In fact, Zinacantecans are probably the people most studied and written about by anthropologists in the whole of the New World. It is therefore impossible here to sum up what is known about them. Readers interested in more ethnographic details than this book can provide will find many studies of Zinacantan listed among my references.

The *municipio* is the smallest politically autonomous territorial unit of the state-federal system of Mexico. Indian *municipios*, however, are more than that. They are ethnic units that form a part society, that is, the peasant sector of a nation-state, but a part society with a distinct whole culture: with distinct forms of native government, language, kinship systems, economic adaptation, and local religion, and with very visible markers of cultural distinctiveness. One such marker, for example, is clothing, the style of which varies from one Indian municipality to another, but overall is very different from the clothing of the national population. Tax (1937) was the first to notice the remarkable set of distinctions that characterize the Indian *municipios* of Mesoamerica. Zinacantan is a prime, beautiful example of a peasant municipality that is also a distinct society, an ethnic enclave, a special kind of rural place, or, as Frank Cancian called it in his perceptive book of photographs (1974), *Another Place.*

The municipality is located in the central highlands of the state of Chiapas, an area crossed by the complex mountain chain of the Sierra Madre. Between the old state capital of San Cristobal las Casas and the border town of Comitán, in the middle of the mountain range, there is a series of small interconnected plateaus and valleys of high altitude, with a population density relatively high for intermountain regions. In one of these, very near San Cristobal and cut through by the Panamerican Highway, is Zinacantan.

The municipality contains 117 square kilometers, and is located at an altitude of approximately 2100 meters above sea level. Nearby mountains of religious importance, such as Tzotehuitz, reach nearly 3000 meters. The climate has two seasons, a dry and a rainy one. Ninety percent of the precipitation falls between May and October, and practically all of it falls between March and November. For ecological factors in the region the best reference is George Collier (1975).

Within the municipal boundaries lives a population of about eight thousand Zinacantecans. Of these, between 400 (permanent residents) and 1300 (including temporary residents) live in the municipal capital or town of Zinacantan Center. The rest of the population lives in hamlets of various sizes, scattered about the *municipio.* There are fifteen major named hamlets.

Zinacantecans are primarily subsistence corn farmers, but they also grow other crops for consumption and sale: wheat, flowers, beans, barley and fruits. They have chickens, pigs, cattle, and sheep, and are also renowned as skillful merchants, richer than many Indians of the other municipalities of the region.

Zinacantecan social life is focused on and centered in the family unit, living as a separate household, which has patrilocal and patrilineal recruitment rules. Beyond this localized, small domestic unit which controls its own agricultural lands, there is a descent group, nonlocalized, which also has a patrilineal bias.

Public life is regulated by a complex civil-religious hierarchy, which is a classic form of Indian government well described in the Mesoamerican literature. In Zinacantan, however, there are marked differences in wealth among families, and an incipient class system, circumstances that affect the functioning of the civil-religious hierarchy. The richer, more established patrilineal family groups tend to dominate the appointments to offices in both the secular and the religious branches of the government ladder (see Cancian 1965, 1972). Zinacantecans also have their own system of common law practice (Collier 1973).

Two other aspects of Zinacantan are remarkable. The first is the complexity and richness of its public ritual life, which has been explored in much detail by Vogt (1969, 1976) and Rosaldo (1968). The second is the resilience of its people, their independent character, humor, pride, and sense of self-worth. These attributes of personality and culture appear clearly in Zinacantan's oral literature. Although Zinacantecans are peasants, small farmers close to the earth and its sufferings, they have quite an extraordinary repertoire of folktales. Robert Laughlin has collected an astonishingly large and beautiful assemblage of Zinacantan tales, which will be published in a work now in preparation. They range from pseudohistorical accounts of ancestral times to tales made up of recent gossip, from sagas of the actions of supernatural heroes to stories of the humble doings of small cunning animals. The language and topics also range widely, from the prosy and carnal to the lyrical and idealized. Among the tales collected over the years are a few about the hummingbird. The poetic one which this book investigates was one of the earliest recorded and transcribed. It was first published in 1969, in Evon Vogt's major volume on Zinacantan.

"The Hummingbird," a poem containing mythical symbolism rather than a complete myth per se, is related in this book to its original prehispanic structural antecedents in Mesoamerican mythology, as derived from contact-period primary sources.[1] The importance of the historical perspective is dramatically highlighted in the case of this poem-myth. Although some of the elements of the symbolic code and structure are embedded in the contemporary Zinacantecan's life, their meanings could not have been unlocked without an understanding of the key symbolic references and transformations that have been lost to contemporary Zinacantan and are buried in the colonial past. The key to "The Hummingbird" is a complex multivocal symbol, of the type Victor Turner (1966: chap. 1, especially pp. 29–32) calls "dominant" symbols and Freud (1965) "nodal" points or symbols. This symbol, a primordial solar metaphor, represented in embodied form in the gods Huitzilopochtli and Tzcatlipoca, is of prehispanic origin.

The Zinacantan Project researchers were apparently unable to elicit a native exegesis of the meaning of the poem's mythical symbols. In particular, "the symbolic references to large size, the whiteness, and the term 'one leg' are obscure" (Vogt 1969: 331). Since research in Zinacantan has been conducted over a long period by many excellent anthropologists, and their collective data gathering has been of extraordinarily high quality, it can be safely assumed that no such exegesis exists, at present, at the *manifest levels* of the structure.

Given Vogt's detailed ethnographic documentation on other matters, however, once the historical key of the poem is known, it is possible to generate a reconstruction of the mythico-symbolic struc-

---

1. For a brief account of sources, see Nicholson 1968:223–225. For longer, detailed discussions, see Wauchope, *Handbook of Middle American Indians*, vols. 12–13. Jimenez Moreno (1968), Wolf (1959), Sanders and Price (1968), and Heizer et al. (1971) also present a synthesis of evolutionary trends.

ture of "The Hummingbird" and to unlock the original covert meaning of symbolically obscure passages.

A historico-structural interpretation cannot explain the social or cultural significance of these symbols today. I was able to discover *some* of the extant parallels in contemporary Zinacantan. I am quite certain that these do not make up a complete inventory of possible relevant interpretations which have meaning for contemporary Zinacantecans, although other symbolic associations that have contemporary cultural significance can probably be produced in the present ethnographic context by further field work now that the poem's nodal symbol has been unlocked.

The English text of the poem follows. Line numbers are given as referrants for my later interpretative discussions. Appendix 3 provides the text in Tzotzil, transcribed and generously made available to me by Robert Laughlin. The transcription meets the orthographic conventions agreed upon by anthropologists working with Zinacantecan materials.

The Hummingbird

The hummingbird is good and big.	1
So that's the way it is;	2
There were workers in hot country.	3
They were burning bean pods,	4
The fire could be seen well, it was so tall.	5
The hummingbird came,	6
It came out,	7
It came flying in the sky.	8
Well, it saw the fire;	9
Its eyes were snuffed out by the smoke.	10
It came down,	11
It came down,	12
It came down so that they saw it was big.	13
Don't you believe that it is little, it is big.	14
Just like a dove its wings are white,	15
All of it is white.	16
I say they tell lies when they say that the hummingbird was little.	17
The men said it was very big.	18

Then they recognized how it was,   19
For none of us had seen it,   20
We didn't know what it was like.   21
Yes, it says "Ch'un ch'un" in the evening,   22
But we didn't know what size it was.   23
But they, they saw how big it was.   24
They saw that it was the same as, the same size as a hawk,   25
Having to do with the father-mother (*Totilme'il*)   26
"One leg" as we call it.[2]   27

The text certainly appears arbitrary on the surface, full of absurdities and nonsequiturs. The hummingbird, one of the smallest known birds, is said to be as large as a hawk. Hummingbirds, usually multicolored and iridescent, are here described as white. Why? The poem's bird comes out, but from where? Was it in hiding? It also comes down. From what height? Why were its eyes snuffed out by smoke? Why did it come flying out in the sky at such an inopportune time, when men were making fire? Is there a relation between the two events? Moreover, if the hummingbird, against all expectations, was so big, why could only the workers in the hot country see it or recognize it? Why had no one, in fact, seen it before? Why had a little bird so common in the area never been seen by Zinacantecans before, so that they did not know what it was like?

The mysteries continue. What does a hummingbird have to do with the father-mother, the ancestral gods of the Zinacantecans? Is this divine association in any way connected with the other mysteries and surprises? Finally, why is a hummingbird, a creature with two wings and two legs, called, of all things, "one leg"?

One could add other minor riddles. Why was the fire tall? Why were the men in hot country burning bean pods? As with the manifest surface of dreams, irrational incoherence appears to reign. But, does it? Freud long ago showed us that the manifest surface of a dream is just a thin skin. Under it lie many layers of highly organized meanings, symbol-messages connected logically to each other

2. Reprinted by permission of the publisher from Evon Z. Vogt, *Zinacantan* (Cambridge: Harvard University, Belknap Press, 1969), copyright © 1969 by the President and Fellows of Harvard College.

in complex chains. Through the mechanisms of conversion, adjacent synchrony, diachronic overlap, merging of similars, displacement, overdetermination, resolved contradictions, identification of opposites, and so on, the dream acquires its manifest texture, its symbolic disguise. Through the uncovering of these same mechanical linkages, with careful "decoding," the hidden meanings can be made manifest. It is only when several layers of skin are peeled off, exposing the dream's flesh, that the links between signified and signifiers can be perceived, and their often simple, straightforward logic revealed.

Myths and rituals have been shown by Turner and Lévi-Strauss to be composed of complex symbolic links which, like those of dreams, are multivocal and arranged in manifest and deeper layers of meaning.[3] Could it be, then, that the symbols of myth and ritual operate with the same mechanics? Keeping in mind that dreams are primarily idiosyncratic personal experiences and myth and rituals are experiences at the collective level, might we say that dream symbol : person : : myth (or ritual) symbol : society? Freud thought so.

It is not necessary, in accepting this view, also to accept Freud's theory of wish fulfillment in dreams or to agree with the theory of

3. There are many other parallels between dream analysis and symbolic analysis in the anthropology of oral literature and myth. Both Turner and Lévi-Strauss borrow heavily from Freud's methods (although Turner specifically parts company with Freud on interpretations based on sexual symbolism). Freud's decoding procedures, his ideas about associations by homology, homonymy, composite figures, displacement, and other processes of the condensation and conversion of dream symbols (for example, overloading of meaning, overdetermination) are heavily used in anthropological symbolic analysis under somewhat disguised names (for example, multivocality). Freud's insistence on the similarity between the decoding of dreams and the decoding of language rules, and on preserving the cultural context of symbols (unlike Jung) echoes anthropological canons. Certainly, Lévi-Strauss's ideas about the manifest and latent levels of meaning in myth come directly from Freud's dream levels (Freud 1965:168). But even more detailed procedures (for example, Freud's use of step-by-step analysis of the superposed segments of dreams that have parallel content or meaning, a method that can be used for myth) are followed throughout *The Raw and the Cooked* and *From Honey to Ashes* (see Freud 1965, particularly pp. 136–174, 313–376). Freud himself clearly saw the relation between dreams and myths when he said that myths were the "wish-fantasies of whole nations, the age-long dreams of young humanity" (Freud 1963:42).

sexual repression. We need only agree that myths and rituals, like dreams, need decoding, and that a similar procedure can be followed—that is, that myths and rituals appear to have obscure meanings because, like dreams, they are made up of symbolic cryptographs. Freud proposed that to uncover and decode the meanings of a dream it is necessary to delve into the individual dreamer's personal history. Because the symbols of a dream are embedded in the dreamer's past experiences, in the psychic traces of these experiences, the decoding process consists in part of uncovering and unraveling the historic threads of the dream's symbols in the patient's symbolic paradigms.

Given the parallel multivocality of myth and ritual, we could hypothesize, as an operational device, that myths and rituals are embedded in a society's collective history, and the cultural process that gave birth to the meanings. As the psychoanalyst becomes the archaeologist of his patient's mind, the anthropologist can become the archaeologist of his society's culture. But for the cultural anthropologist, unlike the real archaeologist, few materials remain that can be dug from the ground. The stratigraphic layers are in the culture itself, in media which are sometimes ephemeral.

I hope to demonstrate in the rest of this work that, in fact, this "archaeology of symbols" is productive of coherent meaning, and that "The Hummingbird," treated in its historical context, can be decoded. Perhaps from the small base of this example and others of its kind, we could, with caution, move into a comparative history of myth symbolism. I will pick up this query in the final pages of the book, after my major task is accomplished.

am asking not how he sees his kind of "structuralism" as opposed to "history," but a more restricted question: how does he see the use of historical data analysis *as a tool* of structural analysis?

Lévi-Strauss seems at first glance to have an ambivalent attitude about the use of historical analysis as a tool of structuralism. On careful reading, however, it becomes clear that he is, like Radcliffe-Brown, unwilling to fall into the trap of conjectural history, but not opposed to the idea of using sound historical documentation. His position can be summarized from two separate statements he has made related to the problem.

In *The Raw and the Cooked* (1969) he rejects historical events as an explanatory device because "the door would be thrown wide open to arbitrary interpretations" (p. 147). This statement could be misinterpreted as a rejection of historical evidence. Clearly, however, that was not his intention, for on the following page he states that "it is certainly our right, even our duty, to take into careful consideration conclusions that ethnographers arrived at by means of linguistic and historical research, and that they themselves hold to be sound and well-founded" (p. 148). Moreover, he himself uses "historical" explanatory devices (e.g., p. 309).

In *The Savage Mind* (1968a, especially chap. 5), Lévi-Strauss argues that symbolic systems move over time from motivation to arbitrariness (pp. 155–157). Arbitrariness is introduced into a symbolic system—which at some point of origin had a coherent structure—by the ravages of human history: demographic changes, wars, epidemics, famine, changes in number and size of descent groups, political conquest, acculturation pressures which lead to the social death of priesthoods. That is, losses occur in the structure because societies are never truly static. In summary, symbolic systems suffer from what the general system theorists have called *progressive segregation* or *transition from wholeness to summativity* (Hall and Fagen 1956). One need not invoke the dubious "zero-time" point of origin; it can be argued that symbolic religious structures in fact respond to both major systemic processes: (1) a movement toward arbitrariness

CHAPTER 2

The Methodological Base

Since the publication of Jan Vansina's *Oral Tradition* in 1961, the importance of using the historical method for the analysis of folklore materials has been clearly established in anthropology. Vansina's major concern, however, is to illustrate the usefulness of folklore and mythical texts in reconstructing historic processes. In this work I propose to use the reverse procedure, that is, to show the usefulness of historical texts in reconstructing the process of symbol formation in myths. In a sense, this other side of the coin is implied in Vansina's work. Both procedures deal with the isomorphism of historical and symbolic aspects of culture.

Since Turner and Lévi-Strauss are the two scholars whose contemporary contribution to religious symbolic analysis in anthropology towers above all others, it is perhaps necessary to clarify how they evaluate the use of historical methods. Turner (e.g., 1967, 1969) following in the steps of Freud, appears willing to utilize any decoding procedure which, within the canons of anthropological elicitation and documentation, can prove heuristically useful in uncovering latent meanings. For example, in his work on Ndembu color symbolism, he dedicates a section to historical archaeological evidence (1967:84–88). In his most recent book (1974a) he has successfully used historical and symbolic methods of analysis in combination with each other.

Lévi-Strauss's public debates with Sartre on the role of the historical vision in science are well known. J. A. Barnes (1971) has carefully dissected the arguments and counterarguments of Lévi-Strauss's view of historical versus nonhistorical time, synchrony versus diachrony, cyclic versus nonreversible time, and the role of history in anthropology. For the purposes of this work, however, I (that is, progressive segregation) as well as (2) a movement toward further elaboration and integration (what general system theorists call *progressive systematization* [ibid., p. 227]). Eugene Hammel (1972) has cogently argued that symbolic structures tend to acquire coherence of form and meaning over time. His argument specifically derives from Lévi-Straussian structural analysis of a historically known set (Goldilocks and the Three Bears). The same position has been advanced in the past by art historians and literati; for example, the "rise and fall" of literary styles follows structural processes of progressive systematization and segration.

The presence of both processes of evolution in Mesoamerican prehispanic religious structures has been demonstrated by archaeological and anthropological research. The Mesoamerican symbolic structures emerged in incomplete form as early as the Early Classic Horizon (Teotihuacan, Monte Alban) and perhaps even earlier, in the Pre-Classic Period (Joralemon 1971). They reached their full-fledged form at the time of the Spanish Conquest (ca. 1520), and have since been partially transformed by loss, syncretism with Catholic symbolism, and other historically and anthropologically documented processes (see Caso 1966, 1967, 1968; Edmonson 1967; Madson, 1967; Mendelson 1967; Ingham 1971; see also footnote 1 to Chap. 1).

The Mesoamerican materials strongly support Lévi-Strauss's view that history (time) erases structure, or, rather, that historical losses in the symbolic structure hide, over time, the structure's total meaning. Because of the Spanish conquest and Catholic missionizing, aided by concerted and punitive religious repression, much of the elaborate and elegant structure of prehispanic religion was destroyed. Without a dedicated priesthood to keep the total symbolic structure alive in its elaborate esoteric form, portions and whole sections of the prehispanic system were lost. Present-day Mesoamerican peasants (including the Zinacantecans), can provide us with interpretations of only those symbols which are meaningful in their contemporary social context. The associations that were the

esoteric, privileged knowledge of ritual specialists, poets, philosophers, and priests [1] were dissolved in the struggles of history and fell
under the impact of the ravages of the Christian Conquest and the
concomitant social decapitation of the priestly class by the colonial
regime.[2]

Given this basic increase in "arbitrariness" of prehispanic structures since the conquest, a study of contemporary Mexican mythology (or Mesoamerican religious ideas in general) should not exclude
from the analysis any proper historical documentation that may fill
gaps in the present system. In the Mesoamerican context, obviously,
these historical data are amazingly rich. They range from pictorial
manuscripts (codices) with attached texts of the relevant myths and
rituals, to a kaleidoscope of other related materials (for instance,
archaeological sculptures for which the symbolic meaning is
known). Such sources can provide the missing links for the analysis
of symbolic structures that have been telescoped, shortened, simplified, or left incomplete in the contemporary record. It is with this
assumption in mind that I began the analysis of "The Hummingbird."

With the analysis now completed, I believe it is possible to say

1. These were known as *tlamatine(me)* in Nahuatl, together with shamans, divin-
ers, and other religious specialists collectively (Sahagun 1907, vol. 8). The word can
be glossed as the "whole-knowing" or "the whole-seeing" or "the knower (of things),"
"the perceiver." It was also the word with the general meaning of "intellectual." Leon-
Portilla (1971) refers to them as poets and philosophers. My interpretation is that they
were in fact a collective class of "theologians." The image of the religious specialist as
"all knowing" or "seeing" has been preserved in contemporary Zinacantan, where
shamans are called seers and the curing ceremony a "vision."

2. I am not arguing that peasants, tribal primitives and similar groups need a
specialized priesthood to keep their symbolic systems alive and well. In the face of
much evidence of the complexities of symbolism of very primitive societies (for
example, see Munn 1966), it would be naive to support this view. What I am arguing
is that a system of such complexity as that of prehispanic Mesoamerica (and others
such as the Buddhist and Greek pantheons and Hindu ritual and calendrics), which is
constantly refined and expanded by a specialist class of "theologians," cannot survive
intact the disappearance of that class. The peasantry may preserve those aspects of
the structure known by them and most meaningful to their agrarian lives. But some
refinements of the esoteric domains (for example, detailed horoscope prediction, or
accurate astronomical calculations) tend to fade without their nurturers.

that "The Hummingbird" demonstrates the heuristic value of Lévi-Strauss's view that history erases the dynamics of structures and that true historical interpretations can solve some of the dilemmas of structural analysis. Some of Lévi-Strauss's own interpretations of South American mythology, however, have been criticized by many for their haphazard methodological quality (for example, Maybury-Lewis 1968; Bamberger 1973). I should point out, in this context, that the structural method employed in this book has been "tightened up" in two directions, in order to meet the requirements of rigorous anthropological verification. The first is the preservation of ethnographic context, within the tradition, established by Fred Eggan (1954), of controlled comparisons. The second is the preservation of source context, whether from an informant, a text, or an exegetic passage. I am not sure just what words in South American myth Lévi-Strauss translates as "demiurge." I have not taken such liberties with Mesoamerican translation. Following the maxim that, at best, *tradutore = traditore*, I preserve original wordings as literally as possible.

Lévi-Strauss's materials from South America are sometimes quite meager, so he has let his fancy fly. I am less imaginative and more rigorous. A psychoanalytic rule states "the best interpreter of the dream is the patient himself." I have adapted it for myth analysis: "the best interpreter of the myth is the culture carrier."

Unlike Lévi-Strauss, I do not profess that myths think themselves into men. This is in itself an obscurantist metaphor, which can have no foundation in the observation of empirical reality. On the contrary, myths are cultural products, which have been created by real live men within the canons imposed by their cultural axioms, and which have entered the public domain as social properties. This position is, I think, the thrust of Freud's and Bacon's observations on the topic. Therefore, mythical materials (be they tobacco, planets, social groups, or wild jaguars) are treated here as culture-bound symbols. To be compared, therefore, myths or transformations have to be grouped by ethnic origin, as sets, according to some specified definition of social and cultural boundaries, and they have to be shown, for comparative and analytical purposes, to be in fact related historically or socially in terms of origin (see Turner 1968b, 1973).

I have one final disagreement with Lévi-Strauss and other scholars who have worked on myth and symbolism, with the exception of Victor Turner. Each has held a pet theory of the "origin of symbols and myth meanings." Freud and his followers, working from the basic discovery of dream symbolism and sexual repression in the West, saw secret messages of sexual conflict, psychological rivalries between adjacent generations, repression of antisocial desires, and so on, in every major myth they studied, from Oedipus to the totemic visions of Australian aborigines. Durkheim, *au fond* more interested in man as a member of a social group than in man as a fanciful daydreamer or a secret neurotic, interpreted myth and ritual as the outcome of man's perceptions of his own social milieu, the organizational principles of the social order becoming the guiding lines for drawing the divine images. Hence his dictum: God is Society. A roster of nineteenth-century philosophers following in the steps of their Greek masters, a handful of archaeologists busily measuring the Egyptian pyramids, and a varied coterie of folklorists, poets, and essayists, all came to the study of primitive religions with their own preconceived theories: for example, that symbols in myth deal primarily with astronomy, or with peasants' moral concerns, or with language games, or with irrational fantasies, and so on.

Spencer and Max Müller, for example, believed in the combined theory that primitive myths involved the veneration of natural phenomena, planets, and geographical features, because the ancients had illogically confused the names of these objects with the things named.

Cassirer (for instance, in *Language and Myth*) placed much emphasis on the language base of myth, as does Lévi-Strauss. Cassirer in his most lucid moments realized that myth as well as science is based on logical synthesis, manipulated by language, but at other times, with grand stubbornness, he insisted that words, symbols themselves in origin, become the whole original substance of myth.

Later in this book I shall discuss the importance of language-derived mythical transformations, but I shall also show that many other prehispanic transformations were based on analogies of sight, touch, and smell. Thus, if earlier authors were right that myth is the child of a "disease of speech," it follows that it is also the child of the disease of all man's sensory apparatus, a visual, olfactory, tactile disease. Lévi-Strauss, who often follows Cassirer without saying so, takes more comfortable refuge in the analogy of language structure derived from modern linguistics. But the seeds of the same grand stubbornness are there, couched in the language of formal science, structural linguistics, and computer games.

In general, it can be argued that the proponents of all theories that deal with sacred symbolism as if it had a single source, assume a unique solution, a single answer to the question: whence do man's sacred symbols come?, and then proceed to "prove" their theories by selecting, from the wealth of mythologic symbolism, the evidence that fits their assumptions. In doing so, they disregard the richness of the symbolism they study, they reduce the ranges of meaning, simplify, narrow down semantic space. George Eliot, in her most brilliant novel, *Middlemarch*, gave us a humorous and mordant picture of such an analyst in her figure of the antihero, Casaubon, who was writing a book called "The Key to All Mythologies," which he could never finish. When anthropology was younger and more naive, we were all Casaubons in search of our key. Now that we are adult and, we may hope, wiser, we must abandon the desire for such simpleminded "neat" analysis and accept the complexities of the worlds we study. Fortunately, doing so does not mean abandoning by the roadside every theory proposed in the past.

None of these single-origin theories is yet dead, and for good reason: each has a kernel of truth in it. Santillana and Dechend (1969) have put forward perhaps the most elequent modern argument for a primitive form of astronomy as the basis of myth. Lévi-Strauss argues for the dominance of the oppositions of nature and culture, from honey to ashes, from natural specie to socialized man, from raw to cooked, from incest to ordered genealogy.

But although modern anthropologists have not abandoned these partial truths, they have certainly much improved on their earlier versions by applying eclectic judgment and the refined analysis of sound ethnography. Spiro, in much of his work (e.g., 1952, 1966, 1967), follows a Freudian line of thought illuminated by the canons and concerns of anthropology. Geertz is Durkheim's best modern interpreter (1960, 1966), and his sensitive treatment of symbolism (1972) is far removed from the biased analysis of earlier scholars. Victor Turner, in particular, has tried to relate the multivalent quality of symbols into an eclectic theory, in which sensory perception, ideological canons, and socio-structural constraints as well as other varied phenomena all serve as sources of religious symbol formation (see, for example, his statement in *Science*, 1973).

One of the marks of quality which characterizes the new approaches to the study of religion (and one to which Lévi-Strauss does not always adhere, although Turner, Geertz, Spiro, and other major figures do) is the preservation of ethnographic context. Lévi-Strauss, like Cassirer, Van Gennep (1960), and the "sacred cow" himself, Sir James Frazer (1911), is a noncontextualist. We cannot deny, however, that in spite of himself, Lévi-Strauss has produced the most significant recent contribution to myth analysis. If nothing else, his technical vocabulary—e.g., concepts such as transformation, code, and operator, which he borrowed from linguistics to apply to myth—will remain with us for a long time.

Because in this book I focus strongly upon symbolism with patterned meanings of directionality, ethnoecology, processes of seasonal change, and agricultural activities, it may appear that I myself have a simple answer, that I believe these are the invariant, real metamessages. Nothing is further from my position. I have no ready-prepared favorite theories, no single magical scheme. Rather, I have a profound conviction that a careful reading of the myths, even at their most manifest level, leads one to discover that multiple significant messages, each structured in its own patterned order, occur simultaneously. That is, there are many layers of meaning corresponding to different domains of messages, transmitted within the same symbolic fabric of the myth. All these meanings, without definite proof to the contrary, should be treated as equally significant to the myth makers and symbol tellers. The job of the anthropologist is not to decide which meanings are primary and which are secondary, but to show how the levels of meaning of each structure logically interlock, and how the potential messages of each and all of them are transmitted by each structural component. Even when a symbolic structure appears to have a dominant message, this should be considered in the context of the total set of messages, as well as demonstrated in the context of comparison of all the symbolic structures of its type. That is, one should attempt to clarify, by logical procedures and standard anthropological methods of verification, the meaning of the poetic language in which the symbols are embedded.

I think, as Turner does, that it is in the nature of symbolism and mythmaking that multivocality, condensation, and multiple human concerns about the nature of reality are woven together. Not only do the moral and natural orders fit into each other in skillful transformations. Scientific discoveries, orectic perceptions as well as ideological convictions, deep-seated psychic contradictions, the obviously socially manifest as well as the obscurely repressed, are all threads in the warp and woof of mythical cloth.

Thus by no means should we allow the analyst to interject his own imaginative symbolism into the materials of his research. I see myself as witness, intelligent audience, rather than as actor in the play of mythology.

Lévi-Strauss himself has argued that the levels of myth represent multiple dimensions of man's experience. At times he appears to prefer certain of these levels for their explanatory value in the context of the myths he is examining. He also tends to favor certain metaphors. However, as Boon has concluded (1972:129), to attribute to Lévi-Strauss the idea that myths have some built-in priorities of metamessage is an opinion based on "many readers' persistent expectation that he will eventually label some level of experience—such as 'social organization' or 'ideas'—primary or causal, which . . . he never does." It is because mythical texts have so thoroughly integrated all levels of reality (integrating experience by using all the available sensory codes as tools of intellectual discourse) that the ultimate product is a bricolage of these levels, a structure of structures, an ordering of different orders. I am not as sure as Boon that Lévi-Strauss does not see culture as the signifier, and other levels of symbols as the signified, exclusively. But he is certainly more on the side of the angels on this issue than other people are.

Previous schools of mythical analysis, on the contrary, have chosen different levels as "keys," "prime movers," "causal," or "focal points." Boon, again, has given us a lucid exegesis of this argument:

There are a finite number of ways of "explaining" the basis of varieties of texts. Theoretically, a series of levels can be abstracted out of experience—psychological, emotional, rational, social, metaphysical, biological, humanitarian, material, ethereal, romantic, mundane, religious, goal-oriented, and so forth—and any one or ordered set of these levels can be designated as primary, of which the "text" is declared a function. Different "schools of thought," then, are only the phenomenon whereby different levels of experience come to be marked as primary (p. 112).

One can argue, however, as Boon does, that Lévi-Strauss appears to avoid this pitfall, by stating that man's mental ability is the only unifying factor. "His relegating 'cause' to *l'esprit humain* is one way of denying primacy to any of those levels of experience we abstracted above. Note, however, that this is *not* to say the 'levels' are not there. It is this denial which makes his stance more general than that of, say, Freudian theory, Weberian theory, or Marxist theory, at least as popularly understood" (p. 113).

If Lévi-Strauss does not argue for level or code dominance, what is he then proposing instead? The answer, Boon asserts, is a theory of meaning in myth in which all possible levels of meaning are combined and recombined in a giant symbolic game as old as the ages. The integrating key is man's ability to play with synesthesia, the phenomenon of transferring one sense feeling to another, and to use it as the background for symbolic constructs. Synesthesia, expressed as metaphor, metonymy, homology, simultaneity, contiguity, isomery, homoplasy, and so on, links symbols. Linkages occur by means of similarity, opposition, parallelism, transmutation, juxtaposition, the use of *pars-pro-toto*, or other mechanisms. All these are the operators, in the logical sense, which create the mythical codes and develop their relationships. Thus experience is integrated at all levels by metaphoric switches, metonymic grammatic rules, transformation from level to level of meaning. *Transformation* has at least two distinct semantic uses in Lévi-Strauss's work. First, it means the magical transformations that the myth texts attribute to their actors. Second, it means the logical transformations, in the structural sense, discovered by the analyst (see Piaget 1972).

Unfortunately, we end up with a loose, weak theory about the human mind rather than a coherent, strong theory about symbols. We can neither interpret nor explicate the symbol systems of individual societies by utilizing Lévi-Strauss's general hypotheses, which are not contextually derived and which apply only to a vague entity called the character of universal mythology. Like Jung, Lévi-Strauss weakens his position by claims to universality and haphazard methods of data collection.

Some aspects of Lévi-Strauss's methodology can be used for the Mesoamerican case, others cannot. Some of his theoretical insights apply impeccably to Mesoamerican symbolic data. Others can be proved incorrect on the basis of Mesoamerican ethnography. Let me give an example.

In Mesoamerica, we find a system in which the natives have utilized more than thirty distinct levels or codes derived from concrete classification of experience. The system is internally ordered, with unit-symbols at each level or code fitted into the structure of oppositions, classes of such symbols arranged as sets, and, built from each set, the core image of each one of the signifiers which define mythical divine figures (that is, the "gods"). In other words, the gods of the Mesoamerican pantheon were sets of linked metaphoric-metonymic transformations, taking identifying symbols from different codes derived from empirical observation and the dissection of the

Chart 1. The formal syntagmatic-paradigmatic structure of the pantheon

Divine hierarchies	Internal ordering of oppositions in a class (A...Z)			(opposition between gods)			
Classes (1...n)	A	B	C....	Tlaloc	Chalchiuitlicue	Xochiquetzal	Z
Set level 1 (element)	symbol a 1	symbol b 1	symbol c 1	falling water	surface water	sky-air	
Set level 2 (plant)	symbol a 2			corn	corn	lovely red flowers	
Set level 3 (animal)				snake	snake	quetzal bird	
Set level 4 (sex)				male	female	female	
... (age)				old	old	young	
... (face)				snake eye, jaguar mouth	flower headdress	beautiful headdress	
... etc.				etc.	etc.	etc.	
Set level ... n							
	god [A1 ...n]	god [B1 ...n]	god [C1 ...n]				god [Z1 ...n]

Paired external isomorphisms (transformations of a god)

continuous flow of reality. Thus every god was built of a set of symbols made up, for example, of a vegetable code symbol, an animal or zoological code symbol, a planetary symbol, and many others. (Appendix 1 provides a list of some of the symbols and levels of code transformation for a single deity, Huitzilopochtli.) These levels were ordered hierarchically, with some symbols dominating over others as distinct markers of each "god." Not all divine beings were clearly defined and integrated, for reasons discussed below. In a general sense, however, the Mesoamerican deities were nothing but a fantastically complex, metaphoric-metonymic myth set. All the divine pantheon together, the set of sets, represented the ultimate "bricolage."

But although in a universal mythic bricolage ultimately *all* combinations are possible, they did not develop in Mesoamerica in this fashion. Some complexes or sets of symbols were fixed by the theological wisdom of the mythologizers, who in this society were members of the elite, erudite specialists, priests who determined and interpreted the sacred truths for the masses. These men, called by the Aztecs *tlamatinime*, and in Yucatec Maya apparently *balam* (priest, sorcerer, prophet), ultimately served as distillers of the cumulative symbolism, selectors, fixers of the structure. By creating a pictorial writing system, freezing the images in stone and other permanent materials, they interrupted the flow of imagery, creating more or less immovable symbolic paradigms, far from arbitrary, selected with delicate logical care out of the totality of potential symbol combinations. Later on, with the introduction of the European alphabet, the imagery was fixed in written texts such as the *Chilam Balam* books, which were still in use two centuries after Cortez entered Mexico. Thus certain images became quite stable, although there were some additions and refinements over time, some local structural variations among different regions of Mesoamerica, and some variation of detail from one symbolic expression to another. (For example, one finds parallel structural variation between codices dealing with the same symbolic texts, such as those in the *Borgia Codices* group, and variations between *Chilam Balam* versions, such as the *Chilam Balam* of Chumayel and Tizimín.)

At the time of the Spanish conquest, the whole of Mesoamerica shared a distinct religion, unique in its basic armature and gross cryptographic detail. The dominant divine images, the calendar, the ritual cycles, the iconographic materials from which the deities were made up and identified, the myths of their origins, travels, doings, and powers, were pan-Mesoamerican (see Jimenez Moreno 1968, Caso 1968, and Kirchhoff 1968, for illuminating discussions of these points).

Curiously enough, Mesoamerica, the geographic and cultural bridge between South America and the Northwest Coast (the two areas which Lévi-Strauss analyzes in detail in his *Mythologiques* [1968, 1969, 1971, 1973b]), was ignored in his theory and its rich evidence unused, except for minor isolated references to single myths, which are taken out of context (for example, 1973b:382). I believe that Lévi-Strauss could not have phrased his conclusions in the same form if he had taken Mesoamerica into account. But the complexity of evidence from Mesoamerica as well as the enormous amount of existing documentation for its religious systems meant that the area did not lend itself well to the context-free form of analysis that he prefers.

One can hardly criticize a man who has written such monumental works for not covering enough ground. Thus, Edmonson, in his 1973 review of *L'homme nu*, remarks upon the absence of Mesoamerican materials, but passes no judgment on the resulting gap in the analysis. But one *must* point out that much of Lévi-Strauss's argument dealing with the universal nature of myth will need revision in the future, in the light of the mythology of nontribal Mesoamerican peoples. Lévi-Strauss deals primarily with tribal societies, from small bands to chiefdoms, but he also uses data sporadically and indiscriminately from nontribal societies, and from areas other than the New World (for example, from Classical Greece and medieval Europe). But, if any nontribal complex system is relevant for his analysis and for his theoretical conclusions, it is the Mesoamerican system. Mesoamerica is crucial for two reasons. First, it is the natural geographic land bridge between the systems that form the core of Lévi-Strauss's work (South America, North America). Second,

Mesoamerica is the cultural bridge on many counts, other than the mythology itself, and it is likely to be the logico-structural bridge in terms of the mythic transformations and armatures that he proposes, such as, for example, the transformation between metaphors about food and metaphors about clothing, both of which occur in the same myth frames in Mesoamerica.

The crucial modification of his theories, however, I believe, will come in the interpretation of the mythical concept of time. Lévi-Strauss, being a noncontextualist, eliminates space, time, and language as significant variables. Because he collected his materials haphazardly, from different historical periods and different authors, time becomes a nonvariable in the analysis. But, tautologically, he then concludes that one of the functions of mythical narrative is to obliterate time. In Mesoamerican religion and symbolism, however, unlike the tribal situations he knows best, time is not only not eliminated, but the whole mythic structure is deeply concerned with time as a major armature prop.

The Mayanist Spinden stated the case elegantly when he said that the Maya "had discovered that time is neither an endless flowing nor a senseless whirligig, but an intelligible interrelation of changing states throughout the universe. They had directed their attention to the repetition of phenomena, and had found that time is change possessing natural regulations even though it passes forward to become the measure of history, natural and political" (1957:369).

The Mexican scholar Leon-Portilla (1973) has even argued that among the Maya the whole armature of the mythology depends solely upon the depth of their vision of time. Although I myself feel quite unhappy with the characterization of any symbolic armature in terms of a single factor, there is more than sufficient material already analyzed in the literature to show that time, in Mesoamerica, is one of the ordering principles behind the mythical structure. In fact, it is clear from the extant codices, the so-called Historic Codices (see Robertson 1959, 1964 for a definition of codex types), such as the Bodley or the Mexica *Tira de la Peregrinación*, that the mythic text passes unobtrusively into historic linear time, in uncomplicated fashion, linking the myth's telescoped past with the historic past.

The passage between the two "pasts" is blurred, but it also is certainly linear. In other words, in Mesoamerican culture myth and history were perceived not as two distinct time-space modes, but as a single continuous one. Mythic time and historic time can be separated only by the analyst, after the event, deducing when one became the other on the basis of precision of dating, accuracy of events reported, and measure of duration. Hence, on the basis of historiographic criteria, one can argue that the earlier historical sections of a Historic Codex tend to have more abundance of mythic sacred events, while the more recent sections have greater historical precision, being more secular in content, more exactly datable from other evidence such as archaeological research. It can also be argued that the Highland Codices treat the time sequences in such a way that time becomes progressively more crowded, from periods of long duration reported in few events in the earlier sections, to periods of short duration reported in many events in the final sections. But this change in perspective is, of course, what Lévi-Strauss himself argues that our own historical vision produces! We start with a capsule description of prehistory and end with an overdetailed history of the nineteenth century. On those same grounds Lévi-Strauss attacks Sartre for his overemphasis on the value of history for giving meaning to social process (1962, chap. 9).

Leaving aside, as a scientific problem, the complicated issue of the transition between mythic time and historic time, we still have the issue of the native's perception of time as an experience of linear duration reported in normative cultural idioms. In this sense, Mesoamerican cultures seem to have had a multiplicity of culturally determined, social times. For example, the Mayan "long count," although ultimately a cyclic astronomical conception, gave such linear depth to the accounting of secular historical events that it cannot be treated simply as frozen mythic time. Georges Gurvitch (1958, 1964) argues persuasively that those social time images may be regarded as both multiple and cross-culturally testable.

In this book, however, we will not be concerned with such problems of analysis because I am dealing with information from a single cultural tradition, and the historical dimension of symbol processing can be dated more or less accurately by detailed evidence drawn from texts of known dates of origin and evidence from other sources such as archaeological or chemical (carbon 14) dating.

The time span covered in this analysis is primarily that between the time of the Spanish conquest, ca. 1520, and the period during which the contemporary ethnographic data were collected, ca. 1950–1970.

The space dimension is that of Mesoamerica, delimited by Kirchhoff's original culture area boundaries, which as far as I know have not been challenged in any major fashion by more recent evidence (Kirchhoff, 1952; Kroeber, 1939).

Moreover, within Mesoamerica there are two major subareas, the cores of which are the central highland plateaus and the territory of the Lowland Maya. Zinacantan is located in the interface zone between the two, in the southern Chiapas highlands. Its language, Tzotzil, is Mayan. Culturally, on many counts, it belongs to the traditions of the central plateau (Nahuatl, Mixtec, and so on), of the valleys of Mexico, Puebla-Cholula and Oaxaca. Connections between the Chiapas highlands where Zinacantan is located and the valley of Mexico are known to have existed in the period of Tula domination, 1100 A.D. Nahuatl-speaking groups apparently entered the Chiapas region in the process of migrations and population relocations which followed the decay of Tula as a major urban center. This same process resulted in a diffusion of cultural influences to the south and east. Archaeological evidence of these migrations shows up not only in the Chiapas highlands but also in such distant places as Chichen Itza in Yucatan and the Guatemala highland plateau. Linguistically, these movements resulted in the presence of Nahuatl-speaking Pipil in San Salvador. Their occurrence is reflected in mythico-historic texts such as the *Popol Vuh*. There is also direct evidence from more recent times for the contact of Nahuatl-speaking groups with the Chiapas highlands themselves. First, there is evidence of late contacts from Tula, and second, there is evidence that the Aztecs had established a garrison in Zinacantan itself just before the Spanish conquest (Calnek 1962). Calnek believes (personal communication) that at the time of the conquest there were Nahuatl speakers in Zinacantan. This theory will tie up with the evidence of the hummingbird symbolism, which in its fullest form appeared among the Mexica-Colhua, who were Nahuatl speakers.

Hence, I have used for this analysis ethno-historic data from both the Mayan and the Highland subareas of Mesoamerica. Whenever possible, I have used the work of other Chiapas experts in related disciplines such as history (for instance, Klein 1970), and of Mayanists (e.g., Roys 1949a and 1949b; Thompson 1934, 1937, 1962, 1965a) and the evidence of Mayan primary sources (for instance, the *Popol Vuh*). However, many of the examples I shall cite will be from the Highland versions of the cosmology, myth, and the like, because the analysis of the Highland religious materials is much more advanced than that of the Mayan materials. This difference exists in part because of the sheer quantity of the evidence for the Highlands particularly at contact time, in part because of the better preservation there of detailed manuscript materials in the European tradition of the early sixteenth century (for example, Sahagun's works), and in part because of unsolved problems in the decipherment of Mayan writing and the matching of Mayan and Mexican sacred iconographies (see Coe 1966; Knorozov 1965; Anders 1963; Rendón and Specha 1965; Kelley 1965; see also Wauchope, vols. 12 and 13).

All the connections between symbol meanings and transformational levels that I use in analyzing "The Hummingbird" occur in ethnographic contexts that I shall explicitly state. The interpretations or decodings are not mine in the general sense; they are so only in their application to this specific study. A long tradition of documented analysis, starting in the sixteenth century with Sahagun and Duran and continuing with Edward Seler and his followers in Germany and Caso, Nicholson, Thompson and others in Mexico and the United States in the nineteenth and twentieth centuries, is the backbone of this analysis. Preserving the source and ethnographic contexts means specifically that I do not invent or reinterpret the meanings of symbols; I simply show the logic of those that have been decoded by others in the past. When interpretations are my own, I have so indicated. It also means however, that I limit myself to a set of data that comes from within the same well-known and well-defined culture area, that of Mesoamerica.

For information on contemporary Zinacantan, I have restricted myself to published sources, with two exceptions. The Harvard Project has produced much material that has not yet been published and over a dozen Ph.D. dissertations. I did not consult these, and therefore I do not claim to be a Zinacantan expert. However, Evon Vogt kindly allowed me to read the manuscript of his new book, *Tortillas for the Gods.* I have also used some information provided by two Zinacantan experts, Victoria Bricker and Robert Laughlin, in personal letters. These are identified in the text as personal communications.

A search through the unpublished literature could have rewarded us, I am sure, with supportive evidence. However, it would have required a length of time incommensurate with the task and the limited purposes of this work.

If my analysis is sound, further field research and examination of unpublished materials should support its conclusions. If my "key" to the "Hummingbird" poem is correct, it ought to "open" other data as well.

Before the mythological poem itself can be anlayzed, it is necessary to explain the basic frame of the prehispanic religious symbolism and discuss the extant structures that survived the process of cultural change over the last four centuries. This is the topic of the following chapters. I hope that this may be in itself a second contribution to Mesoamerican studies, since no equivalent structural statement is to be found in the contemporary literature. Nicholson (1971) comes closest to a modern structural overview, but proceeds from more canonical anthropological categories of data classification (for example, cosmology, the deities, and ritual).

We are now ready to return to the past, taking a magical trip over five centuries.

CHAPTER **3**

The Prehispanic
Transformational System
and the Hummingbird's
Roles in It

Prehispanic religion was a complex socio-cultural system. At its base was an elaborate symbolic structure of the type that Lévi-Strauss has characterized as transformational. The action system was legitimized by a mythical superstructure, an ideology which suffered, in Cassirer's words, "from a hypertrophy . . . of the classifying instinct" (1946b:16–17), and illustrates to the full the ability of myth to "argue with itself and acquire dialectical depth" until "if it is at all resourceful," it will "eventually exhaust all the possible codings of a single message" (Lévi-Strauss 1969:332). This "single message," however, was an ambitious protean task, a "quest for the interpretation of reality," as Cassirer said, which combined a theology, a charter for ritual, a writing system, an elaborate agricultural schedule geared to the varying seasons of Mesoamerica, ethno-science, an exact astronomy, a series of topological notions about the time-space continuum which involved complex mathematical permutations and cycles, and a method of horoscope prediction and divination.[1]

1. The complexity of the goals of what we call prehispanic Mesoamerican religion introduces a further problem into the never-ending debate of Western thinkers, including anthropologists, about the distinction between science and religion. From the early colonial Catholic priests, careful ethnographers who nevertheless spoke about superstition and heathenism (for example, Sahagun, Duran), through Levy Bruhl and his "illogical primitive," all the way to Lévi-Strauss and his distinction between the scientist and the bricoleur, anthropologists have searched for viable definitions that would differentiate between two Western folk-categories lifted to the ranks of philoso-

Once a cross-cultural comparison of mythico-symbolic systems has been established and has matured, Mesoamerica, with a very few other systems (for example, Hinduism) will be found remarkable for the large number of dimensions of juxtaposed taxonomical levels which have figured simultaneously in creating the total structure of its religious thought. As Lévi-Strauss has suggested (1968a:151), the use of computers would be required to reach anything we could call a full analysis of such complex systems. The South American symbolic transformations explored by Lévi-Strauss himself seem poor and meager in comparison with those of Mesoamerica. It is perhaps because of this complexity that no one has yet attempted a full structural analysis (Nicholson 1971:395). However, several generations of scholars have succeeded in putting together many pieces of the mythological puzzle. Besides the primary contact sources, which are extraordinarily rich in native exegetic materials, and Seler's monumental work, we also have some partial analyses of transformational levels, taken three or four at a time (see *ibid.*, pp. 405 and 408, Tables 1 and 2; Caso 1967; Beyer 1965). This work has been possible because in most religious contexts not all the transformational levels were used, but only a few key ones, usually occurring in stable combinations, and some of these were fixed by becoming part of Church dogma. Thus, in spite of the incompleteness of prior analyses, Mesoamerican scholars have been able to lay bare the

phy: science versus religion, and their acolytes of technology versus magic, sorcery, and witchcraft, ritual as instrumental versus expressive behavior, technique-oriented versus symbol-oriented action, and so on. Since Mesoamerican religion, without a doubt a transformational system, included an exact science of astronomy, a writing system, a calendar, and a sophisticated medical code, when and how does the bricolage become science? In Hegel's vocabulary, when does "understanding" become "reason"? Perhaps there is no fundamental reason for separating the two, except in the context of social institutions. It appears that Western man (including philosophers like Cassirer and anthropologists) suffers not only from the delusion that he is in a fundamental sense different from the animals (thus the invention of the soul), but also from the false belief that his system of ideas is fundamentally different from those of other cultures. The consequence of this latter delusion is the axiom that "if it is theirs, it is superstition, if ours, religion; if it is theirs, it is religion, if ours, science." The problem is this: shall we continue using a distinction which has over and over proven logically irrelevant and empirically untestable and which may be based primarily on ethnocentrism?

major operators, constitutive units, and taxonomical levels of transformation.

Much of the dialectical depth of the symbolism has been reduced or oversimplified, however, and as a consequence, some of the analysis appears naive in its attempts, for example, to "reduce" the gods to single unitary meanings. This oversimplification can be blamed in part on sixteenth-century scholars, who, in their anxiety to understand the complexities of a system so foreign to their traditions, attempted to "translate it" in terms of their own religious symbolism. These phenomena are an interesting parallel to the work of early linguists and philologists who, before the advent of structural linguistics, attempted to understand "primitive" languages with the frame of Latin grammar.

I have made use of analyses by modern scholars, but have attempted to place their results in the context of the transformational structure as a whole. The consequence of this procedure is an analysis that suggests that the Mesoamerican transformational system contains over thirty separate coded taxonomies or classes of symbols. The taxa were selected and combined across classes; that is, a symbol was picked from each class and combined with symbols obtained from the other classes, and thus cross-class symbol clusters were formed. Each deity was defined by one of these unique clusters of cross-class, cross-taxonomy symbols. Each cluster functioned as a distinct transformational unit, which was personified in a deity. Although I do not by any means provide a complete list, what follows is my attempt to clarify the literature and simultaneously give the reader a preliminary understanding of the classes that have direct bearing on "The Hummingbird."

The most significant aspect of the transformational system for an analysis of "The Hummingbird" is the nature of the religious pantheon. The prehispanic "gods" were personified deities, superhuman beings who had as individual characteristics and attributes one or two items from each transformational class or taxonomical level. Thus, each god had thirty or more attributes that defined, distinguished, and represented him. The gods were not totally personified as discrete entities, however. Rather, they were clusters of ideas, with a logical order, "sentence matrices," in which each "word class" was a transformational level. For each god many sentences were permissible in terms of canonical religious grammar. For gods of great antiquity, such as Tlaloc, many of the primary attributes were fixed. Newer gods had more fluid characteristics. All the ideas the gods represented, however, could be combined, merged, unfolded, inverted, and so on, into each other by varying the specific "words" (that is, items on a class or transformational level) in the divine "sentence matrix." For example, the god of wind could be pictorially represented with some of the body features, face painting, or paraphernalia of the gods of death to indicate the idea of the wind in his "angered" form as hurricane or tornado, or with black cutting weapons of the gods of war to indicate cold northern winds.

The merging and overlap of divine images did not simply reflect an "improvised" or "unfinished" religious pantheon. It was in fact the pantheon's very nature. Prehispanic religion (and I believe this is true also of that of contemporary Mesoamerican Indians) was truly pantheistic. Scholars have usually treated this issue in an oversimplified fashion, arguing, for example, that although prehispanic peoples were polytheistic, there is clear evidence that they also conceived of a single unique god (for instance, Hunab Ku). This evidence has been treated as if it shows these groups to have been in some sort of transitional stage between polytheism and a more "advanced" religion, monotheism. This view is "evolutionism" at its most naive. In fact Mesoamerican cultures were neither polytheistic nor monotheistic. In their view, as in those of all pantheistic cultures, reality, nature, and experience were nothing but multiple manifestations of a single unity of being. God was *both* the one and the many. Thus the deities were but his multiple personifications, his partial unfoldings into perceptible experience. The partition of this experience into discrete units such as god A or god B is an artifice of iconography and analysis, not part of the core conception of the divinity. Since the divine reality was multiple, fluid, encompassing the whole, its aspects were changing images, dynamic, never frozen, but constantly being recreated, redefined. This fluidity was a culturally defined mystery of the nature of divinity itself. Therefore, it was expressed in the dynamic, ever-changing aspects of the multiple "deities" that embodied it. For didactic, artistic, and ritual purposes, however, these fluid images were carved in stone, painted into frescoes, described in prayer. It is here, at this reduced level of visualization, that the transient images of a sacralized universe became "gods," with names attached to them, with anthropomorphic attributes, and so on.

A grasp of these ideas is important for understanding the later syncretization of Christian symbols and sacred personages with the old religion, which has led to the present-day "hybrid" religion of Mesoamerican Indians. How is it possible, both anthropologists and theologians continually ask, that Indians so readily accepted the Christian religion but continued their old rituals, their attachment to ancient symbols, native gods and authoctonous notions, for over five centuries? The answer is that this is a natural response for a culture with a pantheistic view of the sacredness of the universe. Because reality is one and many, the addition of new images such as the Christian saints or Jesus himself simply expands the repertoire of sacred "words" that can be fitted into the divine "sentence matrix," already defined as simultaneously complex, ultimately unknowable, ever-changing, and unitary.

To understand the aspects of the pantheon that relate to "The Hummingbird" we must now examine the transformational levels that I have isolated. What follows is not an attempt at complete coverage, but rather a substantial outline of major features and classes. Experts in the field may possibly find that some of their favorite observations have been ignored here. I can only say in my defense that in a work of this length it is impossible to do justice to the wealth of the prehispanic imagination.[2]

In the following chapters I have divided the prehispanic symbolic

2. Experts will no doubt recognize the enormous debt this analysis owes to the works of Sahagun, Duran, the anonymous Mayan writers, and the great German scholar, Edward Seler, and to those of A. Caso and H. Nicholson. Unless a specific point is made, no detailed references will be given. Taxonomies or classes in some instances carry names I have supplied, when none was available in the literature.

classes into fundamental components. These are not, in any basic
sense, ethno-scientific categories, but simply obvious analytic devices at the symbolic religious level. I start with the most primitive
nature categories, that is, those categoric levels of taxonomic classes
shared by all societies at all evolutionary levels) The natural
orders—the classes that deal with observation and classification of
the natural environment—exist even in the most primitive symbolic
systems, although their content may vary greatly. No society can
survive without a basic understanding of its ecological niche. On
another level, no society survives without a minimum understanding
of regular, patterned processes, best exemplified by cyclic predict-
able events such as the change of seasons and the annual movement
of the stars. Therefore my analysis proceeds to a section on cosmic
symbols and ideas. In subsequent chapters the discussion becomes
increasingly culture-bound and particularistic. First we move into
the realm of social structure symbols, kinship, and related phenomena. From there we go on to an even more specialized area of
knowledge, that of the Mesoamerican calendar and its relation to
sacred symbolic domains.

Once we have explored these topics in a systematic fashion, from
nature to culture and from general cultural categories to special
supracultural domains, we can return to our mythic poem with a full
understanding of the environment in which it was created and transmitted over the centuries.

Animal Taxonomies
Volatiles

As we open our discussion, we enter directly into the symbolic
category from which our little feathered image, the hummingbird, is
born.

This class was largely composed of birds (*aves*). However, it has

---

For example, the name "volatile" for the class of birds and butterflies has been used by
various scholars. But the class I call "walkers or mammals" has never been so named. I
have derived these classes from their appearance in mythical contexts and although
they are obviously related to prehispanic ethno-scientific categories, there is no claim
that the two conform exactly. In Chiapas Tzeltal and Tzotzil, however, many levels
are not named (Berlin et al. 1968), and are "covered taxonomies."

been accurately called "volatiles" (= fliers, by Caso 1971:366, among others) rather than "birds" because it also included the butterfly. These animals were subclassified by size, color, flying altitude, behaviour in different seasons of the year, eating habits, sleeping schedule, and so on. Each flier represented a god or gods, in the role of alter ego "messenger" between the earth and upper sky levels. Some birds or fliers were also common theophanic disguises or theriophanies of specific deities. One of the most remarkable symbolic uses of the class was in a series of 13 volatiles, called the Burdens (Nahuatl: *i mamal;* Spanish: *cargo,* Tzotzil of Zinacantan: *yikats,* or *skojob*), which run in a series concurrent with the week of 13 days, in one of the calendar sequences (see below p. 193). The concept of burden was associated with the idea that periods of the passage of time had sacred bearers; there were, for example, day, week, and year bearers. This symbolism is extant in Zinacantan in the idea that religious officials who are responsible for special day and annual ceremonies are said to carry a burden, and the office is also referred to as "the burden" (Bricker 1966; Vogt 1969:604). Another group of 13 volatiles was associated with the layers of the heavens.

The idea of the volatiles as God's messengers is clearly illustrated by the hummingbird, which Zinacantecans and other contemporary Highland Maya people believe to be "the animal incarnation or assis-

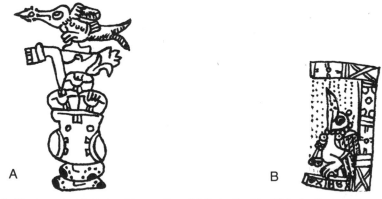

1. The hummingbird in two Maya codices. (A) *Codex Tro* 23a. (B) *Codex Cortez* 19b.

tant" of the ancestral gods (Laughlin 1969:177; line 26 of poem). Also in Zinacantan hawks, moths, blowflies, and butterflies are identified with the ancestral gods; mythically, they are their theriomorphic likenesses (Vogt 1969:299).

Volatiles recurrently appearing in prehispanic mythical symbolism were the butterfly, the owl, the eagle, the turkey, the parrot, and the hawk.

The butterfly was simultaneously a symbol of the soul and a sign for the concept of *olin* (undulant circling, rocking, oscillating or rolling movement, representing the space-time continuum, that is, the passage of time in space, marked by changes in the positions of the planets and the day-night sequences). Butterfly equalled *olin* because of the iconography of *olin* (see section on geometric designs, p. 180). It was also thus identified because of its movements. *Olin* (or *ollin* in other authorities' spelling) comes from the "primitive radical *ol*" (Seler 1963, 1:143), which indicates something round, circling or bouncing like a ball. It also means something that can be stretched or extended from one place to another or across a given space. From the same root come the word for rubber (*oli* or *olli*) from which Spanish *hule* derives, and the verb *oolin* or *olini* = to agitate or move (Garibay 1961). Butterfly-*olin* was also a deity unit (Itzpapalotl).

The owl was associated with darkness because of its diurnal sleeping habits, and with death as its messenger, because metaphorically sleep and darkness = the underworld of the soul after life = nighttime = death. In Zinacantan the bird's voice announces a death in the village. Its sound is that of "scissors cutting the thread of life."

The eagle had multiple associations, but among the most important were those with the sun and war, both of which were also represented by the god Huitzilopochtli. This god in his solar manifestation was an eagle because both the sun and eagles "fly high" in the sky. The eagle also represented the mythical transmutation of Huitzilopochtli from man into god in animal form. Since eagles and hawks are birds of prey = carnivores = killers, they represented warriors, and Huitzilopochtli, divine war leader of the Aztec, was the warrior par excellence. The Mexica or Aztec military order of highest esteem was that of "Eagle Knights," "warriors of the sun," probably in memory of this mythical transmutation. Huitzilopochtli, according to the myth, had been a brave human, leader of the Mexica tribe. After his death, he became a god in the form of a mummy inside a bundle, from whence his bones spoke to the Mexica, directing them in their migration southward (Gonzales de Lesur 1966). He told them:

Verily I shall lead you where you must go. I shall appear in the shape of a white eagle, and wherever you go you shall go singing. You shall go only where you see me, and when you come to a place where it shall seem to me good that you stay, there I shall alight (come down) and you shall see me there. Therefore in that place you shall build my temple, my house. . . . Your first task shall be to beautify the quality of the eagle . . . (Nicholson 1967:131).

This myth is interesting for several reasons. First, it refers to Huitzilopochtli as the leading god of the Mexica, which is a historical fact. Secondly, in their migrations into the valley of Mexico the Mexica moved south, which is the cardinal direction dominated by Huitzilopochtli. Thirdly, this eagle is white, an important fact in the understanding of "The Hummingbird" poem.

Hawks and other large birds of prey were symbolically equivalent to eagles in many ways. In some of the Mesoamerican calendars, in fact, the day name "Eagle" is called "Hawk." Both are large, high-flying, carnivorous hunting birds (cf. Beyer 1965:37). The god Huitzilopochtli was also thus identified with the hawk, which is the poetic referent of the text in which hummingbird = big white hawk (lines 13, 15, 25, *passim*).

The turkey was the god Tezcatlipoca's "commonest theophanic form and another calendar deity" (Nicholson 1971:412). The turkey symbol today has been replaced, in some Indian communities, by the rooster or chicken. The buzzard (or the vulture) was a day name.

The hummingbird was associated with Huitzilopochtli and with the spring and summer seasons. Huitzilopochtli, whose name has been glossed as "hummingbird-left," was an image of the sun in the

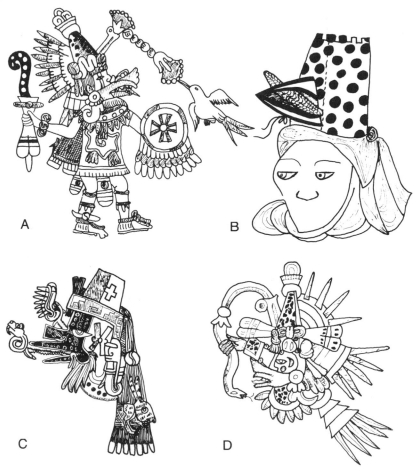

2. Feathered serpent headdress. Note the truncated conical hat with spots, the scarf or beard, and the distended lips or beak. (A) *Codex Magliabecchiano*: The hummingbird drinks from flowers in the headdress of the god of wind (Quetzalcoatl). (B) Zinacantan's contemporary version. (C) *Borgia Codex*. (D) *Codex Borbonicus*.

ascending period of the ecliptic (that is, coming from the south to the north)—the spring equinox and summer solstice periods in the Northern Hemisphere. He was the "sun of the south," because the sun came from the south in its journey northwards in the ecliptic (see discussion of the homophony of south = hummingbird, below,

p. 167). Thus, the south/east corresponded with spring/summer, his season as hummingbird and hawk. Hummingbirds also represented spring and summer. This representation was based on prehispanic ethno-zoology. Prehispanic peoples believed that the real humming-bird hibernated during the fall-winter, the dry period, spending those seasons suspended from a crack in a branch of a perennial tree. With the advent of spring, that is, the beginning of the rainy season, the new life in the sap of the tree woke up the hummingbird, (Duran 1971:72–3). Thus he could be seen again flying around, and meta-phorically, he revived or "came back" in the spring. Thus, the rebirth or return of the hummingbird signified spring-summer, the beginning of the rainy season, and the sun in his ascending journey, all events which in Mesoamerica take place in the same period (see also Clavijero 1917:61).

Hummingbirds in fact do not hibernate in the true sense of the word. Sometimes in the dry season during the day, however, they enter a torpid state to conserve energy because of lack of food (Hainsworth et al. 1970). Moreover, certain types of hummingbirds apparently migrate across the Gulf during the dry season and return in spring to the mainland of Mesoamerica (for example, the North American ruby-throated hummingbird is known to migrate in a nonstop flight across the Gulf of Mexico, and some northern South American hummingbirds migrate to northern Central America [Greenewalt 1960:13]). So hummingbirds well signify, in a poetic way, the rebirth or resurrection of spring, and the coming of the rainy season. As Greenewalt points out (p. 11), "Father Bernabe Cobo, a Spanish priest, wrote in 1653 in his 'Historia del Nuevo Mundo' that the awakening of hummingbirds was used as evidence by the Mexican Jesuits in explaining the mystery of the Resurrection to the Indians."

In Zinacantan hummingbirds are still classified in a similar class of volatiles, which according to some informants also includes the but-terfly and the bat (Acheson 1966:433–454). These three animals are in some ways anomalies. The anomalous character and symbolic meanings of the bat have been thoroughly and insightfully explored by Sarah C. Blaffer (1972) in her charming book, *The Black Man of Zinacantan*. Both Acheson and Blaffer point out that bats, butterflies, and hummingbirds are considered by Zinacantecans to be anomalous animals. This quality places them in a special ethnosemantic category and relates them to each other. Their anomalous quality is related to their mythico-zoological potential for transformations. The bat is a transformed mouse, the butterfly a transformed caterpillar, and a special class of hummingbirds are transformed butterflies. Prehispanic peoples also believed that butterflies and hummingbirds (but not bats) were the transformed souls of warriors (hummingbird → sun → warrior → dead warrior → hummingbird). The contemporary Zinacantecans' mythical "night witch" hummingbirds and the "messenger" hummingbirds, the divine incarnations and messengers of god-ancestors, are paired with bats in the sense that they fly at night. The "witch" hummingbird, a mythical invisible opposite of the real diurnal hummingbird, brings sickness (a punishment for man's immorality). The transformed hummingbird-butterfly (*k'ochol pepen*), interestingly for this analysis, has a "white head and body" and "Zinacantecos believe that *the change takes place sometime in the beginning of August* (summer)" (Acheson 1966:81; my italics). This point is important because it supports my interpretation, reached in other contexts, that the "white hummingbird" symbolizes the transformation of spring into summer; and Zinacantecan ethno-zoology, according to other evidence, also associates the white hummingbird with a summer transformation. Robert Laughlin (personal communication) believes the white hummingbird to be the white-eared hummingbird, *Hylocharis Leucotis*. However, in the poem's text the bird is said to be "all white" and to have white wings (lines 15, 16), descriptions that lead me to believe we are dealing with more than one image.

Blaffer has also pointed out other extensive symbolic parallelisms of bat and hummingbird: for example, both are fliers who suck flowers and who skydive (see Illustrations 2a and 21). She follows

3. A Mayan bat—pottery vessel from the Late Classic Maya Period. The signs ornamenting the bat indicate "death," "night," and "descent" into the underworld (Thomson 1973). Photo courtesy of the Museum of Fine Arts, Boston.

Seler in much of her analysis.[3] Seler noticed, however, that the relation is not simply one of parallelism but also of competitive opposition. Hummingbirds compete with bats for flowers, one coming to suck *after* the other. Unlike bats, hummingbirds were considered by man "inoffensive, were seen with joy and not persecuted or hunted because they could be the soul incarnation of beloved ones" (Seler 1963, 2:72). In Zinacantan, moreover, bats were and are symbols of the opposite season of the year, winter. The most important ritual context in which they appear is in connection with mythical black men, ravens, jaguars, and "moss men," in the San Sebastian *fiesta*, the major ritual complex of Zinacantan in the winter, the dry season. These animals signify the forces of darkness, the under-

3. An extensive bibliography of his works is available in the volumes of *The Handbook of Middle American Indians*.

Table 1. The hummingbird-bat transformational opposition

Transformational class	First symbol	Second symbol
Volatile	hummingbird	bat
color	"white"-light	"black"-dark
order of flower sucking	first*	second
season	summer (August)*	winter (January)
sun	strong solstice	weak solstice

* This ordering makes more sense if we remember that the agrarian solar calendar started in the spring. When the year begins in March, January comes after August.

the hummingbird spends the night in a state of torpidity. Like the sun, he is not seen during the night hours, he does not fly = move in the visible sky.

White hummingbirds, moreover, are quite real. Several genera and species, most of them restricted to northern South America but some extending their range within the tropics, are either white-headed or totally white (e.g., *Michrochera Albo-Coronata, Phaetornis Hispidus*). Interestingly enough, *Hispidus* means "prickly, thorny, rough with bristles or minute spines," which, as Greenewalt notes, is an unusual name for the little bird, and one that uses the same simile that appears in Nahuatl since the word for hummingbird and thorny are Nahuatl homophones. However, the sun's spring and fire image is a blue-green (turquoise) hummingbird, probably the Costa (*Calypte Costae*) which the Aztecs call *Xiuhuitzilli* (fire hummingbird or turquoise hummingbird).

Every culture that creates poetry has its own metaphors for the sun. The Mesoamerican metaphor that equates it with humming-birds, hawks, and eagles, is appropriate in a multifaceted fashion. Birds generally, creatures who move in the sky flying "like the sun," are a simple metaphor. But there is more to the imagery than this. The sun was considered a male, a warrior, a brave young man, and all these birds are "warrior" birds. The eagle and the hawk, because of their carnivorous habits and their beaks and claws that resemble weapons, need no further explaining. What is less known is that hummingbirds are ferocious little creatures, quite fearless and belligerent. Not only do their beaks resemble long sharp weapons; in fact they are weapons. Even in the wild, hummingbirds are known for

world, death, caves, "going down," "sleeping upside
the descending sun = the weak sun = the anomic
winter solstice, when nights are long (see Thoms
Illustration 3). The hummingbird, in contrast, in one of
and all his normal forms, is a volatile of spring and
brightness and joy, of lightness, longer daylight hours,
sun, who wins his battle against the animals of darkness
eras-Holmes 1961). If correct, Blaffer's tentative suggestio
that in Zinacantan hummingbirds could have been conside
(which could be checked with further empirical work) may po
metaphor for the transformation of weak sun → strong sun or
→ summer.

Bats were much more important in Mayan than in Mexica s
bolism. The Aztecs named Zinacantan after the bat and often use
in toponymics (Zinacantan, Zinacantepec, and the like). Howeve
they often appeared to prefer other mythical anomalies for religiou
symbols (the earth monster *cipactli* and the plumed serpent, for instance). The Maya, perhaps because they were more familiar with a
variety of bats, not only mythologized them but assigned to them a
god of their own.

The "night witch" hummingbirds of Zinacantan are most likely
nonexistent mythic creatures or other birds confused with hummingbirds, since the hummingbird seldom if ever flies at night; like
the sun, it appears only during the day. This small creature has, as
Greenewalt has put it (1960:9–10) "the highest energy output per
unit of weight of any living warm-blooded animal" and "while hovering has an energy output per unit weight about ten times that of a
man running nine miles an hour." Moreover, "the hummingbird's
surface temperature is normally slightly higher than ours." Given
these physical characteristics, "nature, with its customary ingenuity,
has found an unusual elegant solution" to the problem of what the
hummingbird does at night, when he cannot feed enough to maintain his energy resources. "She has given the birds the ability to pass
into a state of suspended animation, during which the body temperature drops and the energy output sinks to a very low figure." Thus

their complete fearlessness and disregard for other animals and humans. They are also highly territorial and will defend their grounds "vigorously, whether or not the intruder is of their own family, and quite regardless of size" (Greenewalt 1960:20–21). In fact, "hummingbirds are courageous and aggressive battlers," and a hummingbird "has been known to engage a hawk a hundred times its size, diving at its adversary with well-aimed thrusts of his sharp beak" (ibid.). Since hummingbirds are such successful warriors, a Zinacantecan "man wishing to engage in a fight is believed to gain agility and quicksightedness by eating a hummingbird's heart beforehand" (Laughlin, personal communication).

But there are further analogies which can be easily converted into mythico-poetic truths and which prehispanic peoples built into this bird's symbolism. First, the sun shines, and its color appears to change with atmospheric conditions. On a clear day it can be brilliantly white, red or gold; on a cloudy day it may look a dull coppery blue or even filmy gray. The hummingbird also shines, but its colors change and it loses its iridescence in some light conditions. The coloring and brilliancy are not caused by pigmentation, but by the structure of iridescent bands in the feather. Thus the shining miracle "can be seen only within a narrowly defined set of positions involving the bird, the sun, and the observer" (Greenewalt 1960:173). The colors of the sun and those of hummingbirds are structural phenomena. They depend on matters like the refractive indices and the physical effects of interference in the various substances involved, whether air, moisture, or feather structure. Thus the hummingbird with his unique iridescent feathers, which in Audubon's words are "like a glittering fragment of the rainbow," and the sun are shining objects par excellence, and, equally, will not shine if atmospheric conditions are against them. Furthermore, the hummingbird sun god was male. Only the male hummingbird has spectacular shining colors. In practically all species the female's plumage is dull and even drab.

There is a final important analogy. Hummingbirds fly in a very special way, which mankind has only recently approximated with the invention of the helicopter. They can fly not only up, down, and forward like other birds, but can also reverse, fly backward, and maintain themselves at the same point in space by hovering. To prehispanic peoples, the sun appeared to do these things—and so it still appears to us. First, it reverses its path from solstice to solstice ("flies backward") in the ecliptic, twice. Second, during the solstices, it appears to stop in flight, to hover above in the sky, in the same position. In many world mythologies, including Mesoamerican, there are abundant solstice rituals to encourage the sun to continue and to reverse its flight. There is felt to be a threat of cosmic collapse if it does not.

Thus, the transformation of the hummingbird and the sun into each other follows this logic:

1. Hummingbirds do not fly at night = they are absent from the night sky = sun at night is absent from the sky = sun does not fly at night.
2. Hummingbirds enter a torpid state to conserve energy in the dry season during periods of food scarcity, and can be seen flying upward in the sky mostly in spring and summer (the wet season) = sun flies upward (ascends in the sky) in the spring and summer season (the wet season).
3. The hummingbird shines brilliantly, being the best endowed bird in this regard = the sun is the most brilliant celestial object.
4. Depending on atmospheric conditions the hummingbird's feathers may or may not shine = depending on atmospheric conditions the sun may or may not shine.
5. Male hummingbirds shine = "the sun is a male."
6. Hummingbirds are warring birds, fearless = the sun is a warrior, a brave young man, fearless.
7. Hummingbirds can fly backward, reverse their direction = the sun flies backward, reverses its direction twice in its ecliptic passage.
8. Hummingbirds hover = the sun hovers at the solstices.
9. Costa hummingbirds are turquoise color = sky illuminated by the sun is turquoise color.

And the hummingbird = rain analogy follows from no. 2 above, since both rain and hummingbirds reappear in the spring and are present during the summer, "ceasing to be" in fall and winter. Their apparent demise and resurrection are simultaneous. But in spring the sun goes up, "comes out," flying in the sky, while the rain "goes down," "comes down." In the Zinacantan text the hummingbird does both, exhibiting the behavior of both sun, and rain.

Hummingbirds, obviously by reason of their coloring, were and are in Mesoamerica also identified with flowers, another solar image. Moreover, they are also related to sexual conquest and love. In Zinacantan a man may carry a dead hummingbird tied with a green ribbon when he visits his mistress. Hummingbirds, like the sun, are "hot" and can warm a girl's heart (Laughlin, personal communication). Green or blue-green is the Zinacantan color of good luck. And finally, because of the shape of their beaks, hummingbirds were images of the thorns used in autosacrifice to the sun god. These associations are followed by a unique final one. The "hummingbird god" was a god of the south, and we may ask if this mythic association originated entirely in the homophony of the words for south and hummingbird in many Mesoamerican languages. I believe that another reason exists. The occurrence of hummingbird genera and species and their population density both increase by more than geometric progression as one nears the equator from either direction. A single species is known in northern Canada and in southern Argentina, but the number mounts to 321 species within 5 degrees of the equatorial line either way. In fact, out of approximately 600 species known to exist, 566 live within the tropic zone. If we take the Northern Hemisphere, and within it Mesoamerica, the number of known hummingbird species increases from about 19 at the latitude of the tip of Baja California, to 55 for central and southern Mexico, and 158 for Central America, and their density likewise mounts. Given this distribution, it would not take long for any human group in the Northern Hemisphere to discover by observing its natural surroundings that there is indeed a strong connection between hummingbirds and the southern direction. Of course, for most of South America, the image would be reversed to be hummingbird → north.

It is now clear why hummingbirds were separately identified with the sun and the south. But why was the sun identified with the south? We must now explore this relation to close the symbolic triangle:

$$\text{sun} = \text{hummingbird}$$

south

First of all, the sun never attains the zenith above 23.5 degrees north latitude, the location of the Tropic of Cancer. For cultures north of the equator the northernmost regions of the sky are those through which the sun never passes. This itself identified the sun and south as "belonging together." For people living north of the equator but south of the 23.5 degree parallel, the sun is actually north of their own zenith during part of the year. For much of Mesoamerica, however, this period is extremely short compared with the number of days that the sun (seeming to move over space) is south of an observer's zenith. In Tenochtitlan (today's Mexico City), for the Nahuatl-speaking Aztecs who named the sun after the southern region (see section on names, p. 167, below), the sun was north of the zenith for only a very few days. At 19.25 degrees north, the sun is north of the local zenith approximately 66 days out of the 365 of the year. At the latitude of contemporary Zinacantan (calculated from San Cristobal las Casas, 16.75 degrees north), the sun is north of the local zenith for about 91 days in the year.

Therefore, from three different points of view "sun" is associated with "south"; first, south is the direction of the sun at midday for most of the year; second, the sun is never seen in the northernmost part of the sky, above 23.5 degrees north latitude; third, the length of time the sun is south rather than north of the zenith, depends on how far the observer is located from the equator and how near the Tropic of Cancer.

Therefore, the prehispanic divine image of the dominant sun, and its name in Nahuatl, was "the southern one." It was only the sun in its weakest image in myth which was associated with north and winter. Many other societies north of the equator, in classic and present times, have made the same association. North is often seen as the region of cold, darkness, and winter, and south is, as D. H. Lawrence put it, "going towards the sun."

Prehispanic cultures identified the sun of spring and summer, that is, the rainy season, particularly with the south and east directions because prehispanic peoples marked lines or sides for the cardinal directions, points for the intercardinal ones, and assigned one of each to the four divisions of space and of time (see discussion of the time-space continuum, p. 179, below). North and south were not the polar points as they are for us, but the tropical lines. From winter solstice to summer solstice the sun appears to move from south to north. This was imagined as the movement from a point southwest, to a point southeast, to a point northeast, or, in linear terms, as the movement over the southern and eastern boundaries of the square, flat earth.

And then the sun of summer was seen to arrive in the northernmost position—which corresponds with our view of the matter. But this sun was defined as the southern one. How can this be possible?

This association with south and east is a paradox explained by the intricate relation between time and space in prehispanic thought, a relation in which "movement over space, after it has accumulated" = time. Although the sun is actually southernmost in winter and northernmost in summer, the dominant sun is defined as southern because *south is the direction from which it comes, the direction in which it spends most of its time, and the space, line, and point of origin of its movement.*

The reader should be aware that, unlike us, prehispanic peoples counted time cumulatively, in elapsed rather than current periods. When time is counted thus, the sun that marks its passage cannot be named for what has not happened yet—that is, for the direction it will reach in summer. Rather, it will be named for the direction it came from. Prehispanic peoples, in Teeple's wise simile (1930:35), "counted time as the meter of a motor car counts miles. It does not register a mile until the whole mile has been run, while Christian chronology, like a taximeter, registers a unit the instant it starts." Therefore, the sun is named "southern" because it does not reach its northernmost position until the end of its upward ecliptic journey, which is the summer solstice. The sun was imagined as a humanized being, moving in the sky, and doing the work of keeping the world warm and lighted and nature growing. Since this anthropomorphized sun spent most of its time "working" in the southern sky, this is ultimately why it was a "southern one," a deity of the south. A lovely metaphoric paradox.

The paradox has further complexities, moreover, because prehispanic peoples associated both south and summer with the left hand. Such associations seem arbitrary to us. But if an observer stands at the east, facing west (as the sun as a personified god does every day), the left hand marks south. In fact the Nahuatl-speaking peoples called the sun "the left-handed one," because he spent most of his time "doing his work" on the left hand (that is, in the southern sky). And if the summer sun is defined as southern, and south is left, therefore summer is left.

However, during the late spring and early summer, an observer south of the Tropic of Cancer, if facing west, will actually see the sun on the right-hand side, as it will be north of his zenith. The association of "summer" and "left" again rests on the prehispanic view of time, not on the sun's position on any specific day near the summer solstice. When time is counted in elapsed periods, the celebrations for time periods take place in the end of the periods (as Mesoamericans celebrated the monthly festivals on the last day of the month) and the symbols of its marks are reversed from our point of view of current time; south goes with left and summer, and north with right and winter. Since the sun is the marker of time, it is "he" who defines its symbols by "his" movement, not the human observer on the earth's surface, unable to fly, his feet tied to the ground!

All together, the daily, annual, and ecliptic metaphors combine to make a single metaphor, in which a divine, personified flying sun, hummingbirds, and the south are blended together into a single glorious image of triangular light and beauty.

Victoria Bricker, in a personal communication, has asked why the Mesoamerican peoples did not consistently use the quetzal bird as the symbol of the sun, since they have always made so much of the quetzal's symbolism. There are several reasons why they preferred the hummingbird. First, in my opinion, while quetzal feathers are brilliant, they do not have the particularly iridescent properties of the hummingbird's. Admittedly, this is not evidence. There are, however, sound reasons for excluding the quetzal, as well as the family of trogon birds of which it is a member. All these birds fly in short, rapid, spasmodic patterns and seize most of their food on the wing with their short curved beaks. Thus the flight patterns of the quetzal provide little metaphoric material for comparison with the hummingbird-sun flight patterns: there is no reversed flight, no steady hovering in the air. However, because quetzals fly "in puffs," short spasmodic patterns, they were equated with wind, and therefore were an image of the god of wind (Quetzalcoatl in Nahuatl, K'uK'ulchon in Zinacantan, Kukulkan among the Highland Maya of Guatemala). The food-seizing habits of the quetzal also serve to equate it with "wind." The wind bird carries things "on its wing."

The symbolism of the hummingbird's beak—equated with weapons, warriors' tools, and sacrificial thorns—cannot be transferred to the curved short and wide beak of the quetzal. Quetzals were not warriorlike images, and hence represented a non-warrior, a priestly god, Quetzalcoatl. In many myths about the historic fight between the promoters of human sacrifice and those opposed to it, Quetzalcoatl is the condensed symbol of the people who favored a ritual without human cruelty. Particularly in the Tula myths, he represents those opposed to human sacrifice, and Tezcatlipoca-Huitzilopochtli (hummingbird-eagle) represents those in favor of it. The myth of the triumph of Tezcatlipoca-Huitzilopochtli at the historic site of Tula, related by Sahagun's informants (1969; see, for example, 1:278–291) and Ixtlixochitl (1891–1892), can thus be interpreted as the overcoming of theocratic tendencies by militaristic regimes in the valley of Mexico. This "event" took place at about the time of Tula's period of decadence. The favoring of Quetzal-

Quetzalcoatl as a dominant god in highland Guatemala may point to a different ideological orientation of the elites ruling the Highland Maya and the northern central valleys. The Maya appear to represent "nonmilitaristic" tendencies, the Aztec "militaristic" ones. There is no doubt in my mind that when the *Popol Vuh* evidence is compared with the Aztec mythology, Quetzalcoatl is a more dominant figure in the former. The contrasts in terms of the symbolic code-message arrangements are as follows:

quetzal	: hummingbird (eagle)
: : short, spasmodic flight	: steady, reversed, hovering flight
: : short, wide beak	: sharp, narrow beak
: : pacific (against human sacrifice)	: cruel (war prone, in favor of human sacrifice)
: : theocratic (a priest)	: militaristic (a warrior)
: : Maya of Guatemala	: Aztec (Mexico)
: : Quetzalcoatl	: Huitzilopochtli (blue Tezcatlipoca)
: : wind	: sun

This contrast between Guatemala and Mexico has been preserved in modern symbolism. The national seal of Guatemala has the quetzal bird in its center. The national seal of Mexico shows the eagle of Huitzilopochtli perched on its mythic nopal, where the Aztecs founded the capital of their empire, today Mexico City.

Crawlers and Swimmers

This group of animals used in religious symbolism includes some that belong to our class of reptiles, some crawlers (for instance, worms), and some fish. Those most often appearing in myth, pictorial manuscripts, and sculpture, and as gods' eponyms and associates include the snake, the alligator, and the lizard.

Snakes were ubiquitous symbols. They represented lightning, celestial light rays, rivers, and all kinds of linear or undulant images. They were also, as in many other cultures, symbols of male fertility and phallic symbols. Among the Maya, the duality "sky-earth" was represented by two reptiles, the sky being a giant double-headed snake. This concept probably stemmed "from the fact that the word for sky, *caan*, is a homonym of the word for snake" (Coe 1966:152). I believe that the snake was not the sky as a whole, but rather the Milky Way. The image was double-headed because the Milky Way forks into two branches. The body of the serpent was marked in iconography by the moving planets, since the Milky Way was the starry path in which they were supposed to move.

Another crawler of mythical importance since the early times of Teotihuacan was the snail. The prehispanic peoples saw in the shell a symbol of mysterious things. It represented both the sky and the sea from which it came. The transversed cut shell with its coiled center represented whirlwinds, and the animal closed in his shell was a symbol for the womb, while his coming out was "childbirth" or "life." The empty shell among the Maya was the symbol for "zero" or "naught" (*ibid.*, p. 156).

The list also includes a totally mythical creature, a monster, half fish, half reptile, which represented the living earth. This animal, called *cipactli* in Nahuatl, has been glossed in Spanish as *pejelagarto* (Caso 1967:8), but Sahagun thought it was the *pez espada* (swordfish) and Seler the *caiman* (alligator). In fact, it was a mythical creature, like the medieval dragon or griffin, that combined two species into one.

Contemporary Cuicatec Indians among whom I have done field work identify the earth monster in Spanish as the anomalous *ballena* (whale). Since the Cuicatec are landlocked, it is possible that at some time in the colonial period a Spanish-speaking immigrant who knew about whales made the identification from a native description. The Cuicatec *ballena*, however, with its fanciful green skirt of coiled snakes, imagined as a goddess living in the center of the world's lagoon or universal ocean (as the prehispanic earth monster did), controlling the rivers of the world, appears to be a merging of *cipactli* with the goddess of surface water, Chalchihuitlicue, and Coatlicue, the earth mother.

Another mythical animal of major importance among both Maya and Highland Mesoamerican groups is the "plumed serpent," the quetzalcoatl. The complex name can also be glossed as quetzal-snake, flying snake, bejeweled or precious snake, that is, a snake with bird attributes. It also means precious twin or quetzal twin, because *coatl* = snake and twin. This animal represented the god Quetzalcoatl, its homonym, whose image of divinity included the planet Venus, wind, fertility, and life. Metaphorically, wind = breath = life (Seler 1963, 1:68). He was a twin because Venus appears as two sibling stars, one in the morning and one in the evening. In Zinacantan, this mythical creature appears in the Saint Sebastian rituals disguised in its dark transformation as a raven, which is appropriate for a winter aspect (Vogt 1969:542).

The prehispanic class I have called "crawlers," is also recognized as such in Zinacantan ethno-zoology (Acheson 1966). Victoria Bricker (personal communication) has pointed out to me that the ritual impersonators called "raven" or "plumed serpent" at the Zinacantan festival of Saint Sebastian are dressed as "feathered serpents" with green velveteen breeches and a bird headdress and wings, but the bird headdress is not painted black like a raven. Instead it is spotted, and it carries a corn cob in its mouth (see Vogt 1969:542). This apparent contradiction (black = not black) is an old prehispanic sacred paradox. The bird is a raven (= black bird = winter aspect of the deity) in shape, but *also* the feathered serpent (= Quetzalcoatl = K'uK'ulchon) in coloring. The headdress is shaped like the head of a raven, but the impersonator is dressed and painted like a quetzal with bluegreen and red spots on the dress, resembling the crimson underspotting of quetzal feathers. That the Zinacantecan feathered serpent and the prehispanic are one and the same symbol can be easily observed in the iconographic designs of the headdress and other sartorial features. Distinctive features of the head of the prehispanic image are preserved quite faithfully in the contemporary one: the distended lips or beak mask, which covers the lower part of the face, now in Zinacantan featured as a beak at the bottom of the headdress; the truncated conical hat; the spots on the hat, sometimes portrayed as circles over a light background, at others as jaguar skin spotting; and a ribbon, beard band or scarf wrapped around the headdress (see Illustration 2).

The image is exquisitely complicated because K'uK'ulchon represents the proven fertility of the land (the corn in the beak, the blue-green color), and the crops in the postharvest period (the corn in the beak) and because the raven is believed to have gotten "used to cracking maize" (Vogt 1969:309, myth of origin); to have announced that the earth was dry after the deluge (= end of rains) (*ibid.*, p. 311); and to have given man corn in ancestral times by stealing it from the other gods, carrying it in his beak (*ibid.*, p. 313). There is, then, a merging of complicated symbol-images in the Zinacantan Saint Sebastian rituals, which take place during the winter period when the rains have stopped ("the land is dry"), corn is harvested, dry, and ready to shell ("crack"), and the year's fertility has been proven by the new harvest. The fertility image of K'uK'ulchon is celebrated as the wind-raven-quetzal-feathered snake which brought fertility, the corn.

But the festival takes place in December. Since this is the winter solstice period (= dark = black), the dry season (= raven announcing land is dry) and the time when the harvest is in (= fertility of crops), the symbol of the bird which is both black and responsible for having given man corn and that of the feathered serpent are merged in the iconography of a single ritual impersonator. The merging of symbols parallels the merging of ecology, astronomy, and agrarian schedules and events in the winter.

The dual image is carried in different codes. The raven is transmitted in a verbal code (that is, the name of the impersonator), and an iconographic zoological shape code: the bird-shaped headdress which clearly looks like a raven (see, for example, photos 181, 182, 183, in Vogt 1969). The quetzal-serpent with its fertility meaning appears in a verbal code (the second name of the impersonator) and in a zoological chromatic code: the blue-green breeches, the blue-green-red spotted elements of the impersonator's dress. The fertility aspect of the raven and its mythic role in giving man corn are expressed in an iconographic botanical shape code: the corn cob in the beak of the raven-shaped headdress. Both the feathered (flying) serpent and the raven are expressed in the shape code of the "wings" of the impersonator. All the codes juxtaposed—chromatic, textual, formal, anatomic, iconographic, and verbal—meet in a single impersonator at a single specific point in the space-time continuum: the winter ritual, the dry, postharvest season of the winter solstice. Thus, the (black) raven feathered-serpent (blue-green-red) of contemporary Zinacantan is as multivocal and complex as that of its antecedent prehispanic image, Quetzalcoatl. This color-animal-name paradox itself is prehispanic, since one of Quetzalcoatl's names was "he who is feathered in black," although the image of the god was painted in other colors (Sahagun 1969: Volume 1, Book 3, appendix to chap. 7). There are no black quetzals, unless they transform themselves into ravens! In other Highland myths Quetzalcoatl, disguised as a black ant rather than as a raven, stole the corn. The prehispanic image of Quetzalcoatl wore a cape of raven feathers from which the name "feathered in black" derived. Raven or ant, he is both black and not black!

Venus-Quetzalcoatl as morning star was also the wind god in two aspects: an annual and a daily one. As annual wind god he represented the equinoctial wind storms just before the beginning of the rainy season, which "sweep the path" for the sun to ascend in its ecliptic journey and also for the rain gods (Sahagun 1969: Book 1, Chap. 5, p. 45). As daily wind god he represented the early dawn wind and the morning star, which "sweep the path" for the sun to ascend in its daily journey through the sky. Thus, he was called the "sweeper of the path." Venus is known today in Zinacantan by this exact name (Vogt 1969:316). But the wind-Venus-god has been transformed into a Chamula Indian girl. Why? First, women are usually the sweepers in everyday life in Zinacantan. Men are "sweepers" only on ritual occasions. Second, Chamula is a *municipio* with lands to the east of Zinacantan, the direction from which the sun and the morning star appear! Chamula girls dress in black, the color of ravens (Robert Laughlin suggested this last point to me). In the Zinacantan myth about the girl this point is made explicit by calling her "the awful ugly black Chamula" (Vogt 1969:317).

The combination of different animals, that is, the use of a mythic bestiary for symbolic coding, did not occur only with the feathered serpent = raven image of Quetzalcoatl. Other gods were also built of superimposed animal symbol codes. A clear example is the rain god, Tlaloc, called Chac in Yucatan, and the *Tlaloque* (Mayan: *Kanbel*), his assistants. The *Tlaloque*, small transformational images of the god, were depicted as small animals who live in water, frogs or lightning-rod snakes. With the latter symbol they are still known in Zinacantan (Vogt 1969:302), where they are called *janbel* or *chauk* (lightning).

The major god himself, in the highland iconography, was portrayed (*a*) holding a lightning snake in his hand, which represented the visual image of a lightning flash descending, and (*b*) as a face mask that had two eyes resembling goggles, made up of two coiled serpents, and a fierce "jaguar-shaped" mouth. The eyes repeated in the visual code the image of rain lightning, the snake. The jaguar mouth symbolized thunder, a visual transformation of an auditory code symbol. Thunder sounds like the roar of the jaguar; therefore, the rain god has a mouth (= voice, metonymically) like a jaguar. The merging of a visual metaphor (lightning = snake) placed around the god's eyes and a phonic metonymy combined with a visual metaphor (thunder = jaguar's roar, voice = mouth, therefore sound of thunder = mouth of jaguar) was shown on the pictorial and sculptural face of the god. These two iconographic symbols provided the distinctive features of the Tlaloc face mask. The Maya gave the rain god a large dripping nose, like that of a person who has a runny head cold. Here, rain is seen as a giant case of the flu!

Animals could be transformed from one major symbol code to another, e.g., from the zoological to the vegetable code, as in the following complex example. Snakes represented fertility not only as phallic symbols but also because the umbilical cord resembles a snake. This image is used effectively in the *Fejervary-Mayer Codex*, to signify different kinds of childbirth. One of a series of pictures shows a "goddess" in the postpartum stage. She has breasts bulging with milk and the wrinkled belly of a woman who has just given birth. She holds in her hands the baby she has just delivered from her womb, or rather, she is pulling at it by means of the umbilical cord, which is still attached to it. The baby has blue coloring, like a baby who died in childbirth, strangled by the cord, and the cord around the baby's neck is a snake. Another image shows a live, healthy baby, his skin the normal color, and here the umbilical cord is transformed not into a snake but into a symbol of joy—it is the long stem of a plant with a lovely flower at the end. Here the zoological code for the symbol indicates fertility in its negative aspect, represented by the snake—an ambivalent animal—which may look like an umbilical cord, but can also kill humans with his poison or by wrapping himself around their necks, as the umbilical cord can kill babies. In the botanical code, the stem and flower represent the unequivocal aspect of fertility, the joyful side of giving birth. Comparable examples of animal-animal, or of animal-plant transformations, of transposition and replacement of codes, are innumerable in the pictorial representations.

Four-Legged Walkers or Mammals

The "walker" class includes four-legged vertebrates familiar in the Mesoamerican landscape. All the prehispanic images are those of wild animals, except for the fattened dogs which, besides the turkey, were the only domesticated creatures used as a major source of protein. In contemporary Indian mythology and symbolism, domesticated European-imported animals also appear, particularly the bull, which plays an important part in ritual in Zinacantan, as it does all over Mexico (Vogt 1969:520, 522–531, 535–536). These animals, like the volatiles, are classified by size, habits, "temperament," eating proclivities, color, speed of movement, and so on. Favorites in myth and as day-name signs are the deer (a forest image) and the dog. The dog was a messenger of the gods of death and the guardian, like the Greek Cerberus, of the underworld entrance (see Beyer 1965:440–442). The monkey represented "unfinished imperfect men." These were men of an era before a deluge, who are still remembered in Zinacantan.

The jaguar was sometimes associated with the gods of the underworld and the night, and with witches, sorcerers or priests (meta-phorically jaguars = carnivores = soul eaters = witches or knowers of dark mysteries = priests). This symbolism is still extant in many Mesoamerican communities including those of the Chiapas high-lands. The jaguar is also, in the auditory code, the voice of thunder and the voice of the earth deities (the noise or rumbling of the earth during earthquakes).

The rabbit was associated with a complex of related ideas which included the moon. Its image is said to appear in the full moon. The maguey beer (pulque) "rabbit" gods were lunar gods. They were also gods of fertility (and as such, related to the moon as menses) and were linked with Huitzilopochtli.

The association of maguey beer with the moon and fertility can be easily understood by those acquainted with the Mesoamerican drink. I am not aware that an explanation of the link exists in the literature, but one can be seen in the context of a contemporary Cuicatec myth, which I collected in the town of Concepción Pápalo. In this myth, the goddess of pulque, Mayahuel, or perhaps the vir-gin maiden Xochitl (see below p. 82) appears as a Cuicatec woman who "lived alone" (that is, who was unmarried). She invented the drink (see *Diccionario Porrúa*, 2:1502). The god Patecatl makes his appearance as a strong, well-muscled man—or is he perhaps the old king of Tula in disguise? He was, prehispanically, the god who pro-tected the herbs, woody substances, and other vegetables that were added to maguey sap to hasten the maturing of the beer. One of the briefer versions is given in full:

Pulque was invented by a woman of Pápalo. This is a good place for maguey because it is cold. But every night a man from Lightning (mountain) came over to drink the pulque and made it "drooly" (see p. 83). He was strong, tall, well muscled. The woman hid to find out who was ruining her pulque. He came in one night and asked, "Who is here, good night?" But no one answered because the woman was hiding. Then he asked, "Is there a little pulque to drink? A little bit?" He crawled into the *tapanco* (false roof of the house used for storage) where the pulque was. The woman was scared and said nothing. The Ancestor drank and drank and drank once more of the pulque until he became drunk. Because he was from another part of

Lightning Mountain, he made the pulque drooly while drinking. Now, when they cut open the maguey plants to make pulque, and when they prepare the pulque jars, they put garlic and coriander and sometimes chile and make sure that the man from Lightning Mountain does not come and make it drooly.

This myth contains much that cannot be explained without a long analysis mostly irrelevant to this book. It forms part of a set of Cuicatec myths dealing with ecology and the directional associations of mountains in the Cuicatec district, which mark a quincunx pattern (see later discussion, pp. 97–98). This particular myth contains information on two of the mountains (the myths are told as oppositional pairs).

The contrast of directions here is between Pápalo Bell Hill (a female mountain) in the southwest corner, and Lightning (a male mountain) in the northwest corner of the mountain quincunx. As in other myths, the sex of protagonists is southwest = female, northwest = male. Other familiar contrasts are also found here: women "cook," men eat their "cooking." An unusual feature of the symbolism is that in most Cuicatec myths women are the destroyers or polluters, while in this story the male has these roles. The myth relates to other myths about men interfering with women's "jobs" and vice versa. The sexual symbolism is exaggerated in comparison to other Cuicatec myths, because pulque is a white, viscous liquid which is identified with milk and semen. When ready to drink, it looks and tastes slightly like sour skimmed milk. But when it ferments past its prime, it becomes thicker and develops a smell, consistency, and appearance strikingly similar to human semen. Again, the maguey plant, to release its juice (from which the beer is made) is cut open in its center (its "vagina" or "mouth") and left with an opening (that is, the plant loses its "virginity"). Some Indians say the maguey "is castrated."

Mayahuel, the goddess of pulque, was conceived of as a woman full of milk (she had 400 breasts). Xochitl, the human female who invented pulque in some other versions of the myth, was a maiden, later ravished by one of the kings of Tula. Among the Cuicatec today, maguey is a feminine plant and pulque is a feminine juice (milk of a mother goddess). When pulque comes to resemble semen, it is spoiled. In the same fashion a virgin is "spoiled" (= drooling), Cuicatecs say, after her first intercourse.

"Drooly" is a literal translation. The meaning of the word is quite complex. Its denotation, like that of "to drool" in English, is to let saliva flow from the mouth, to dribble a thick, viscous liquid. By metaphorical extension Cuicatecs apply the concept of "drooling" to other body orifices and fluids. After sexual intercourse a woman "drools" semen from her vagina as she drools blood during menstruation. But in this tale "drooly" has yet another set of connotations. To drool also means to court or woo to excess. A man who insists on excessive gallantry or on making improper advances to a woman is called a "drooler." Here the reference is to his incontinence. The expression condenses, symbolically, the equivalence of body orifices and their secretions. Fresh maguey beer equals milk. Maguey beer past its prime equals semen or saliva. The equation reads mouth : saliva : : vagina : semen after intercourse. Drooly pulque, then, means "pulque with the consistency of saliva or semen."

Lévi-Strauss's favorite images of food and sex appear in this myth, developed to their fullest. Garlic, coriander, and chile, strong-smelling substances used by women in cooking (= culture), also serve as prophylactics for preventing evil and disease (= wild nature). These same substances are used to flavor the pulque and make it stronger. Here they act as a "chastity belt" for the pulque, which should remain "virgin" (untouched while fermenting or maturing) until ready to be drunk, or it will spoil. In the same fashion young girls should not be "spoiled" (made to drool = lose their virginity) before they are mature and ready for marriage and can legitimately become mothers.

The same symbolism occurs in the older versions of this myth collected in the sixteenth century. In one of these versions, pulque was also, as in some of the Pápalo versions, invented by a female human being, a virgin, who discovered the honey-like sap of maguey by accident. Her name was Xochitl, flower, which links her with Xochiquetzal, the image of a goddess of youthful sexuality, patroness of flower arrangers, prostitutes and embroiderers. Like the woman in the Pápalo myth she was the victim of male interference. She was said to have taken the honeyed liquid to the king of Tula against her father's wishes. The king "forced" her (in another version he married her), and from the sexual union the last king of Tula was born. Because women of pleasure are in a sense equally "forced," their goddess was Xochiquetzal (Ixtlilxochitl 1891–1892).

Moreover, this version of the myth had the same symbolic ritual associations. Pulque was considered a powerful drink, dangerous because it caused drunkenness and thus sexual license. But it was also considered an inducer of fertility. It was given to pregnant and lactating women, and its use was forbidden for youngsters (virginal persons). Warriors were given it to drink to increase their potency, here not sexual but military.

Thus woman's sexuality and her fertility were linked with pulque. But it was also a negative symbol (a taboo) of premarital status, and young persons were forbidden to drink it at the risk of their lives. In a late eighteenth-century farce, produced by Nahuatl-speaking Indians, the same symbols appear. Victoria Bricker (1973:194–195) reports it as follows:

As late as the eighteenth century, some Nahuatl-speaking Indians were producing a farce which resembled the prehispanic performances in several respects (Paso y Troncoso, 1902:313). One of the characters, a stooped or hunchbacked old woman, pretends to be pregnant. Her grandson imitates coyotes and dogs. The farce begins with the deformed old woman announcing her craving for agave sap, which she carries in a gourd: "I have a desire, a longing, a craving for thick [agave] sap . . . which will prevent me from having a miscarriage" (Paso y Troncoso, 1902:314; my translation).

She does not want her grandson, Peter, to drink the juice, so she tells him that the gourd contains poison for dogs. Having told him this, she leaves the stage, groaning with pain: "Look, I should think first of the child that I have conceived. I have very sharp pains in my hips. Perhaps I am going to have a miscarriage" (Paso y Troncoso, 1902:315; my translation).

Peter cannot resist tasting the bowl of juice she has left behind, and he likes it so much that he drinks it all: "Ah, ah, is that ever good and sweet!

That is why dogs like to eat it, and that is why they die. God will it that I do not transform myself into a dog. Here is a truly sweet death. This is the end. Let's scrape the bowl" (Paso y Troncoso, 1902:315; my translation).

Then he thinks he is dying: "I have sought for myself a violent death! Oh! How unfortunate I am! It is my gluttony which carries me away. Please God, that I may still live on earth! It seems to me that I am already getting numb, that my eyes are clouding over. . . . I am dying, I am already dying" (Paso y Troncoso, 1902:315; my translation).

Peter's grandmother returns and asks where he is. Peter replies, "Grandmother, I am only holding onto my soul by the skin of my teeth: I am already dying" (Paso y Troncoso, 1902:316; my translation).

The old woman asks what happened to him, and Peter lies: "Grandmother! Twelve hundred dogs came. They began to eat the poison which you left down there; because the food seemed to be so very tasty, I immediately wished to taste a little bit of it" (Paso y Troncoso, 1902:316; my translation).

The old woman scolds him: "Imbecile, scamp, glutton! You have eaten the thick sap that I crave! Now if I feel the craving of a pregnant woman, what will I eat?" (Paso y Troncoso, 1902:316; my translation). And she hits him with her stick. The act ends with the old woman chasing her grandson around the stage.

This farce has obvious sexual innuendoes, using the metaphor of thick maguey beer. The old woman is saying that she craves pulque (= semen), that is, sexual intercourse. She claims it will prevent a miscarriage. I cannot say whether Zinacantecans have exactly the same belief, but the Cuicatec and many other Mesoamerican Indian people believe that when a woman is in the first stages of pregnancy she should have frequent intercourse because the added semen "strengthens and solidifies the fetus" (amaciza la criatura). Many Zinacantecans believe that several acts of coitus are necessary to induce conception, and sexual intercourse is permitted until the last months of pregnancy. The idea that the fetus is "soft" is expressed in their view that it has the consistency of corn gruel (atole), another milk-semen metaphor, since atole is a dense white liquid. A pregnant woman who does not have frequent enough sexual intercourse, and does not maintain relations with her husband, is believed likely to have a miscarriage, because there is not enough of the father's substance to solidify the growing fetus.

The joke in the farce is, of course, that the woman is a grand-mother, and craves pulque not because she is a young fertile woman or a nursing mother, but because she is a lecherous old lady.

Again, her grandson is not supposed to drink the stuff. First, he is a grandson (= young, presexual). Second, a man drinking old thick pulque is a metaphor for homosexuality. "He likes old pulque" is a euphemism for "he likes semen," that is, he likes men as sexual partners. The references in the farce to dogs and coyotes affirm and reinforce the symbolism because dogs in Mesoamerican folklore are said to be not only irresponsibly promiscuous but also indiscriminate about the sex of their partners. To say that a "woman has dog" in many Mexican communities means that she is sexually insatiable and, perhaps, a lesbian.

In the farce both grandmother and grandson are ridiculous sexual figures. They are funny because they are inadequate sexual part-ners. The grandmother is too old to engage in sexual intercourse, the grandson too young. The farce is a structural transformation of the same moral that appears in the sixteenth-century myths and the contemporary Pápalo myth. It deals with the inappropriateness of engaging in sexual intercourse outside the normative age range. It says that it is legitimate for young mature males, such as warriors, to do so or for fertile young women, those who are pregnant or nurs-ing, and are married. But it is illegitimate, dangerous and/or ridi-culous for a person who is either prefertile (the grandson), or post-menopausal (the grandmother) to engage in sexual activity. We must also remember that the moon, pulque, milk, atole, and semen are all white.

There is another link between pulque, mother's milk, female fertil-ity, the moon, and, ultimately, rabbits, the symbol with which we started this discussion. First, a woman's fertility and ability to pro-duce milk is said to derive from her menses, and woman's men-struation is, according to Mesoamerican Indians in general, regu-lated by the moon month cycle of approximately twenty-eight days. The relationship of the pulque gods based on rabbits, to fertility and the moon is obvious, and clearly follows the same set of analogies which prompted prehispanic peoples and contemporary Indians to make the equivalent associations, in a semantic circle: mothers' milk/semen = menses = moon = rabbit seen in the moon = fertility = pulque = milk, and so on.

The relationship between Huitzilopochtli, the hummingbird god, and the rabbit as a symbol is not directly dependent on this lunar complex. It is explained instead by the god's association with the calendar quarters, since south was his dominant direction and also that of the calendar sign-name "rabbit." Why such an association? South, as I explained above, was identified with summer and rabbits (a humorous image of extreme fertility that we share in our own folk imagery), and summer, the fertile season of the year, were linked together (according to the prehispanic conception of space-time) to form one of the four year signs which were the names of the year's cycles. Rabbits and summer together were also associated with one of the four cardinal directions, one of the inner planets (the moon), one of the day names, and so on. Perhaps because of these cumulative, multiple, multivocal transformations, rabbits developed into a god complex of their own, the Ometochtli god and Cetzontotochtin gods ("two-rabbit" and "four-hundred-rabbit" gods; Nicholson 1971:419–420) which were, of course, gods of pulque!

I believe that, like Zinacantecans, the prehispanic peoples also distinguished certain other classes of animals—for example, insects, arachnids. These, however, appear to have been of minor importance in their religion, and were not often depicted as the protagonists of mythical dialogue. I do not know how many definable classes the prehispanic peoples recognized. One exception to the mythic lack of dominance of small animals was the placement of bees according to Mayan mythology. A bee was assigned to each quarter of the space-time continuum (*Chilam Balam de Chumayel*). Zinacantecans recognize the animal categories of walkers and crawlers which they distinguish from flying creatures or volatiles, but apparently they place butterflies, flies and other insects or flying animals, including bees, in a general category of animals which is sometimes classed separately, sometimes merged with birds. Further investigation is required to discover how far their ethnozoology corresponds to the zoological mythology. (For a prehispanic picture of the animals of the southern sky see Illustration 4.)

Mankind

Man was defined by prehispanic peoples, as he is today by Mesoamerican Indians, as part of the natural order. First, human souls were in part made up of animal-spirit and other cosmic images (the *nahual*), called *chanul* in contemporary Zinacantan (Vogt 1969:371–373 and *passim*). In fact, man appeared on the earth to replace previous and inferior orders of humanity which had failed to meet the gods' demands for appropriate behavior. In an interesting twist of what we could call a prehispanic "theory of evolution," man had replaced other animals. Previous universal eras had seen more primitive races of humanity, herbivores subsisting by gathering seeds, such as acorns, pinyon nuts, and the seeds of aquatic plants. The prehuman race of mankind had become fishes, monkeys, dogs, butterflies, and turkeys, representing all the classes of animals. These myths have been partially preserved in Zinacantan in the myth of the Flood, in which an imperfect race of men ate berries and nuts

4. The eagle, celestial snake, and rabbit, symbols of the south. *Borgia Codex*, p. 5, center-right section.

and became monkeys (*ibid.*, pp. 308–316). The present race of mankind, however, was superior, a better creation of the gods. Thus it was placed only one step below ancestors, cultural heroes, and gods, and above all other animals, in the ladder of power, merit, and perfection. Thus man himself was a transformational category, occupying a special niche in the mythical system. While lower orders of animals ate one another and plants, and man ate all of them, the gods ate men to subsist. This basic idea of an arrangement of the living orders of the universe as a phagohierarchy was the theological justification for human sacrifice. Man was, however, not separated from the animal order but was an intimate part of nature, because his soul parts were animal-spirit beings or aspects of the cosmos and nature (whirlwinds, lightning, and so on).

In one of the many cosmogonic myths, the common mass of mankind had been created by Quetzalcoatl and the hummingbird-sun god (*HDLMPSP* 1941:209–212). In Zinacantan, the sun is also an ancestral parent, and is called *ch'ulk'ak'al* (holy heat or holy sun) or *chultotik* (holy father).

The vital heat given by the sun god was located in the human soul. This soul aspect was called, in Nahuatl, a man's *tona* (or *tonal* or *tonalli*). In Zinacantan today it is called *chulel*. What man possessed was a small replica of the *tona* of the creator gods themselves, and creator-parental gods, such as Tonacatecuhtli (the father god), Tonacacihuatl (the mother goddess), and Tonatiuh (the genitor sun), carried the lexeme *tona* in their names. Thus man was an aspect of the sacred life of the cosmos, connected to it through his spirit. As such, he was consciously responsible for the continuity and balance of the cosmos, which he promoted through rituals. The soul of man related him to the universe in a sacred interaction. This belief is still held today in Zinacantan (see Vogt 1969:369–371).

Symbolic Plant Taxonomies
Domestic Plants

The category of domestic plants with connections to myth included the important plants cultivated in Mesoamerica in prehistoric times. Two major cultigens of symbolic importance were the maguey plant and corn, both "solar" plants. The relation of maguey and sun has already been explained. Corn, the staple of Mesoamerica, was related to the sun because the agricultural schedules of corn were regulated by solar calendrics. Corn was offspring of earth and sun. In Zinacantan, as in other Mesoamerican communities, the corn is said to have a divine protector soul, a snake, called its "mother" (*me'ishin*). She appears to be the daughter of the rain god, who is also "Lord of the Earth," a principal deity of Zinacantecans. He is given offerings on the third day of May, at the beginning of the rains, during the Holy Cross rituals (Robert Laughlin, personal communication). She created the red variety of corn when she wiped blood from her nose with a white corn cob. She appears in the *Popol Vuh* texts under the name Blood Girl. Today she can be a flower, or transform herself into a snake or a girl (Laughlin, personal communication). In the Nahuatl myths she was a goddess combining all these attributes. Her name was Xilonen, from the same root as the Spanish Mexicanism *jilote*, that is, the "flower" or tassel of the corn plant, or the tender green ear.

Amaranth, particularly the seeds, was also used extensively in ritual contexts during holy days, including those of solar deities like the hummingbird god.

This class had one peculiarity. Many plants were classified internally, with subdivisions for each stage of growth from seedtime to harvest. The most significant of these subcategories was (and still is) the complex one for maize. Corn was not only symbolically distinguished according to seed or kernel color, size and shape of cob, and other physical characteristics, but also as different personae: "flowering corn," "ripening corn," "dry corn cob," and the like. The symbolic significance of corn kernel colors and the size and shape of cobs, particularly for divination purposes, persists today in peasant Mesoamerica, including Zinacantan (Vogt 1976). The vocabulary of Zinacantan for stages of corn growth is especially rich (Vogt 1969:48–50). The stages of maize growth in prehispanic times were symbolized each by a different deity, some female (for example,

Xilonen = flowering tender corn) and some male (for example, Centeotl = the corn cob). These names have been glossed by Nicholson
(1971: Table 3) as "young maize-ear-doll" and "maize-cob lord." In
the codex *Fejervary-Mayer* (pp. 33–34, top section) there is a set of
pictures of four divine stages of the growth of corn. Three are depicted as males, but the "pregnant" plant with full corn cobs is
pictured as female. Each of the four corn deities of the *Fejervary-
Mayer* corresponds to a cardinal direction, and to one of four periods
of time, probably the year's seasons.

Powerful Plants and Plant Parts

This class included plants with special properties which were used
extensively in ritual: hallucinogens, such as the seeds of Santa Maria
or morning glory (the Aztec *ololiuhqui*), peyote, hallucinogenic mushrooms, tobacco, maguey from which beer is made, and copal, a resin
incense burned for ritual. The Maya of the early colonial period also
used frangipani flowers (Maya: *nicté*) as an aphrodisiac. This idea
was derived from the shape of the flower, which resembles genitalia.

Apparently, with the single exception of copal, all these plants of
major symbolic, mythical, and ritual importance were directly con-
sumed by humans, for the purpose of altering body or brain functions. In addition, a form of copal made from the seeds of the *pirú* or
pepper tree was used to add to maguey beer, which became "in-
censed." This powerful mixture was said to be a potent medicine
which could cure venereal disease (*Diccionario Porrúa*, 2: 514).

Many other plants which are not hallucinogens but have medici-
nal value of some sort (rue, willow leaves and bark, and so forth)
appear to have been included in this class, but the information available to me is inconclusive. The "powerful plants" have been studied
in detail by Schultes (see, for example, 1972). Thompson (1970) has
covered the topic of tobacco among the Maya. Most of these plants
are still used among Mesoamerican Indians for religious purposes.
Since colonial times alcoholic drinks made by distilling maguey beer
or sugar-cane alcohol have been included in the roster. Tobacco and
alcoholic beverages are particularly important in Zinacantan ritual

today as offerings to the gods and for human consumption. Other Indians (for instance Cuicatecs, Mazatecs) still use mushrooms and morning glory. In northern Mexico the list of ritual substances includes peyote.

"Flowers"

Many flowers were used for religious purposes by the prehispanic peoples, both in the context of ritual and as mythological symbols. Flowers were distinguished by shape, color, locale in which the plant grew, and other attributes such as their perceived beauty, texture, and "temperature."

The "flower" itself was a nodal, multivocal symbol, of major significance in prehispanic religious ideology. It named one of the calendar days, it represented live or sacrificial blood, it signified ornaments, poetry, beauty, articulate speech, vegetable nature, sophisticated thinking, philosophy, joy, love, games, sexual pleasure, venereal diseases, and a multitude of related convergent images (Sahagun, *Florentine Codex*; Leon-Portilla 1971; Seler 1963, 1:26, 156, and *passim*). Several gods which were complexes of these ideas relating to fertility in vegetation were named "Flower": Xochiquetzal (precious flower, female, or flowery bird, or flowery plume, or euphemistically, the goddess as beautiful as flowers or quetzal feathers), Macuilxochitl (five flower, male), Xochipilli (flower prince). The intricacies of flower symbolism have persisted in Zinacantan, as Laughlin (1962) has elegantly demonstrated.[4]

Specific flowers were identified symbolically with single ideas. For example, marigolds, perhaps because of their disagreeable smell, were flowers of the dead. It is also true that marigold plants flower most abundantly in the autumn, which in the space-time continuum and ritual calendar was the period for the ceremonies celebrating the dead and ancestors, and were therefore the most easily available flowers to use for offerings to the dead.

The category of flowers as ritual symbols also included plant

4. Vogt (1976) also contains an extensive analysis of Zinacantecan flower symbolism in ritual.

parts, which we do not consider flowers. In prehispanic times these formed a single symbol complex (as they still do in contemporary Zinacantan). Among these "flowers" were tender pine boughs, leaf sprouts, moss, and thorns. Huitzilopochtli, for example, was symbolized by flowers with thorns. In the sacred bundle that represented the god wrapped in many cloths were maguey thorns, symbols of the blood sacrifice to the god. In the *Tira de la Peregrinación*, sacrifices to Huitzilopochtli take place on top of thorny xerophitic plants, in this case maguey and viznagas (a kind of spherical cactus; see Illustration 5). In the foundation myth of Tenochtitlan the god appeared as an eagle perched on a thorny nopal cactus. Maguey thorns were also used for autosacrifice to Huitzilopochtli. Moreover, his direction, south, was called "the land of the thorns," which

5. Sacrificial victims of the god Huitzilopochtli, lying over viznaga and maguey plants. The god is being carried in his bundle on the back of a human bearer whose name is Black Snake. He is giving orders to his people and wearing his hummingbird headdress. *Tira de la Peregrinación Azteca*, section 4.

6. The hummingbird god drawn in the European manner, circa 1579, with the nopal plant. Plate 3 from *Book of the Gods and Rites and the Ancient Calendar*, by Fray Diego Duran. Copyright 1971 by the University of Oklahoma Press.

makes the thorn image clearly multivocal. The south was a "land of thorns" because prehispanic peoples believed it was a desert plain, overheated by the sun's great proximity.

Trees and Bushes

Certain trees were selected as symbols because they possessed attributes that Mesoamericans considered remarkable: strength of wood, longevity, position in the landscape, and so forth. Among them were the palm, the mesquite, the willow, the native oak, and the ceiba or silk-cotton tree. The flowers of the silk-cotton tree apparently provide hummingbirds with food, and this tree was a dominant symbol in Mayan mythology, as it is today in the Chiapas highlands (Holland 1964).

This category also included some mythical, imaginary trees, such as the jewel tree of the *Borgia Codex* (p. 49). Since specific mythical or real trees were associated with the cardinal directions, gods which were attributed to these directions in the space-time continuum were either mythically related to or were transformations of these trees (see *Codex Fejervary-Mayer*, p. 1). Huitzilopochtli had a palm, but was also associated with the silk-cotton tree (*ibid.*). Other trees, plants, or "flowers" which occurred in myths also acquired special associations with certain gods.

Corporeal Taxonomies or Classes
Sex

According to principles of classification based on man's animalmorphism—part of which would be what Tylor (1920) called animism—all the classes of the natural orders were distinguished by sex (male, female, or hermaphrodite). Mountains, caves, and other features of the landscape were personified and defined as having a specific sex. By metonymic linkage the sex of a deity and that of its mountain were the same.

The majority of the deities' apparitions were defined as either male or female. Many, moreover, were defined as actively sexual, as married couples. This principle governed the divine hierarchy of beings from top to bottom. The top deity itself was a duality, the male and female principle combined, the pristine image of the reproducing heterosexual parents. These two aspects of one god were Ometeotl (Ometecuhtli) and Omecihuatl ("two lord" and "two lady," or rather, dual lord and lady or, in a sense "the couple of deities"). They were also called Tonacatecuhtli and Tonacacihuatl, "our flesh lord and lady," or "lord and lady of our sustenance." In one of the Mayan versions, the *Popol Vuh*, they appear as "begetter of children" and "conceiver of children," or "creator" and "maker." As fire (heat) genitor and progenetrix, they were also seen collectively as "mother and father gods."

It is under this last name that they still exist in Zinacantan, imagined as the ancestral couples from which Zinacantecans descend to the present, and call the Totilme'iletik, from *totil*, father, *me7il*, mother, and *etik*, plural. One of these ancestors is the sun-father. Six other ancestors with their spouses took up residence in the mountains which delimit the sacred territory of Zinacantan, marking the sacred directions. The twelve mountains are arranged in six male-female pairs. The numbers apparently derive from local mythology about the original founders of the municipality (see Vogt 1969:298–

299, also discussion and map of mountains, pp. 375–390), but they overlap with a directional paradigm of sacred mountains and crosses. The mountain-deity system is replicated in the principal cross shrines in the central hamlet of Zinacantan, of which there are also twelve (*ibid.*, p. 388).

This pattern of assigning deities to specific mountains and giving them a sex is of prehispanic origin. Each major mountain marker in the Highland cultures indicated the divine territories of communities of city states and was the "home" of a deity of a specified sex. In the folklore of Mexico City, the two imposing volcanos Popocatepetl and Iztacihuatl are still imagined as a male and a female. They are a favorite illustration in popular calendar art. Present-day Cuicatec Indians also assign deities to mountains, give the mountains a "sex," and use them to define the limits of sacred territories.

Some of the most famous associations between mountains and deities, the myths for which have been preserved in the colonial written literature, are those for the valleys of Mexico and Puebla. One example, the volcano Malinche, was occupied as a home by Matlalcueye, the mother goddess of the Tlaxcaltecans, who was a transformational image of the goddess of water known in Nahuatl also as Chalchihuitlicue.

The most significant of all the contemporary associations between mountains and deities is that of the hill of Tepeyac, Guadalupe, which in prehispanic times bore a temple to the mother goddess Tonantzin and is now the site of the Catholic basilica to the Virgin of Guadalupe, the divine image of motherhood par excellence for all Mexicans (Wolf 1958; Turner 1974a:166–230). She is particularly dear to Indians because she is herself an Indian.

These mountains were not chosen in isolation, but were arranged in symbolic sets. Thus, for example, in the rituals of the Aztec month of Tepeilhuitl, women were sacrificed on five female mountains located in a ring around the city of Tenochtitlan. This ring was followed, in counterclockwise sequence, in a ritual march.

The mountains associated with deities and rituals in the Cuicatec region today also form mythic sets. These sets are arranged as geometric, cognitive paradigms, selected for their approximate position at the cardinal and intercardinal directions and points, alternating the sexes of the divine couples. Waterholes are similarly arranged, the paradigm approximating the actual geographic locations on a Western-style map. The Lowland Maya of prehispanic and colonial times also designated waterholes (sinkholes, *cenotes*) as sacred markers. An example from my own data shows how the Cuicatecs from Concepción Pápalo visualize the arrangement of the mountains in the district. Of all the mountains available, Cuicatecs select some only: the ones "which count." They assign to them gods who live in them, sex, colors, and other transformational code symbols. When all the mythic contrasts are mapped, a quincunx figure emerges, the points of which are sacred mountains, marked in Illustration 7 by sex and name. It is obvious that there is a relation between the positions of the mountains as informants describe them and as they appear in mythic contrast, and the actual locations. Sex is attributed according to height; the male mountains are all higher than the female mountains "because males are taller than females."

This example led me to suspect that the mountains and waterholes of Zinacantan are equally arranged as sets. The evidence I was able to muster from published data and from personal consultation with Evon Vogt suggests that this hypothesis is correct, although further research is needed to test the completeness of the imagery.

The waterholes of Zinacantan Center appear to be arranged in a paradigm as follows, with north approximately at the top of the page:

Nio7 (female)		Ya7ahvil (female)
Pat toj (male)	Popol Ton (male)	Ton tz'i7kin (male)
Ninab chilo7 (female)		Vo7ch'oj vo7 (female)

Each waterhole is linked with a mountain or sacred shrine, the sex of which it shares.

Similarly, in the Zinacantan rituals of visiting mountains, and in ritual prayer, the mountains appear in sequence, seemingly following the criteria of location and sex. For example, in the prayer for waterholes which Vogt (1976) reports, the names are listed as sets in

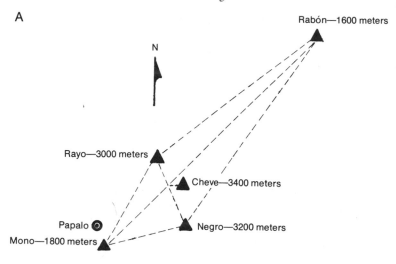

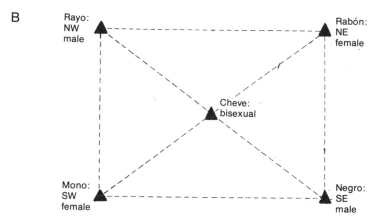

7. Arrangement of the quincunx of mountains of Papalo. (A) Locations according to Western-style mapping. (B) Locations by mythic contrast.

this order: (1) three male mountains and three female mountains at the south and east edges of the sacred quadrilateral paradigm of Zinacantan, (2) two male mountains (senior and junior) and a female waterhole ("Saint") in the northwest corner, (3) two male mountains (senior and junior) in the southwest corner, and (4) the four major saints in the altars of the Zinacantan Center churches, three male and one female. The paradigm then includes a route S → E → NW → SW → center, ten males, five females, the four corners of the world and the center. The prayer includes, near the end, the invocation to these sacred beings to "Observe us here ever, encircle us here ever. . . ."

In curing rituals, again, mountains are selected for visits following various patterns of combination. "The most common order is San Cristobal, Mushul Vits, Sisil Vits, and Kalvario" (Vogt 1969:433). These mountains form a small quadrilateral unit near Zinacantan Center, and two are male, two female.

I have not been able to determine from published materials whether other mountain patterns used for ritual or prayer in Zinacantan follow equivalent paradigms. I suspect, however, that similar patterns may be used in other contexts. Obviously only further research can test this suggestion. If my hypothesis is correct, other groups of mountains that are chosen for ritual ought to be similar in orientation and have similar sex associations. It should be noted, however, that what counts in the pattern is not the "actual" geographic location as we see it on a map or measure it with a compass, but the relative positions of the mountains in a set vis-à-vis each other, that is, their being seen as a paradigmatic set. This distinction is important because our ideas about exact measurements do not allow for the rough and ready method of measuring by eye practiced in the native culture. Furthermore, I suspect, on the basis of published evidence, that the mountains form sets of units in which each unit itself includes three subunits: a waterhole, a senior mountain, and a junior mountain. However, this pattern is incomplete—either in Zinacantan paradigmatic symbolization or in the data available to me.

The role of the parent gods, that of normal, sexually mature adults, was not the only one manifested in the traditional iconography. Unlike Western society, where sexual deviants and anomalies are ignored, avoided, or rejected, Mesoamerican Indian culture seemed to recognize these roles and incorporate them as part of the human-sacred experience. Some of the deities had ambiguous sexual attributes, and some, in fact, represented bisexual or homosexual, beings. The typical example is the complex of the so-called "goddess" Cihuacoatl ("woman-snake") and Tlazolteotl ("filth deity"). This deity has usually been interpreted by students of Mesoamerican religion as one of the fertile mother-goddesses. In my opinion, the evidence is abundant and clear that she also represented in some of her aspects an inversion of normal female sexuality, by means of several combined images of female infertility, male homosexuality and other forms of sexual incapacity or deviance. Seler, in particular, made many mistakes about the sexual symbolism of the deities, probably because there was much Victorian repression of a personal kind in his interpretations. Thus, he labeled practically any sexual image as "fertility" or as indicating "the pleasure of the senses," when in fact some mean dripping menstrual blood, others mean the act of coitus, death in labor, and so on. Images of opposed attributes, sexual "purity" and "pollution," normal and abnormal sexuality, he also blanketed all together under the general category of the sexual symbolism of "fertility." He does not seem to have had the same problems with Thanatos (death, aggression) that he had with Libido or Eros!

Cihuacoatl was said in sixteenth-century myths (by Sahagun's informants) to have a tail, and a fake baby, which was not a baby at all but a flint knife wrapped up in a bundle. Her name "snake woman" suggests the tail, since the snake can be seen as a tail, but it also suggests the penis; thus, Cihuacoatl is "a woman with a penis." In some codex paintings (*Borgia* group) she is drawn with the snake coming out from under her skirt and between the legs. Often the skirt is actually a male loin cloth. She was related to other images of multiple deities of abnormal sexuality, the *cihuapipiltin* or *cihuateteo*. Cihuacoatl and Tlazolteotl had distinct subdeity images, the general category of cihuapipiltin. One of these was an image of the "abandoned mistress" or "unloved wife." She is pictured in the codices with wild hair, her head turned to look backward, unhappy, and with tears in her eyes. The Aztec called her Ixnextli, which means "with the eyes full of ashes." She represented failure in marital love, an unfinished adult, immature sexuality, *and* dirty things, symbolized by a bowl full of excrement she held in her hand. She was also related to the deer, and wore a deer headdress (for example in the *Borgia Codex*, p. 59, central figure at the bottom). In contemporary Spanish-speaking Mexico she still exists under the name La Llorona (the crying woman). One of her relatives was another *cihuapipil*, who had reversed head and abnormal feet. She appeared in the shape of a man's lover at crossroads and in the western sky, to scare libidinous men. She also had wild hair. Pictures with this representation can be found in the *Codex Vaticanus*, where she is naked above the waist and wearing a male loincloth on the lower part of her body. As I will show below, these divine morbid images are still alive in the religion of Mesoamerican Indians.

The *cihuateteo*, in a general sense, were deified women who had died during pregnancy or in childbirth, that is, women who had been incapable of normal sexual reproduction. They were also the stars of the western sky. This deity complex was associated with Mictlacihuatl, "death-woman," or "the lady of Mictlan, the land of the dead," goddess of the underworld. All these "female" figures belonged to the direction of darkness, sunset, the west (Cihuatlampa = land of women). It was from that direction that they appeared at night. They were souls of "female warriors." Male warriors belonged to the easterly direction. Cihuacoatl's temple in Tenochtitlan was in the dark region, the northwest of the city called Coatlan ("snake land") after her. Her home was Tlillancalco, the "black house" or "house of darkness." She and her assistants were also responsible for "black diseases," and for killing children. Those born on the day of these goddesses were "perverted," had "vices, drunkenness, corruption." Women born that day were "like dogs" (that is, promiscuous and gossips) (Sahagun, *Florentine Codex*, Book 6, Part VII:161–165, III-2, Part V and VI:81, 107, 108).

Since the images of the fertile mother goddesses have been confused with the totality of Tlazolteotl-Cihuacoatl, contemporary analysis of this divine image which sometimes represents anomalous sexuality has been muddled. Contemporary evidence for this symbol still exists both in the Cuicatec region and the Puebla-Nahuatl area, and in a modified structural pattern she also exists in Zinacantan. Among the Cuicatec, she is called by the Nahuatl name Matlacihuatl or Maxtlicihuatl (homophone of Mictlacihuatl) and the Spanish name Mujer Enredadora. Her Nahuatl name means several things. A *maxtli* is a loin cloth, a male garment which is wrapped around the genitals (as the figure appears in the *Codex Vaticanus*). The first part of the name is also a word for net, snare, or trap. Thus, she is "a woman who wears a man's loin cloth" (perhaps an euphemism for penis), or "a woman who ensnares." The Spanish name means exactly that, "ensnaring woman."

Her femaleness, however, is only a disguise to trap men. The Matlacihuatl appears to drunkards, and to adulterous, promiscuous, or homosexual men, and tries to trick them and seduce them. She appears in the guise of a man's sweetheart, but is not the real beloved. She is a fake. If she offers food, a man can recognize that she is a fake because her food is not salted, which means she is a thing from outside the range of civilization, culture, or society. Salted food = cooked food : : unsalted food = uncooked food : : uncooked food = wild : : cooked food = normal, cultured, civilized. If a man puts salt on the food the Matlacihuatl brings, it is transformed into wild and rotten things. Tortilla cakes become oak leaves, turkey meat becomes rotten white wood, sugar cane beer becomes muddy water. Wild or rotten uneatable things : Matlacihuatl : : good cooked food : real woman. She is wild in other ways too: her hair, like that of wild animals, idiots, mad persons (who are outside the realm of culture), or bewitched people, cannot be combed down and is constantly tangled. Normal cultured humans : combed hair : : abnormal (wild) humans : tangled hair.

She has two other characteristics that directly define her as sexually abnormal. Her feet are reversed, the toes pointing backward, a visual euphemism for homosexuals, who among the Cuicatec are sometimes called "reversed walkers." Moreover, instead of a vagina, she has "a hole like a mouth in the back of her neck." This is a complicated symbolic inversion. In the Cuicatec language the anus is literally "the mouth of the buttocks." The hole in the back of the neck multiplies the Matlacihuatl's sexual anomalies. Instead of having her genitals in the lower front part of the body, she has them at the back and in the upper section. The front-back reversal is the obvious image of sodomy, which is reinforced by calling the hole in the back of the neck a "mouth," as the anus is also called. This image is reinforced by the reversed feet, also a symbol of intercourse between sodomites.

Moreover, the myths ascribe other anomalous attributes to her. If a man is seduced by her, he becomes pregnant and produces a "baby resembling feces." This reversal again points to men who act like women, and sodomy, since the product of the anus is feces, not babies.

If a man is wise and refuses to be seduced by her, he can use a defensive strategy to cope with her advances. He can light a cigarette, and put it inside the hole in the back of her neck. When it burns her, she becomes a snake and runs away to hide in the grass. The cigarette seems to stand for another multivocal symbol. First (as any Freudian could tell!), it is a penislike object, introduced in a vaginalike hole. But it is also the inversion of the natural sexual act. The cigarette burns her, giving pain rather than pleasure—it cooks her. It also normalizes her, or rather sends her back to the wilderness where she belongs, by transforming her into a snake. Her final transformation into a snake (another penislike image) is the ultimate assertion of her nonfemininity.

In addition to this array of symbolic inversions, Matlacihuatl has a further abnormality. She chooses to appear to men at times when it is forbidden to have sexual intercourse (during the middle of the day) and in places where it is inappropriate to do so, for example, when a man is walking along a public road or working in a corn field.

Matlacihuatls are also called in Cuicatec "black ladies," which links them with their structural antecedent, the Cihuacoatl aspect of inversion. They are, moreover, responsible for having brought into the world the "black disease," *tifus exantemática* (in Nahuatl called *matlazahuatl*, a sacred pun on Matlacihuatl).

The set of symbolic inversions may be summarized as follows:

Normal woman	*Matlacihuatl*
Reproduces by being fertilized	Fertilizes the male
Produces babies	Men produce a baby resembling feces
Has a clitoris	Has a tail (penis) like a snake
Wears a *huipil*	Wears a loin cloth
Cooks and salts her food, which is part of normal diet (turkey meat, tortillas, beer)	Serves unsalted food, which becomes inedible rotten and wild things (oak leaves, rotten wood, muddy water)
Wears neat braids	Keeps her hair tangled
Feet and toes point forward	Feet and toes point backward
Has a vagina, a hole in front lower part of her body	Has a "mouth in back of her neck," a hole in back upper part of body
In intercourse receives a male penis, a pleasurable experience.	Receives a lighted cigarette which burns her, a painful experience.

Cihuacoatl's negative images are elaborated extensively in the Cuicatec version of this supernatural being. However, I suspect that many of these images were already present in the sixteenth century since the codex pictures show the same physical attributes. Olivera (1969) reports a myth from a town in the valley of Puebla, where the same images of a "female with a tail" and of sodomy also occur, in a different region of Mexico and a different mythic context. Here she is called by her old name of *cihuatlpipil*. Moreover, Cihuacoatl lives in the house of darkness, a black house, while the Cuicatec figure, too, is black, lives in a dark cave, and afflicts with a black disease. Furthermore, the Matlacihuatl likewise "lives in the west," the sunset region. Her cave is a barranca west of the villages, often called Barranca of the Dead.

The reader may ask why I have indulged in this long digression about a prehispanic Nahuatl deity and a contemporary Cuicatec one. How is it relevant to the symbolism of Zinacantan? The answer is that this same supernatural creature appears in Zinacantan's myths under several names. She is also a complex of beings. Her closest equivalent, as Robert Laughlin pointed out to me, is the Xpak'inte7. Second, she is the Charcoal Cruncher. But there is also a structural variant for both of them, which is male, not found in the Cuicatec area.

The Xpak'inte7 is the perfect twin of Matlacihuatl. Although her name has no exact translation, she is an "evil female spirit" (Laughlin, personal communication). "She takes the appearance of a man's wife to lure a hapless drunk into a clump of magueys. The back of her head is hollow. Her hair is made of poisonous caterpillars. When the drunk touches her sexual parts they turn into excrement. When he strikes her she turns into a tree" (*ibid.*). She is the spirit of a stillborn fetus (Blaffer 1972:105). She also turns into rotten things and excrement when she is exposed (*ibid.*, p. 7). Thus, here too she is associated with wasted sexuality and misbehavior: drunkenness, abnormal pregnancy, sodomy, excrement, rotten wood. Not only is her myth alive in Zinacantan, but she is known throughout southern Mesoamerica under various local names, walking with reversed feet (*ibid.*, p. 150). The male version is called Long Hair or Feet Turnabout, and one of his faces is backward. Robert Laughlin tells me he appears in the rituals of winter under the name Mossman.

The Charcoal Cruncher is the modern Ixnextli, deer headdress and all! The Charcoal Cruncher (prehispanically called "the one with the eyes full of ashes") is a "black being," cold like the dead, who eats a dead, burnt thing: charcoal. Vogt (1969:332–340) reports a long myth about her. She too is an image of female sexual abnormality, expressed as a series of inversions, transpositions and reversals. The Zinacantan Charcoal Cruncher, unlike her peer the Xpak'inte7 or the Cuicatec-related figure Matlacihuatl, is "married," but her sexual abnormalities are there, although more carefully hidden. Her abnormal tail and neck symbols are mentioned only once in tales about her. One of Robert Laughlin's female informants said that the Charcoal Cruncher belonged to the male sex.

But the Charcoal Cruncher, as described in the central myth about her, is an abnormal person indeed: instead of food she crunches charcoal. Her head has been separated from the body, by means of salt (cooking her), and it roams alone. Her husband, rather than remaining loyal, makes a coalition with his mother against her (again a symbol of unsuccessful marital love and sexuality, since he has not transferred his libidinal attachments from mother to wife). The Charcoal Cruncher tries to have a child, but the baby fails to nurse. The man (spouse) rubs *salt* (semen?) *on her tail and her neck*, to bewitch her and get rid of her. At the normal time for going to bed, she gets up. At the time for chatting or making conversation, she dozes and nods her head. Instead of entering houses through the door, she jumps atop walls. Unlike good women, successful wives, who are clean, her head is filthy from sleeping on the hearth full of ashes and eating charcoal. Finally, her unattached head fastens itself to the man's neck, so that ultimately people think *he* is a "double-headed hermaphrodite, with long hair." Like the Cuicatec Matlacihuatl, her long hair is also wild, unruly and uncombed.

In despair, the man tricks her into going to the woods (wildness), where he offers her "wild awful fruits" to eat, and the loose head ends by attaching itself to a wild thing, *a deer* which passes by. The deer enters a cave, where the she-head is eaten by a coyote. The man kills the deer, buries the headless body, and humanity is rid of her.

I have paraphrased this Zinacantecan story to highlight its similarities of inversion to those of earlier myths. Thus, although Mesoamerican peoples recognize the existence of sexually anomalous beings, they certainly do not approve of them. They identify them with wild things, things of darkness, sickness, infertility, death, trickery, animals, and behavior that would be inappropriate in normal, sexually mature, adult humans. Both physically and morally, the Cihuacoatl, Ixnextli, and *cihuapipiltin* of yesteryear and the Matlacihuatl, Xpak'inte7, Llorona, and Charcoal Cruncher of the present are companions in imagery and destiny (see also Blaffer 1972 for other Mesoamerican variants of the Charcoal Cruncher).

I suspect that the image of Cihuacoatl in Zinacantan has been divided in the process of syncretization. The bad aspects appear in the contemporary image of the Charcoal Cruncher, destroyed by salt. The sacred, good aspects (for instance, her association with salt in the aspect of Huixtocihuatl, salt patroness) have been transferred to the Virgin of the Rosary, patroness of salt. The Virgin of the Rosary in Zinacantan, like Cihuacoatl, belongs in the western quarter of the space-time continuum, where her chapel is located. Later I shall discuss this set of associations in more detail.

However, the majority of the sacred divine images were defined as sexually normal. Besides the divine parental couples, there were adolescent, sexually appealing gods and goddesses, as well as child-like ones. Xochipilli and Xochiquetzal, for example, both spring-summer divinities, were images of play, sexual attractiveness, the fertile season and the spring of a human life. They symbolized beauty like that of the flowers after which they were named. They represented youthful sexuality, the normal sexuality of the young growing human. These images have been syncretized today among Mesoamerican Indians with the images of the young Jesus and other male saints, and those of young Mary or other female saints.

Sexual imagery was and is also used to speak of the places of origin of ethnic groups, which were identified with caves or wombs, original vaginas from which came forth the ancestors of the prehispanic nations (for a comparative case, see Myerhoff 1974:139). In the codices, these are often imagined as flower-shaped or as caves with the shape of multichambered wombs. There is evidence that, in fact, the people "emerged from caves," in the sense that the earlier inhabitants of New Spain, like all prehistoric peoples, actually once lived in caves and rock shelters, when they were still hunters and gatherers, before the invention of houses and villages (see MacNeish and Peterson 1962, for a Chiapas case; see also NacNeish and Byers 1967: vol. 1). In the *Relaciones de Texcoco* there are several references to this topic (Pomar 1941:7–55).

Thus, their myths about the days before the discovery or invention of agriculture, weaving, cooking (in other words, culture), when they lived in caves, are actually oral history statements, remembered by the local traditions, about the period in which culture as they know it now came to be. This is the culture of a settled agrarian people who live in villages. However, the mythic cave-vaginas, the maternal wombs from which their culture emerged, also constitute another multivocal image, which reflects other culture traits. First, it reflects the fact that many prehispanic towns were built around early cave settlements, and indeed some cities of the Mesoamerican urban complex grew around these original settlements, while the caves became sacred precincts, temples, or specially sought-after ritual centers for worship (Heyden 1973; Thompson 1959).

There is also conclusive evidence that prehispanic peoples, like their modern counterparts, carried out a large number of rituals, and sometimes buried their dead, in caves near their settlements or in cavelike chambers in their pyramids (= manmade mountains). Thus, these caves are imagined simultaneously as womb-vaginas and as mouths that swallow dead souls, entrances to the underworld from which man once emerged and to which he returns after a short journey on the earth's surface.

The landscape of Mesoamerica, much of it limestone, is dotted with caves and depressions, or "sinkholes." These dark places, with dripping stalactites and jagged stalagmites, often with subterranean rivers opening into them, wet, dank, full of echoes and mysterious noises, are in fact today places of worship. Often important archaeological remains have been found in them, showing that they have been used for sacred purposes since prehistoric times. It is not surprising that contemporary Indians continue to perceive them with awe. I myself, entering one of these caves, felt an overwhelming sense of the esoteric and arcane and fell into a mood of shadowy thought.

Zinacantan Indians share this symbolism, and much ritual activity centers around caves, which are also seen as vaginal entrances to the universal womb of the earth. The Zinacantan caves are "symbols of fear and uncertainty, symbols of special intensity. The cave is a place where people are swallowed up" (from a Laughlin manuscript quoted in Bricker 1973:57). It is in one such cave, underneath the "senior large mountain," Bankilal Muk'ta Vits, the most sacred mountain of Zinacantan, that the house and corrals for the soul counterparts of Zinacantecans are kept by the deities (Vogt 1969:371–383).

Cave-wombs, burial holes, are not always objects of fear. Although their inhabitants are indeed fearful creatures, Black Men with long penises, carnivorous jaguars, the ambivalent Lord of the Earth, these are also sometimes treated in ritual as images of laughable, incompetent, and ridiculous precivilized men. Simultaneously they represent the mysteries of origin and reproduction, of a dark ancestral past, and the superiority of living, civilized, cultured Zinacantecans for whom sex is a tamed, domesticated aspect of life. So in the humor plays of ritual, they are treated as sources of laughter and ridicule, and the cave-vaginas and Black Men-penises figure in hilarious puns and word games which are manifestly about sacred beings but obviously also about obscene topics, jokes about sexual intercourse, about incredible sexual anatomy and even more incredible sexual feats (Bricker 1973:65–67, 114). Zinacantecans, like us, are equally impressed with the mysteries of sexual reproduction and capable of taking the whole issue with a sense of humor. Sex is at once sacred mystery and beauty and profane joke.

Stages of Growth and the Ages of Man

Stages in the life cycle were recognized in all things. The Aztecs distinguished four basic stages: childhood, youth, adulthood, and old age (Duran 1971: 113–114). In Zinacantan today the same distinctions are made. The stages are: *ʒunen*, until weaning, near age three; *krem* (male) and *tseb* (female), until marriage; *vinik* (male) and *ʒantz* (female) until near the age of forty-five; and *mol* (male) and *meʒel* (female) for respected old persons (Vogt 1969:182).

The prehispanic gods, like men, had been born and could die, and they too passed through life stages. In fact, they were symbolically born, grew up, and died every year in the calendrical ritual cycle of holy feasts, just as in the Christian calendar Jesus is born every Christmas and dies at the end of Lent. In some codices the gods are pictured with their calendrical birthdays connected to their bodies by umbilical cords, to symbolize their humanlike life cycle.

However, every god had an age which was dominant as his symbolic marker. For example, Toci, "the mother of the gods," signified adulthood, while Huitzilopochtli was a male at the top of his youthful powers, a *telpochtli* (youthful male) idealized as the model warrior (*oquichtli*). His name was thus a play on the words *opochtli* (left-handed), *telpochtli* and *oquichtli*, all concepts that were part of his image.

The prehispanic yearly ritual calendar was arranged in linear fashion according to the logic of the growth and age-stages of the transformational system. The year's ritual cycle moved through four quarters. The beginning of the year was the period of the spring equinox = start of the rainy season = the birth of maize (that is, the beginning of the planting season) = sacrificial rituals of children, and the celebration of childlike and young gods (for example, *Tlaloques*) = symbols of small animals (for example, frog, hummingbird). The second quarter celebrated youth, the period of the summer solstice = maize at the flowering stage = flowers = sacrifices of young men and female virgins = celebration of youthful, sexually appealing gods (for example, Xochipilli). A third group of rituals celebrated adulthood and the fertile married state = autumnal equinox = the full corn cob before the harvest = woman's labor in childbirth = male warring and hunting activities = the homestead, a symbol of marriage = the celebration of married pairs of fertile gods of parental age and postpartum goddesses (for example, Xochiquetzal—an image of youthful motherhood as well as of adolescence—Coatlicue, Camaxtli) and their newborn baby gods or "returned" gods (for example, Huitzilopochtli). The rituals of the fourth quarter were concerned with old age = the winter solstice period = old or defeated sun = end of the rainy season = end of harvesting and the hunting season = barren = dry = wrinkled = rituals for old people = celebration of elderly gods and postmenopausal goddesses (for example, Ilamatecuhtli). The penultimate month of the year was named for these "wrinkled ones." The last month, named Resuscitation or Resurrection, was the overture to the new birth and year.

Table 2. Transformational periods of the prehispanic ritual calendar cycle
which follow the age-growth cycle

	Months included (18 of 20 days)			
...nsformational ...ss	1st quarter (5 months)	2nd quarter (4 months)	3rd quarter (4 months)	4th quarter (5 months)
...asons	Spring	Summer	Autumn	Winter
...n position	Vernal equinox— southern sun ascending	Summer solstice— southern sun victorious	Autumnal equinox— northern sun descending	Winter solstice— northern sun, defeat & recuperation
...ter	Rain begins; irrigation canals shut off; dry season ended	Season of strong rains	Rains diminishing	Rain ends; opening of irrigation canals; dry season
...riculture of ...ize-growth ...le	Begin planting 1st maize crop; earth's vegetation cover revives	Flowering of maize & other plants; flower and reed harvest	Solid corn cobs; begin harvest of major maize crop	Post-harvest hunting season
... group rituals	Childhood sacrifices and offerings; child-growing rituals	Adolescence, youthful virginity; phallic games	Adulthood, fertile married state; sacrifices, rituals, & offerings for family homestead	Old age, ritual sacrifices and games of old women
	Presexual	Potential sexuality	Realized sexuality	Barren = postsexual = postmenopausal
...dinal direction	East	South	West	North
...inant color	Blue-green (turquoise)	White	Yellow	Red
	Cane (or reed)	Rabbit	House (home)	Knife (flint)
...s—general ...gories ...brated	Childlike or small gods (e.g., *Tlaloque*), Earth renewal gods (e.g., Xipe Totec)	Youthful, sexually appealing gods (e.g., Xochipilli), game and flower gods	Adult, fertile gods, parental gods with newborn gods (e.g, Coatlicue, Huitzilopochtli reborn)	Postmenopausal, elderly gods (e.g., llamatecuhtli)

...te: Time grain, amplitude, rate and synchronization were not exact but fluid. Stages were roughly dis-...ished from the continous flow of time, growth, and change. Thus, periods were unequal, some ritual ...s were longer or shorter than those at other transformational levels, and ended later or started earlier ... young virgin sacrifices started in the fourth month). For definition of time grain, synchronization, and ...r terms, see Lynch 1972. Dominant colors are given according to Duran 1971, plate 35.

Thus, Huitzilopochtli, the blue-green "baby" hummingbird, born at the end of the dry season, came back with the new year, flying in the sky. In the poem he is first imagined as the small (= childlike) hummingbird resurrected in spring (east), then transmuted or grown into the mythical big (= grown) white eagle or hawk (south), which symbolizes the growth of spring into the summer period and the ascending (= growing) sun. This period coincides with the beginning of rain and of the planting season. How the symbolism fits Zinacantan today will be discussed in the last sections of this work.

Zinacantecans exhibit one major concern that ties together age and the sacredness of the universe. All sacred beings, as well as human officers of the village, secular and sacred objects, such as mountains, drums, and the images of Christian saints, the sun and moon, siblings in the nuclear family, and so on, are classified hierarchically as senior or junior to each other. The pairing of senior-junior sacred dualities is of prehispanic origin. For example, in Huitzilopochtli's rituals, a small junior sculptured image was carried in the procession. The senior-junior distinction is implicit in the duality aspect of all deities.

Parts of the Body

Parts of the body were transformationally related, by mythopoetic analogy, to other transformational levels, for example, to day signs and to gods' signs. One of the most elegant and amusing examples of these associations occurs in the *Borgia Codex*, p. 17 (Seler 1963; see illustration 8). The god of all directions, Tezcatlipoca, the omnipresent (referred to here as god of the body parts), is depicted with the twenty day-name signs of the month, attached (metonymically and metaphorically) to parts of his body and clothing. The humor and irony of the metaphors is astonishing. For example, the day-name sign "Movement" is placed on the tongue near the cheek. Out of the mouth comes the word or speech symbol pictured as the day name "Flower," which makes sense if we remember our own expression "flowery speech" (see Leon-Portilla 1971: 447–451, esp. 450, discussion of the concept "flower and song"). The feet are the day names of the earth symbols "Jaguar" and "*Cipactli*," since feet touch the earth. The hair is "*Malinalli*," the day name twisted straw. The bowels are the day name "House," while the stomach, which "chops up food," is represented by the day sign "Knife." The front end of the loin cloth is the phallic snake. The back of the loin cloth

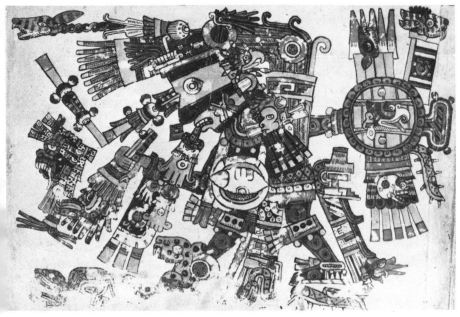

8. Tezcatlipoca with the twenty day signs attached to parts of his body. *Borgia Codex*, p. 17.

contains the symbol of the day name "Wind." Seler, a true Victorian, interpreted this last sign as "insinuating" that the loin cloth "waves with the wind" when a man walks (Seler 1963: 207).

The classification of body parts was also attached to the gods' images. For example, Huitzilopochtli was associated with the left hand and left-handedness (homonym of part of his name). In the body transformations shown in the *Borgia Codex* he is alluded to by the day sign of a bird of prey. The bird's head is centered in a shield (= warrior) that the god holds in his left hand. Tlaloc was often identified simply by his round eyes, which look like goggles; postmenopausal goddesses were identified by their dry hanging breasts.

Body parts were also related to the earth as a living thing. For example, the center of the earth was the umbilicus, mountains were its back, and the underworld the bowels. Zinacantecans today also use the body parts as earth symbols (for instance, the navel) and as symbols for parts of the house. Miller (1974) analyzes in detail a Mayan mural which portrays with subtle imagery the body symbolism of the universe, particularly the umbilical cord and navel which represent the celestial axis from pole to pole and the center of the universe. The contemporary Chontal Indians seem to have developed a body taxonomy into a complex subsystem that pervades other symbolic domains; thus ritual offerings of wood are laid down in bundles, the spatial arrangement representing body parts (Carrasco 1960).

Sickness

Prehispanic peoples had a sophisticated medical science and pharmacopoeia which dealt with the taxonomy of illness and its treatment. From the religious point of view, sickness was utilized in a transformational subsystem, which had associations with cardinal directionality and with the gods. Thus, water diseases (for example, "amniotic water," or pregnancy diseases), or death by drowning, belonged to the water gods of the eastern paradise. Xolotl and Tezcatlipoca, both gods depicted with body deformations, were protectors of handicapped or deformed people. The god Xipe or red Tezcatlipoca controlled eye diseases (see explanation in the discussion of the planet Mars, p. 144, below). The divine hummingbird of Zinacantan can be eaten to cure epilepsy (Robert Laughlin, personal communication). I believe this last to be a case of allopathic magic: a bird which has perfect control of its movements is used as medicine for a disease that has as its main symptom uncontrollable movement.

Among contemporary Cuicatec Indians parts of the body and diseases, together with the cardinal directions and year periods, form a system of transformational interchanges. The combination of symbols from each of these codes is the cognitive core of the divinatory rituals of shamans. Moreover, the parts of a house and those of the body are another transformational subsystem, the roof being the head, the door the mouth, the walls the stomach, the hearth the heart, and so forth. The body-house taxonomy is also extant in Zinacantan.

Furthermore, certain ritual roles were performed by individuals in public cults, "as the result of a vow, often in order to be cured of a disease connected with the god being worshipped" (Carrasco P. 1971a:359). In contemporary Indian Mexico this symbolism has been transferred to Roman Catholic saints. Many of the saints are said to cure specific illnesses, for which they are "controllers." Mexican church altars are full of small silver offerings in the shape of body parts left to thank a particular saint for a cure. Grateful patients will also vow to supply the saint with flowers and wear the saint's typical clothing for a period of time, such as a year.

It is important to note that the prehispanic system of medical treatment was thoroughly bound up with the religious system and cosmic symbolism. This union has been preserved in the present-day medical systems of Mesoamerican Indians, including the complex curing rituals and symbolism in Zinacantan. Vogt (1976) treats these symbols in detail.

We must now pause, and move from the surface of the earth, with its animals, plants, mountains, and human beings, to a higher sphere of phenomena: the cosmos. New mysteries and surprises await us there.

CHAPTER **4**

The Cosmos

In Mesoamerican thought, the divinities encompassed all the mysteries of the universe, small and large. In the preceding chapter I focused on the small symbols of everyday life—the environment of man's daily existence, the house, man's own body, the animals he knew, the plants he cultivated, the landscape he inhabited. Beyond man the world extended in infinite grace and grandeur. Mesoamerican culture, in this mytho-poetic vision, gave much thought to the mysteries of such cosmic arrangements. It ordered the elements and deified them in a complex transformational taxonomy. This macrotaxonomy included subtaxonomies of winds, water, fire, and other elements and primary forces of cosmic nature, as well as major celestial objects, stars and planets.

Natural Phenomena—The Elements
Winds

The prehispanic class of winds has not yet been fully analyzed or understood. Wind as a general concept was a day name and a god, *Ehecatl*. However, "wind" appears to have included a classification of winds by four directions of origin, season of the year, velocity and such other variables as their beneficial or harmful quality for man and his habitat. Some named winds were singled out as religious symbols, among them small winds (*aires*) which could bring disease, and strong easterly and northerly winds (hurricanes) which accompanied rains. The strong winds were sometimes identified with the god of the morning star, Quetzalcoatl Ehecatl, god of the east, according to Seler, but also were symbolized in the gods of the four directions of storms and of rain, and winds which were said to occur only during the equinoctial periods.[1] A special windstorm that produced waterspouts, whirlwinds, and tornadoes was a key image of the god Tezcatlipoca, from whom Huitzilopochtli unfolded as one of his quadripartite sections. The relevance of this relationship will be seen later in this work.

Several of the other major gods who had direct cardinal associations or transformations also unfolded into four or five aspects, sometimes each with a different name and associated with a different time period, and a different cardinal direction and color. The "unfoldings" in the myths are expressed in many different rhetorical devices, such as: "the god divided into . . ." or, "he changed into . . ." or, "he doubled himself into . . ." or, "he was truly four . . . ." The myths also spoke of four brothers or sisters who were really only one deity. Another common rhetorical device is to list the divisions of the deity by enumerating its sequential names. In the codices, the "unfoldings" are usually pictured literally on sequences of folded pages. (Codices were not like our books; they were either rolled strips or pages folded in accordion fashion. To move from one picture of a god to another, one must literally unfold the pages, or "unfold the god's images.") There are several other pictorial devices to indicate similar divine transformations. I will illustrate with some famous ones.

Sets of the four aspects of a god represented the cardinal directions and four undefined units of time. The usual arrangement was from east, to north, to west, to south. Another common pattern follows the order west, south, east and north. For example, in the *Borgia Codex* a divinity is pictured unfolded into four world bearers or cosmic supports. He appears (on the upper parts of the pages) as follows: page 49 is west; page 50 is south; page 51 is east; and page 52

1. Dr. Phillip Wagner, a geographer and Mesoamericanist, tells me that in many regions of Mexico in fact the equinoctial periods produce what have been called "equinoctial storms" (personal communication, 1973). These are actually hurricane and cyclonic storms that originate in the east, the Gulf of Mexico, and sweep over Mesoamerica. Their existence explains the association of spring and summer with east plus southeast (the Gulf) in prehispanic thought. The major period of cyclonic activity is from May to October (Comision del Papaloapam, 1956). The period from November to April, in contrast, is characterized by subtropical calms.

is north. Sometimes there were five rather than four unfoldings, which appeared on five sequential pages in the codex. The fifth or new dimension represented the center in space and the totality of time. This space-time position usually came last in the page sequence. However, it sometimes appeared in the third position, reinforcing the idea of centrality.

On the lower sections of pages 49 to 53 of the *Borgia Codex*, the five aspects of a deity are represented as divine regions of the cosmos. Page 49 is east; page 50 is north; page 51 is west; page 52 is south; page 53, the last, is the center. However, not all such representations are on sequential pages. Sometimes the painter of the sacred book utilized the page spaces in a different way. The second most common style arranges the aspects of the deity in the four corners of a single page, which are read counterclockwise in boustrophedon fashion. When the five aspects are pictured on a single page, the fifth occupies the center of the drawing. On page 28 of the *Borgia Codex*, windstorms and rain are deified following this pattern. Page 27 of the same codex depicts five aspects of the god of windstorms and rain in space-time. Each image of the god at a corner of the page, represents one cardinal direction, one year name, the associated colors, and other symbols that were used to divine the characteristics of the year the god meant to send to mankind. The order is bottom right, top right, top left, bottom left, and then the center. The center picture shows the same god inside a rectangle, in his image as the rain which comes straight down from the sky above. To indicate that the center does not correspond to any year in particular, but to all time, on top of the god there is drawn the image of "unmarked" or "liminal time," the "boundary of night and day": a divided circle, with one half showing the sun and the other the starry sky. The total picture reads as follows:

Place on the page	Time period & position	Direction	Color of god	Divinatory value based on associated symbols in picture
Bottom right	year Cane, first position	east	black	headdress of *cipactli* (the earth) and cloudy sky; a fertile year

Top right	year Flint, second position	north	yellow	headdress of death and fiery sunny sky; a drought year
Top left	year House, third position	west	blue	headdress of monkey, the "man" who died in deluge, dark heavy clouds; a flood year
Bottom Left	year Rabbit, fourth position	south	red	headdress of buzzard, fiery sunny sky, rotten corn eaten by mice; year of plagues and failure of the corn crops
Center	out of time, all time, fifth position	center	striped white	no year-marker headdress, the circle of celestial liminality

Some pictorial manuscripts unfold the aspects of a deity in unusual patterns of visual display. In the *Cospi Codex* (also called *Bolonia* or *Bologna*), there is one of these rare divine sequences. A section of the codex is dedicated to the time periods and spatial travels of the planet Venus. The image of the planet is depicted as the god Tlahuizcalpantecuhtli in his fierce aspect. He is angrily throwing darts at his enemies. His appearance is fearful indeed, because he is wearing a skull mask with fangs. He unfolds into five directions and periods, each with complex related symbols, as follows:

Place on the page	Time period	Direction	Color of god	Enemy facing	Element
Bottom of first page	first	east	greenish black	yellow Centeotl of the west	corn
Top of first page	second	west	white	Chalchihuitlicue of the east	surface water
Top of second page	third	center	yellow	mountain of war the central city of warriors	earth
Bottom of second page	fourth	north	reddish	royal hummingbird of the south	sun fire
Bottom of third page	fifth	south	blue	jaguar of Tezcatlipoca of the north	blood

Top of third page: empty

The unfolding of a god into separate four-sided or five-sided manifestations was most typical of planetary deities, but also occurred in connection with deities which represented elements of weather, such as wind and rain, and symbolized meteorological values used in weather prediction. The predictions were based on diadic oppositions of the visual values. For example, in the *Cospi* picture just described, the deity and his enemies appear in dual sets of oppositions. The east god, black, is opposed to the west of the same god, which is white. The enemy of east is west, the enemy of west is east. The north god, red, is opposed to the south of the same god, which is blue. The enemy of north-red is south-blue (the hummingbird). The enemy of south-blue is north-red (blood). Reading down the element column in sequence, the pairs represent complementary ideas. Corn is followed by the surface water, which feeds it. Surface water is followed by earth, over which it runs. Earth is followed by the sun that warms it. The sun is followed by the sacrificial blood, which feeds it.

Tezcatlipoca, the whirlwind, in his blue *southern* manifestation was identified with and named Huitzilopochtli. This is a pun on the first part of the name Huitzilopochtli, since the morpheme *huitzil-* here stands for both *huitzilin* = hummingbird and *huitzli* = thorn. The south was "the place of thorns," *Huitztlampa*. And since hummingbirds are often iridescent blue-green (the color of a sunny daytime sky), the equation blue southern Tezcatlipoca (wind, sun) = Huitzilopochtli (sun) is based on south = thorn = hummingbird = blue-green.

Originally, myth tells us, there was only the dual deity, half male, half female, or a mythical pair of gods: Ometeotl and Omecihuatl (also named Tonacatecuhtli and Tonacacihuatl). These were the "mother-father gods," and still exist in Zinacantan under that name (Vogt 1969:298). They gave birth to or unfolded mythically into the Highland complex god Tezcatlipoca (smoking mirror), who in turn had both four and eight aspects. In my opinion, the Maya equivalent was Itzam Na. He was the all-knowing god, the omnipotent one. The meanings of Tezcatlipoca-Itzam Na are multitudinous and protean (see Nicholson 1971:411–412). He ruled the four-sided directions and center of the world; he controlled the destiny of man as god of providence, justice and wealth; he was the universal trickster or teaser of man; he was sometimes imagined as a turkey, at other times as an iguana, often as a jaguar sitting in the central cave of the universe (Tepeyollotl), sometimes as transfiguring himself into a whirlwind or a black apparition. However, Tezcatlipoca-Itzam Na was basically a quadripartite god: as the Christian Trinity is one and three simultaneously, Tezcatlipoca was one and four, and, as a duality, two and eight simultaneously. This was a sacred mystery, which originated in the conception of the space-time continuum, in which the god was visualized as the idea of the horizontal motion of the world directions: each one of his four parts was a different god image, with a different name, age, kinship role, color, and other transformational qualities. The *Historia de los Mexicanos por sus Pinturas* (1941: 209 and *passim*) is one of the text sources dealing with this topic. Nicholson (1971) has a brief but careful account of the major transformations of this fourfolded god in the Highland myths. Thompson (1970) has an erudite discussion of the Maya variants of this symbolic complex.

Each one of the four "Tezcatlipoca" parts ruled a cardinal direction, a planet, a wind, and season, while the god as a totality ruled the center of the directional quincunx. Each direction had a volatile, a moral aspect, a tree, and an "order of birth" (since the quadripartite gods were siblings, mythically, they were born in a certain order). The black center was the second son, the red the first or eldest, and the god Huitzilopochtli, the white or blue one, was the youngest (*HDLMPSP:* 209–210), usually belonging to the south and left (see Illustration 9). That Huitzilopochtli was the youngest testifies to his late introduction into the pantheon by the Mexica. He was the youngest both mythically and historically. (The female deity Tlazolteotl also was four sisters in one.)

Each of the aspects of a fourfold god also had a set of day signs and names assigned to him, and several other transformations. (No complete list has yet been compiled, and it would be difficult to make one, because sources of the mythical versions of the transformations vary significantly—perhaps because they refer to different, unconnected myths, perhaps because in each temple or locality there were differences in subtle points of theology that are reflected in the extant documents.)

9. God bearer of the southern sky. *Codex Vaticanus*, obverse A, section 7, upper-center-right.

The fourfold god Tezcatlipoca had four assistants who helped him to hold up the sky. These *eight* sacred figures together are worshipped today in Zinacantan as the *Vashakmen* (Vogt 1969:303, 304; *vashak* = eight). The end of this name appears to be a homophone of the word *nen*, mirror. Another interpretation suggests that it comes from *men*, an old Maya word for pillar or column. In the latter case, the name would mean eight-column, which is highly appropriate, since these eight aspects support on their shoulders the four corners of the sky and the four corners of the earth.

The totality of Itzam Na, however, has unfolded into the Zinacantecan image of the Yahval Balamil, the Earth Lord, or Lord of the World. Because he is conceived as a superior being, full of power, Zinacantecans imagine him as a rich Mexican. However, like his prehispanic image, he is symbolized by snakes, iguanas, and other earth animals.

Yahval Balamil controls both rains and winds, elements which appear usually in four directional aspects. We do not know if Yahval Balamil today is so divided. However, there are some areas of general agreement, as far as our task is concerned, with respect to prehispanic winds. Huitzilopochtli, the hummingbird god, was the unfolding of Tezcatlipoca assigned to the south and the left side, the rainy season. The south, summer, "the region of thorns," was in many versions a white wind (see Nicholson 1971, Table 1). Color transformations, which are obviously derived from the culture in an arbitrary manner, and which are multivalent (unlike ecological factors or planetary positions), vary enormously according to the prehispanic record as well as in contemporary Indian systems (see Wauchope, ed.: vols. 7 and 8). Since the hummingbird god was the wet season sun, fire, he paired with Quetzalcoatl's image as the wet winds of spring and summer.

Falling Water

Water was divided into two subclasses identified as male and female, one being moving or falling water, and the other surface water. Falling water was the sign and name of one of the days of the prehispanic cycle, "Rain."

Tlaloc, the god of the Mexica with the ringed eyes, called "thunderbolt" in Zinacantan today, was one of the most ancient in the Mesoamerican pantheon and represented falling water or rains, which originated from the caves of the earth, went up to the sky, and came down again. His name indicated these associations since it meant the one who moves the earth or is in the earth (Garibay 1961:310) or the one who makes things grow from the earth. The transformational ideas involving this god and the minor godlings connected with him (the *Tlaloques* or water goblins; *7anheletik* in Zinacantan) included the idea of the male fertility principle, as fertilizing ("moving") the earth. Falling waters were classified by their strength, and particularly by their cardinal point of origin. Many myths deal with four aspects of Tlaloc, one for each direction of the horizontal earth plane, or with the god pouring water from four vessels, one on each corner of the horizontal quincunx of the sky-earth. In Mayan, one of his names was Ah Bakolol, the pourer-of-narrow-neck-vessels. In this image he is pictured in the frontispiece of Spinden's (1957) *Maya Art and Civilization*, from a capstone in the Temple of the Owls at Chichen Itza, Yucatan. There he is holding a tray with the four vessels, which look like elegant glass decanters with long narrow necks. The rain god in many Maya paintings and sculptures is pictured with a dripping nose, symbolizing a head cold. In the image at the temple at Chichen Itza, the mucus is running from his nose in a stream. Rain, here again, is a giant attack of cosmic flu! (These beliefs and myths are extant today among the Cuicatec.)

Damaging rains were distinguished from beneficial rains and were plainly symbolized as such in painting and myth. The most dangerous rains ever known in myth were the deluges that had brought previous eras to an end.

The god of rain was intimately related to the winds of storms and to the hummingbird sun god, because in Mesoamerican ecology rain and hummingbirds reappear in the spring. The Mexica were so impressed with this transformational relation that in the *Templo Mayor* in their capital, Tenochtitlan, they placed the two gods side by side as major temple deities (Duran 1971:154; see illustration 10).

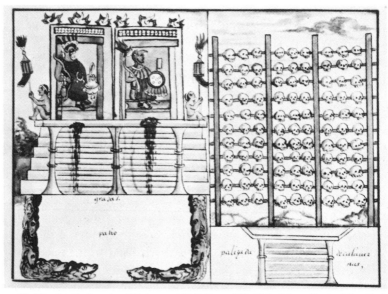

10. The double temple of Tlaloc and Huitzilopochtli. Plate 4 from *Book of the Gods and Rites and the Ancient Calendar*, by Fray Diego Duran. Copyright 1971 by the University of Oklahoma Press.

In an agrarian society that depended for its sustenance mostly on crops planted in spring and in need of seasonal rain, this connection is not surprising. Séjourné believes that the combination represents the symbol "burning water," the union of water and fire (1957:119–124). "Burning water" also means war, and Huitzilopochtli was a warrior god.

Surface Water

The springs, lagoons, rivers, waterholes, lakes, irrigation canals, and other bodies of water on the earth's surface were conceptualized as female and represented by a set of deities headed by Chalchihuit-licue ("she who has the [precious] jade skirt," literally, "she of the jade skirt"). She was the female fertility principle (the precious jade "skirt" is probably a euphemism for the vagina or uterus). The name of an Aztec princess executed for adultery manifests the same symbolism, for she was called Chalchiuhnenetl, "she of the (precious) jade genitals," or "the (precious) jade doll." Chalchihuitlicue was the complement of Tlaloc, mythically his wife, or sister, or both. Both these deity complexes were old agrarian gods. Since surface water (by means of irrigation canals) was used to grow a second crop during the dry season, and the rainy season made possible the major corn crop, these male-female deities complemented each other in the reality of the annual agrarian cycle as well as in myth. The Lowland Maya, who lived in tropical rain forests and did not need to irrigate, paid little attention to this female deity, but instead emphasized divine waterholes (cenotes).

Fire

Fire was seen as the element which provides heat, life, and light. Fire is the force that moves the cosmos, and ultimately will destroy it. Thus the parental gods were fire deities.

The taxonomy of fire is an extremely complex and at present obscure one, which Seler, alone among scholars, appears to have understood well. Fire was also symbolized in a god complex: the Mexica called him Xiuhtecuhtli (Nicholson 1971:412 and *passim*). The Maya called him Itzam Cab, an aspect of the "unique" god Itzam

Na. He was mythically (and archaeological evidence agrees) an old god.

Prehispanic peoples distinguished man-made (cultural) from natural fires. Three major cultural types of fire were sacralized: the slash-and-burn fire of agriculture, which clears the fields for new planting, the cooking fire, and the "New Fire." The cooking fire was represented by three deities. Mesoamerican kitchen hearths had three stones that supported the grill and cooking pots over the flame. These were symbols of the three goddesses of sustenance. Since women did the cooking, the fire deities in this homely position were female. This belief still exists among Cuicatec Indians.

The New Fire was built by religious officiants at the end of every fifty-two years, the prehispanic time cycle equivalent to our century (see p. 195). The New Fire was used to renew all fires that had been extinguished as part of the ritual of *fin de siècle*.

Natural fire was divided into celestial and earth fire. Celestial fire included the fire of the sun and lightning (sky-water fire or cloud fire). Lightning was sometimes represented in deified form as Xolotl (evening star), the ugly twin of Quetzalcoatl (morning star). At other times it was represented as a snake uncoiling in the hand of the god of water, Tlaloc, and in other forms (see Beyer 1965:49–53). Sky-sun fire (light) was carried by Huitzilopochtli in his hand as an uncoiling fire snake. The god of fire's theophany, "blue hummingbird," gave its name to the southern sun (see under god Xiuhtecuhtli, Table 3, p. 174). But lightning and rain were both said to come originally from the earth, while sun fire came from the sky as the light of the daytime (see Vogt 1969:302 for a Zinacantan parallel). Earth fire included burning lava coming out of volcanoes and earthquakes. Mesoamerican peoples knew a good deal about these, since two of the major volcanoes were active well into the sixteenth century (some are active even today). Myths predicted that the end of the present universe would be produced by earthquake fire.

A balance between the kinds of fire was necessary for the maintenance of the world's existence. During the winter solstice period, when the sun was weak ("because" daylight was short), "sun fire"

Chart 2. Prehispanic classification of fires

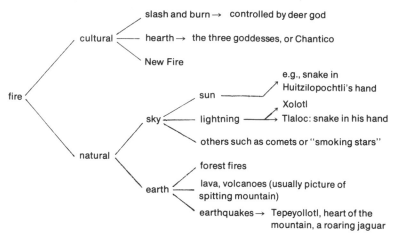

was in imbalance with "earth fire" and the solstice was thus a dangerous period for the universe. One of the reasons why Huitzilopochtli was feasted and celebrated at that period was to coax him, as sun fire, to retrace his journey in the ecliptic and recreate a balance with earth. The reversal of the sun's journey was symbolized in a counterclockwise parade, a ritual called "the race of the sun," which took place near the winter solstice at the time the sun had crossed the zenith into the northern section of the sky. Again, in the spring, when the southern sun as Huitzilopochtli or Tonatiuh started his journey northwards in the ecliptic, he was celebrated because he was conquering imbalance and the forces of destruction inherent in the closeness of the fires of the earth to the sun's fire. When he reached the highest position, he was then the southern victorious warrior. Seler also notes that the hummingbird's nose markings resemble the Mayan fire sign (1961c; and see Illustration 1, above). Robert Laughlin kindly pointed out to me an important story that bears on this discussion. A Cakchiquel tale relates that Zakitzunun, the white hummingbird, was the only animal who dared to aid the Cakchiquel forefather in putting out the fire of the volcano Santa Maria. In this tale, the white hummingbird, a symbol of sky fire, the summer sun, appears clearly in his role of "balancer" of the earth's fire, the active volcano. In "The Hummingbird" he appears as "balancer" of the man-made slash-and-burn fire.

The idea of balance so dear to Mesoamerican peasants (Ingham 1970) pervaded not only the taxonomy of fire and fire rituals but all aspects of the religion and the gods' images. Gods were often depicted in pairs, as dual sets, or in two halves representing the mysteries of ambivalence and balanced opposition. The *Borgia Codex* (pp. 56 and 73) for example has two extraordinarily nightmarish but beautiful composite pairs of images, representing the mystery of the balance between earth fire and sky fire, hot and cold, life and death. Two gods, back to back, symbolize the mystery in each picture.

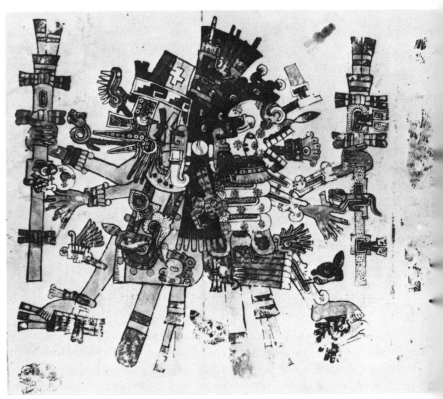

11. Life and death gods. *Borgia Codex*, p. 73.

Quetzalcoatl, here as Ehecatl, the god of wind, meaning wind = breath = life, leans against Mictlantecuhtli, the god of the under- world. He is represented with a skull (= death; see Illustration 11).

Ingham (1971:623) has argued that the calendar was arranged in alternating dyadic oppositions between the elements fire and water. His interpretation suggests possibilities, but it ignores the fact that the gods were not "unique solutions," that is, they did not have fixed unitary meanings. Thus the fire-water calendar he proposes is his own interpretation of symbols, not necessarily a native one, or is perhaps rather one of the many possible native subsystems. It leaves out planets and other elements like wind and earth. For example, he consistently interprets Quetzalcoatl as water, which is not possible in many of the contexts where this god appears. Again, Huitzilo- pochtli (as the fire of the sun) was imagined with his oppositional duality, the four hundred gods (the fire of the stars), but could also be imagined in opposition to the earth, or in conjunction with rather than opposition to water (as in the summer quarter of the calendar).

Fire itself represented heat, power, energy and life itself (*elan vital*), seen as the warmth of a living animal organism. Thus *tona*, the human soul, equaled heat, life, and the sun itself, the source of heat and life. The name of the sun god in Nahuatl is Tonatiuh, and in Zinacantan "sun" and "heat" are equivalent symbols and homonyms.

The Earth

The earth played an interface role in the taxonomical system of natural and sacred orders. The religious representations of earth in the symbolism of prehispanic Mesoamericans embody some of the most complicated, diversified, and exotic of their ideas. In a work of this length is is impossible to describe adequately all the sacred meanings of earth. I will simply give examples of the major ideatio- nal patterns.

To begin with, the earth was conceptualized in the form of many concrete symbols. These symbols were assigned as identifiers or markers of practically all the other fluid divine images. The gods symbolizing vegetation were either deities with earthly attributes or were considered, mythically, the earth's children. The corn divinities belong in both these categories. The dead seed was buried in the earth and resurrected because the earth gave it new life. All other divinities, particularly the domestic plants, were indirect aspects of the earth: her hair, her children, her jewels.

The earth also appears as a planet in the balance of celestial bodies (for example in the myths of oppositions between the anthropomorphic moon, sun, and earth). The earth was thought of in several images in this context. First, when the planets were not visible in the sky, they were believed to be inside the earth's bowels, and were said to have been eaten by the earth, which was here thought of as a monster. The "jaws" were the western cardinal direction. Second, there was a symbolic coding in terms of material culture. The invisible planets had gone to their "house," the interior of the earth, to rest. This "house" was the name of one of the days of the prehispanic calendar. In a third image, the interior of the earth was a "tomb." The planets went there to die, to be resurrected later on, rising in the eastern sky. In the codices, occulted planets visualized according to this metaphor are painted, anthropomorphically, as dead human beings with closed eyes.

Thus the earth was womb, mouth, bowels, and house of the universal deities. The body image was exploited at several levels. The center of the earth was its navel, the trees its hair, and so on. The total body of the visible surface of the earth, the continent "floating" in the ocean, was a theriomorphic deity, the mythic *cipactli* or Tlaltecuhtli. This monster had a corrugated back, like an iguana, a giant frog, or an alligator, which was the metaphor for the mountains and the creviced valleys of the earth's surface.

The deities that, at some coded level, symbolized other elements such as water or fire were also, symbolically, aspects of the earth, because the earth was said to be composed of these elements. Some deities combined several metaphors in one god. Xipe Totec is an example of combinations. His name means "the flayed one," the god who loses his skin, and, in his west-fall period, he represented the earth that had lost its skin—the vegetation that covers it—after the harvest. But Xipe was also the god of gold, a mineral that comes from the earth.

All the deities which symbolized aspects of reproduction, birth, and death had earthly aspects. Symbols of vegetable, animal, or humanoid deities were earthly symbols because the earth was conceptualized as the primordial image of the generating and regenerating principles of life.

But earth was also the universal tomb. Its interior contained the precinct where the bones of the dead and their disembodied souls were kept. The dark dead images of the planets were also there. Astronomically, this "interior" was the invisible southern pole of the sky.

Many different gods were said to be rulers of the earth's interior. In the caves in the mountains lived a divine jaguar, "the heart of the mountains," Tepeyollotl. His roar was the noise of earthquakes. In subterranean rivers lived a rattlesnake, or a divine iguana, or a turkey. Their animal noises were the sounds of the underworld rivers. The guardians of the dead bones were a pair of deities, the lord and lady of death, who also lived inside the earth, on its dark side.

Earth, like all the other ambiguous images of the gods, expressed the essence of mystical ambivalence about man's place in the universe. It was loving and destructive, nurturant mother and carnivorous monster. Reflecting ideas both complicated and anguished, the earth was most often represented as a demonic figure. Coatlicue, the female earth, had two snakes instead of a head, a necklace of cut-off hands, and a skirt of living serpents flowing over her (the rivers). The earth was both human and animal, male and female, a dead and a living thing.

Another separate conceptualization of earth was developed by prehispanic astronomers. The religious astronomical aspect of earth was the plane of the equator, which was imagined as an oscillating flat surface. Its edges were cut by the lines of the equinoctial colures, the celestial tropics and the sunrise and sunset lines. This concept gave an image of the earth as a quadrilateral plane with four sides and four intercardinal points, plus a fifth point at the center. The points of the earth quincunx were conceptualized in the religious pantheon as atlantean figures, four earth-bearer gods, and were marked, astronomically, by four constellations, which stood guard

Chart 3. Examples of the earth's sacred aspects and divine symbols

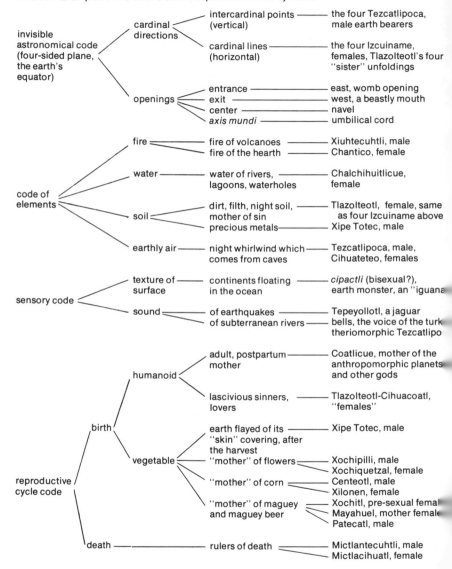

above and were the eyes of the earth bearers looking upon man. One of these star clusters was apparently the constellation that Sahagun (1969, 2:262–263) recognized as the "fire sticks" (see R. Simeon's definition of *Mamalhuaztli* [1963:224]). I do not know which specific constellations were defined as the eyes of the earth's bearers, but possibly among them were the Pleiades and Gemini, which the Maya named "the turtle" and "rattlesnake."

Chart 3 lists some examples of deities and their coded earthly meanings. Since earth as a symbol complex was coded and transformed into practically all the other mythic and ritual codes, it is hopeless to attempt to produce a complete list. I thereby rest my case.

What has been left in Zinacantan of all this confusion of gods? First, the earth's quincunx still functions, as I shall demonstrate later, as a major symbolic paradigm which orders all other symbolism. Second, the earth and sky bearers continue to exist as divine beings, under the name of Vashakmen. Third, several prehispanic deities who represented the earth have been syncretized and condensed into one: Yahval Balamil.

Yahval Balamil, the Earth Lord combines unto himself the prehispanic Tepeyollotl, Mictlantecuhtli (god of death), *cipactli,* and several other earth deities, plus the god of rain, Tlaloc. Among the Tzeltal Maya, Tepeyollotl was called Votan. In Yucatan he was called Akbal, and in all Mesoamerican calendars he was patron of the third day of the twenty-day sequence (see discussion of the calendar below pp. 184–203 and Table 3.). This deity was a dominant Chiapas god, and in his jaguar image still lives in Zinacantan's ritual. The death images of Mictlantecuhtli also appear in the figures of the Blackmen, skeletons that float around, and other Zinacantecan ghostly or scary creatures. Like his prehispanic counterpart, Yahval Balamil is parent to the vegetable deities. In his guise of "thunderbolt" he fathered the snake that is mother of the corn (Robert Laughlin, personal communication). This snake, who is also a young bride and a flower, was the prehispanic goddess Xilonen or Xochiquetzal ("corn doll" or "precious flower"). Moreover, the earth's interior, the mythical cave-house-uterus, still persists among the symbols of Zina-cantan (see Vogt 1969, chap. 17).

Just as prehispanic man was ambivalent toward the earth, so are contemporary Zincantecans. Just as the earth deities were demonic, so is Yahval Balamil. He is imagined now as a devilish greedy Mexican riding around mounted on a deer with iguanas for blinders, and communication with him is still today "viewed with ambivalence" (*ibid.*, pp. 302–303).

Geographical Aspects of Earth

As I pointed out above, many features of the earthly landscape were systematically associated with features of prehispanic religion. Mountains, particularly, had a complex role in mythology and in the system of toponymy (see Illustrations 12 and 13). Deserts, rivers, forests, lakes, waterholes, mountaintops, caves, and the like all had "gods" and "goddesses" who ruled over them and required man's ritual coaxing. Rituals concerned with the *cenotes*, the "mother of the lake," and mountain gods were scattered throughout the annual cycle. Contemporary Mesoamerican Indians have preserved some of

12. Hummingbirds in the toponymic Tepeucila (Hill of Hummingbirds). (A) *Codex Porfirio Diaz*, p. F of facsimile edition. (B) *Codex Fernandez Leal*, p. X obverse of facsimile edition.

13. The bat in Mesoamerican toponymics. (A) In the toponymic Zinacantan, "Place of the Bat" (*Mendocino Codex*, p. 14). (B) In the toponymic Zinacantepec, "Hill of the Bats" (*Codex Fernandez Leal*).

the complexities of these rituals. Among the Cuicatec, for example, cave rituals, mountain ceremonies, and waterhole rituals are quite important. In Zinacantan, waterhole rituals and mountaintop rituals punctuate the ceremonial cycle.

The images of celestial deities at the cosmic level also had counterparts on the earth's surface. Among the Aztecs, Huitzilopochtli was particularly associated with the mountain in the valley of Mexico called today Hill of the Star, located south-southeast of Tenochtitlan, and also with the mountain Culhuacan, from inside which he had spoken to his people, ordering them to carry him on their pilgrimage (*Tira de la Peregrinación Azteca*, 1944; see Illustration 14). I believe "hummingbird" in Zinacantan is associated with the mountain "junior brother," south-southeast of Zinacantan Center (see discussion in section on contemporary structure, p. 221, below).

Celestial Bodies

The class of celestial bodies included identified planets and constellations visible to the naked eye, which prehispanic astronomers studied. Most of their knowledge has been lost, but we know that their advanced astronomy recognized and understood the orbital

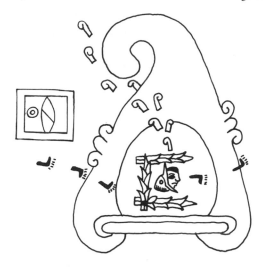

14. The hummingbird god speaks to his people from inside a cave in Culhuacan. *Tira de la Peregrinación Azteca.*

behavior of objects in the sky, both sources of light and bearers of the passage of time. The Maya in particular were astronomers of genius. Prehispanic astronomy was expressed in symbolic religious language. Like animals, plants, and other living things, deified planets were conceived to have gender and sex and to pass through life cycles. These life cycles were, of course, images of periods during their synodical revolutions (around the sun, or in relation to the earth, when visible or invisible to the naked eye).

The major distinctions made in this context were those between the daytime images of the sky deities and their nighttime counterparts, and those between the visible and invisible aspects of the planets. Some deities unfolded into day-night and live-dead pairs. Others appear only as one (when the other aspect of the god is an "invisible partner"). These were "sky-underworld" dualities of celestial objects. But in the codices they are represented as human beings.

The complexities of prehispanic astronomy have been explored by many scholars. Chesley Baity (1973), in her bibliography, includes many major works specifically dealing with Mesoamerica, as well as comparative cross-cultural data. Digby (1972) has given a highly plausible description of a piece of technological equipment that

Mesoamerican peoples may have had to observe solar astronomical movements and calculate them accurately. We also know they had complex architectural structures that functioned principally as celestial observatories. However, together with the scientific, empirico-mathematical investigations, prehispanic peoples created a complex mythic symbolism that they communicated in an astronomical code. The two were warp and woof of the same ideological fabric. Yolotl Gonzales (1975) has a stimulating discussion of the astronomical myths and rituals.

The planets were deified as various gods. The planets found in mythical texts and paintings were, of course, those visible without modern telescopes, the seven planets of antiquity: Sun, Mercury, Venus, Moon, Mars, Jupiter, and Saturn. It is possible that only six planets were actually deified. In several codices a series of "celestial walkers" included only six of them.

The Sun

The subtaxonomy of "suns" included different suns according to solar positions in the day and night, during the annual ecliptic journey, and at eclipses. Each position was a "different" sun god (see Illustration 15). The prehispanic peoples knew the number of days

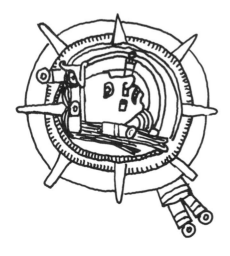

15. The face of the sun god ascending. *Borgia Codex*, p. 23, center-left panel.

in the solar year and used the figure in complex mathematical-calendrical calculations (see the section on numerology, p. 184, below). Their advanced astronomy, however, was deeply embedded in mythico-poetic pantheistic thought and ritual.

The sun at night and during the winter solstice period was the "tired" or "dying" sun. Rituals were necessary to cajole it into moving again. The newborn or infant sun was a god of the sunrise, of the east. The dying ripe sun was a god of the west. The high-flying, "southern sun" was the light of the daytime sky, Huitzilopochtli, and/or Tonatiuh, reigning victorious between the spring equinox and the end of the summer solstice period. As ascending victorious god, the sun possessed many images: the blue-fire hummingbird; the white hummingbird; the eagle or hawk, bird-king of the sky, who flies high; a youthful warrior winning his battle. These images related transformationally to each other, so that, for example, as patron of professions, the sun protected warriors, and as tutelary image of an ethnic group, it was the defender of the Mexica tribe, well-known for its conquering armies.

If for Western culture "the measure of all things" is man, for prehispanic Mesoamerican peoples it was the deified planets. And among the planets, there ruled, victorious and unchallenged, the sun, as his worshippers the Mexica ruled over much of Mesoamerica. The importance of the sun as a "measure of man" is delightfully pictured in the section of the *Florentine Codex* which Sahagun called *Adages* (Anderson and Dibble 1970, Addendum II, vol. 2:81–84). There a working man who saves his earnings is likened to the sun which accumulates warmth; to find one's future spouse is to discover one's sun; to place the sun in the middle (that is, the summer solstice) is to be a mature man; to cause the sun to set is to become old; to overturn the sun is to forget a good custom; to attain the sun is to merit something precious. No wonder, then, that a little hummingbird can indeed be, in the eyes of Zinacantecan man, so very big. He is indeed, today, in various disguises, several Zinacantecan gods, autochthonous sacred personages, and even Christian saints! This point will be demonstrated later, in the discussion of contemporary deities.

The Inner Planets

The "inside visible" planets, those between the sun and earth (the moon, Venus, and Mercury), were among the most important mythical-astronomical deities; perhaps because their movements, their disappearances and reappearances, are naturally more baffling, rapid, and "temperamental," than those of the more distant planets. In any case, the early chroniclers seem to have obtained much more information on the inner planets, particularly the moon and Venus, than on the others.

The Moon

The moon, related to the elements of water and earth, and partner, junior sibling, or spouse of the sun, was a complex deity subsystem. Some images represented specific phases (a half-moon ornamented the noses of the moon deities). The moon's movements and phases gave rise to the lunar month system, which was apparently most important among the Mayan peoples (for whom "moon" and "month" were homonyms). The Copan astronomers, around 682 A.D., calculated the formula for lunations on the base 149 moons = 4,400 days. This gave them an average lunation of 29.53020 days (our present astronomic value is 29.53059).

Some of the moon's divine images in the past were male, some female. Some were humanoid and some were animal (see Illustration 16). As with the sun, different aspects were deified and symbolized as "different" moons. A complex series of sagas or myths about the origins of sun and moon were of major importance throughout Mesoamerica, and many versions are still extant in rural villages. These two complexes of deities and planets have been syncretically identified throughout Mesoamerica (including Zinacantan) with Jesus and the Virgin Mary. The complexities of the lunar calendar have apparently been forgotten, and the peasants have been left with the

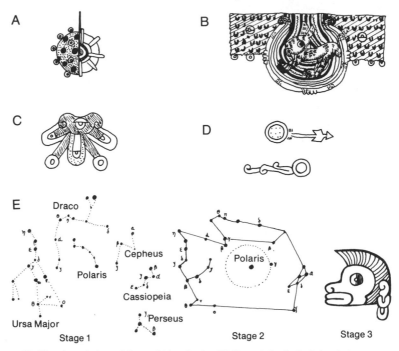

16. Planets and stars of the prehispanic sky. (A) Sunset, the liminal time between sun and stars. *Borgia Codex.* (B) The rabbit of the moon, hanging from the starry sky. *Borgia Codex.* (C) The sign of Venus. *Codex Fejervary-Mayer.* (D) Two comets. *Madrid Manuscripts* 1 and 2. (E) Stage 1: Constellations on a Western astronomic map. Stage 2: Stars in these constellations, linked to show approximation of monkey's head. Stage 3: Sign of the constellation Monkey. From the hypothesis of Beyer (1965).

poetic images minus the astronomy. Much empirical knowledge of the effect of the lunar phases on other events is still used, however: for example, the notions about increased sap flow in plants and trees during a full moon. Also the myths connecting fertility, the moon, and rabbits are still extant throughout Mesoamerica.

Venus

Two major deified transformations of Venus were imagined, one as the evening star, the other as the star of sunrise. Many gods of different names were attached to this planet. Venus was messenger god of the sun's arrival. It was Quetzalcoatl, as the spirit of the eastern wind, and in his morning star aspect. The evening star "twin" was Xolotl, a doglike monster, guardian of the western entrance to the underworld. The Cuicatec Indians still make this mythic link. The evening star Venus is called "the star like a hairy beast," and its image is a fierce dog flying downward, fire pouring from its mouth. Gonzales (1975) believes Xolotl was Mercury, but in my opinion the twinship of Quetzalcoatl-Xolotl is that of the dawn and evening apparitions of Venus.

The observation of Venus's synodical revolutions and the complexity of its cycles in relation to the sun and moon forms the basis of one of the most elaborate mysteries of the esoteric astronomical knowledge of prehispanic religion. Venus's relative distance is 7 (Bode's law),[2] which may explain why its god, Quetzalcoatl, also the god of wind, has the sign 7-Wind assigned to him in the *Anales de Cuauhtitlán*. The *Borgia Codex* interpreted by Seler (1963) covers venusian symbols in detail. As Quetzalcoatl, wind-morning star deified, Venus was the sweeper of the path of the sun and rains. The dust storms before the beginning of the rainy season were the signs of his sweeping activities.

The people of the Puebla-Cholula region worshipped Quetzalcoatl as a major deity. Zinacantecans today call Venus the Chamula girl, the sweeper of the sun's path. Their Maya forebears had also become specialists in the understanding of Venus's synodical passages. The divine symbols were simply mythic idioms for their scientific knowledge.

Mercury

I believe that Mercury, the small planet nearest the sun, was symbolized by prehispanic peoples as the god Paynal, "the swift," "the hasty," who was the sun god's "junior companion." The epithet "swift" is obviously appropriate, given that Mercury's sidereal revolution takes 87.9 days compared with the earth's 365.25. Mercury

---

2. My suggestion here is that some of the important numbers that occur in the prehispanic calendric counts are the same as those derived from Bode's law of the relative distance of planets. This hypothesis is discussed in footnote 2 to Chap. 6.

17. Christ as the sun in colonial Mexico. This stone cross stands in the cemetery of Atzacoalco, D.F. Notice the resemblance of the stylized top to the *olin* symbol. The face of Christ appears surrounded by a collar of thorns, rather than by a crown of them. The collar is made to resemble the circle of rays with which prehispanic peoples framed the sun's face. To increase the effect, all the thorns face outward. At the square base, four bearerlike figures support the column. The body of the cross, like that of prehispanic deities, is covered with appropriate symbols: the column where Christ was flogged, the rooster, a host, and the deity's anagram. Many stone workers used by the Spaniards during the sixteenth century had been of the same profession before the conquest, and they continued to apply their own canons of symbolic design to the new Christian work they were assigned. From this cross and similar evidence it is clear that the identification of the sun with Jesus, which occurs in many Indian villages including Zinacantan, took place early in the first century of the conquest. Photo courtesy of *The Bulletin of the INAH* and of Mariano Monterosa.

was the sun's junior companion because it is so close to the sun that they are never truly "without one another."

Santillana and Dechend (1969) have argued tentatively that Tlaloc, the god with the face of coiled or twisted serpents, was, in his planetary transformation, Mercury. They relate this god to the "intestine faced gods" of the Old World, not by diffusion, but by parallel symbolism. They argue that both in the Old World and in the New astronomers had observed the apparently erratic, tangled, and convoluted orbital movements of this planet, and had likened them to entrails and coiled snakes (*ibid.*, pp. 289–292). Since many gods had multiple associational levels including planets, and all major gods seem to have planetary images, this hypothesis is not farfetched, but much further evidence is needed to establish the identification. However, if proven true, it will also explain why Tlaloc and Huitzilopochtli appeared together in the major temple of Tenochtitlan. Since Mercury is so close to the sun, prehispanic peoples may have assumed that one could not appear without the other being very near, in the same fashion that sun and rain appear together in summer. The closeness must have been a matter of astronomical inference, since Mercury is often invisible.

In tentative support of this hypothesis, we could offer the fact that Tlaloc was also Nappatecuhtli, "the four times lord," which may have referred to the fact that Mercury makes four sidereal revolutions during the solar year or the "earth year." We must point out, however, that scholars do not agree about the prehispanics' knowledge of sidereal revolutions, but only about their knowledge of synodical revolutions.

There is no evidence that Zinacantecans or other contemporary Mexican Indians pay any attention to this planet. They appear to have lost not only the astronomical knowledge of their forebears, but also the myths relating to Mercury. It is obvious, moreover, that this disappearance is a consequence of Mercury's relative lack of importance in prehispanic mythology, in comparison with other planets such as Venus or Mars.

The Outer Planets

As religious symbols, the planets of "the other side of the earth" were both the least discussed by the colonial chroniclers and the most powerful, oldest and most mysterious for prehispanic peoples. It is regrettable that colonial priests knew less about astronomy than prehispanic peoples did—and that most modern archaeologists and anthropologists (including the author of this book) are likewise less knowledgeable! We do, however, know some of the most obvious associations.

Mars

Mars, the visible red planet, was identified with the "bloody gods," the gods of war and hunting, in their forms of the *red Tezcatlipoca, Mixcoatl, Camaxtli*, and others. This planet was thus Xipe = Mixcoatl and/or Camaxtli at the same time (Escalona Ramos 1940). Since prehispanic·peoples thought of celestial objects, and painted them, as "eyes in the sky," in their conception this red-colored planet had "blood-shot eyes," and suffered from eye trouble. Unlike the inner planets, which are always appearing and disappearing (= closing or opening their eyes), the outer planets are visible for much longer periods. Mars, with its orbit close to that of earth, "although at times presenting a markedly gibbous aspect like a nine- or ten-day's old moon, is always more than half illuminated" (*Encyclopaedia Britannica* 1942, 17:998). He may not often close his eyes, but he has eye trouble! Thus was Mars Xipe, the god who, according to the *Florentine Codex*, "visited the people with blisters, festering, pimples, eye pains, watering of the eyes, festering about the eye lashes, lice about the eyes, opacity, filling of the eyes with flesh, withering of the eyes, cataracts, glazing of the eyes" (Anderson and Dibble 1970, vol. 2:39).

Zinacantecans still believe that Mars, the red planet, is a god who hurts the eyesight. Many years ago the anthropologist Trudy Duby Bloom brought a young Lacandon Indian to San Cristobal las Casas, Chiapas, to have an eye operation. I was visiting there at the time.

One afternoon there were several Zinacantecans visiting too, standing around the courtyard. I struck up a conversation with a Zinacantecan woman and remember two things vividly. First, she was worried because she was not sure that a long-haired Lacandon man in robes, who had spoken to her, was really a human being. Second, she was convinced that the Lacandon child's eye trouble was caused "by the spirit who lives in the red star which moves in the sky" (Mars). On this point the Lacandon man who had scared her agreed. He was the father of the sick child, and the same day he told me that he was not sure an operation could help his child because the eye trouble was a disease brought by the "bloody red star."

The Maya apparently had a scientific understanding of this planet's motion. Coe believes that one of the *Dresden Codex* tables deals with the Mars synodical year of 780 days (1966:162).

Jupiter and Saturn

It is not clear from the extant documentation whether these two planets were clearly differentiated for religious purposes, which specific god images were associated with each, or whether these planets represented transformations of gods. Santillana and Dechend (1969) have argued that both Jupiter and Saturn were the god Tezcatlipoca, the major god, omnipresent. Obviously, Jupiter, the largest planet, most often visible, whose illumination variation is so small as to be almost imperceptible can clearly be thought of as the all seeing, omnipresent (in the sky). He is all seeing because metaphorically he never closes his eyes. The commentator of the *Codex Magliabecchiano* and Sahagun thought Tezcatlipoca, the "major of the major of the gods," was Jupiter (quoted in Nicholson 1971:412). Escalona-Ramos (1940) makes the same identification. Interestingly enough, Jupiter's relative distance according to Bode's law is 52, the number of years in the prehispanic century. If prehispanic peoples were aware of this (as perhaps they may have been?), Tezcatlipoca the god and Jupiter the planet would have been astronomical images of the largest, longest passage-cycle of time, a complete "bundle of years," and thus the eternal as well as the omnipresent.

Jupiter and Saturn, either or both, could have been the mysterious god of the high northern sky, the top layers of the heavens. Saturn, with its universal image of an astronomical "cubic outermost sphere," the furthest planet then known in outer space, is also a likely candidate for the fourfold god, Tezcatlipoca. Escalona-Ramos (1940) thinks Saturn was Xiuhtecuhtli (fire lord), and Gonzales (1975) follows Escalona. However, Tezcatlipoca has another image of astronomical interest, deriving from the meanings of some of his symbols. He is the god of waterspouts, whirlwinds, whirlpools, cyclones, tornadoes, *all things that coil around themselves in a spiral motion.* He was also the god of all directions, and thus the god of the celestial "whirlpool," an image which appears in many mythologies around the world. This whirlpool is the "ecliptic world marked by the whirling planets," and embraces "everything which circles obliquely with respect to the polar axis of the equator" (Santillana and Dechend 1969:239). Because of the phenomenon of the precession of the equinoxes, the positions of the north and south centers or poles of the whirlpool vary, since the earth, "falling like a slowed-down spinning top," (*ibid.*), moves with respect to the true celestial pole. The variation was conceived as causing cataclysmic ruin at the end of each cosmic era. This circular movement takes approximately 26,000 years, and *the prehispanic 52-year cycle fits into it exactly 500 times.*

The north circumpolar image was called by prehispanic peoples "The North and its Wheel" (Seler 1963, 1:116). The radius of the projected pole of the earth circling around the true pole has an angle of approximately 23.5 degrees. Within this circumpolar ring, different stars become the "pole star" as the equinoxes precess. Ours is Alpha Ursae Minoris. Around 3000 B.C. it was Alpha Draconis. However, the pole of the ecliptic itself, which "does not move," is not a celestial body: *it is a dark spot.* We must remember that the celestial bodies were for prehispanic peoples equal not only to eyes, but also to mirrors shining in the sky. Eyes and mirrors are always metaphorically equated in prehispanic poetry and myth. What happens to a smoked or smoking mirror? It does not shine: it is black-

18. Tezcatlipoca drawn in the European manner, holding the all-seeing mirror in his hand. Plate 8 from *Book of the Gods and Rites and the Ancient Calendar*, by Fray Diego Duran. Copyright 1971 by the University of Oklahoma Press.

ened, darkened, a dark spot. Thus, Tezcatlipoca, the axis or North
Pole, ruler of all directions, is named after his dark spot in the sky:
"smoking mirror." It is by a similar name ("eight mirror") that Zinacantecans know him.

⎡Tezcatlipoca, the synthesis of all the divine astronomical ideas,
thus included: (*a*) the nearly always visible, largest, slowest-moving
planets, Jupiter and Saturn, (*b*) the stars and constellations near the
polar center, changing with the precession of the equinoxes, around
the dark northern poles of the ecliptic, and (*c*) the Northern Wheel,
which is the only celestial pole visible in the northern hemisphere.
Its *true* center, the ecliptic northern pole, being a dark point, was
Tezcatlipoca as a smoked mirror. Specifically, Tezcatlipoca's body
was the constellation Ursa Major. His "mirror" was the black circle
of the ecliptic pole, which he held in his hand (see Illustration 18).
That is why he was "the heart of heaven and the heart of earth."

The pole star itself seems to have been the image of another god:
the "guiding star," god of traveling merchants, Yacatecuhtli. This
deity's "nose" pointed in the direction of their travels. His costume
was that of a nocturnal deity; he wore a dark blue mantle and had a
black and white spotted face. His "siblings" were probably the other
stars of the Ursa Minor constellation (Gonzales 1975). In addition,
the Northern Wheel was itself the image of a separate deity, Citlalte-
cuhtli (lord of stars), and was also called "the ball game court."
Tezcatlipoca ruled over it as a "ball player" (see Illustration 19).

Tezcatlipoca, in addition, had associations with all the other planets. Being the universal motion in which all the directions take
part, the ultimate core of the celestial plane, the measure of time and
space, Tezcatlipoca unfolded into (or had an effect on the position
of) every one of the major celestial objects. Tezcatlipoca, mythically,
was said to move from one place to another in the sky, in the precession of the equinoxes and planetary orbital movements. He was also
described as several "brothers" occupying different points in space
and time (see Chart 4). Thus in the myths he was simultaneously the
"ever present," "omnipotent" (Jupiter), the center (ecliptic northern
pole), the north (circumpolar stars), and each one of the major visible

19. The god Tezcatlipoca dressed as a ball player, showing his deformed leg. *Borgia Codex*, p. 21.

planets which make up the space-time continuum, the "time machine" or "clock" inside which we live. Because of this arrangement he was also god of all the seasons, summer as well as winter. These relations between astronomical events, celestial objects, seasons, and imagined deities, were metaphorically treated as Tezcatlipoca's aspects or "unfoldings," and as the "kinship relations" between the gods-planets—all siblings, spouses, or parents of one another (see section on kinship, p. 164, below, and Charts 4 and 5).

There were several ritual dancing games that specifically symbolized the ecliptic world and the planetary rotations. The *volador* game, an acrobatic display, is still performed in many Mexican towns, with "Tezcatlipoca" at the center top of a pole and the imper-

Chart 4. Tezcatlipoca transformations, related to kinship, and astronomical values

Black Tezcatlipoca—*Born-in-the-middle sibling*
= Jupiter (major, omnipresent)
= Saturn ("the cubic one," four-sided, originator of time, highest [outermost] justice, north)
= ecliptic North Pole (the center, the dark mirror)
= ecliptic world (the whirlwind, whirlpool, all cardinal directions, the north circumpolar stars), the night sky
= Ursa Major

Mixcoatl-Xipe-red Tezcatlipoca = "Mirror of Fiery Brightness"; Gemini-Fire Drill Constellation (= 2 Reed Constellation-Fire); Mars—*eldest brother of sun"*	Tepeyollotl earth center (Heart of Mountain) (southern pole?); earth = center-horizontal cardinal directions; earth as a celestial horizontal plane; theriomorphic soul companion	Meztli-Tecciztecatl = male moon; *younger sibling of sun,* partner in myth of origin; Coyolxauhqui = female moon, *"sister" of sun* ("wife" of sun?)	Quetzalcoatl-white Tezcatlipoca. Tlahuizcalpantecuhtli, Venus. *"3rd born, sibling of sun"*	Paynal, the Hasty (Tlaloc also?); Mercury—*"youngest brother of sun"*	Huitzilopochli = blue Tezcatlipoca= Sun-Nanahuatl-Tonatiuh; *"youngest brother of Xipe"*

Note: Kinship relations follow primarily the myths in *Historia de Los Mexicanos por sus Pinturas.*

sonators of the planets nearest the earth, dressed as fliers, descending from him. The *patolli* game is another. The most characteristic prehispanic ritual game, however, was the complex Ball Game, the courts for which were situated near or within the religious structures of many cities. In them, the reenactment of the astronomical gyrations, by players who were, of course, real men, took on its most human form.

The Stars and Constellations

Many stars and star clusters visible to the naked eye played an important part in religious symbolism. The Milky Way, today known in many Mesoamerican towns, as it is in Spain, as "Saint James Road," was the road of the zodiac, playing the same mythical role in Mesoamerican astronomical reckoning as it did in the Old World. The Milky Way was imagined as a double trunk tree, a double-headed snake, an umbilical cord connecting heaven, earth, and the underworld, a white road on which the stars and sun traveled, and other related sacred metaphors. The deities of the Milky Way were parental images, dual god-goddesses of sustenance—symbolism that ties in with the double branching of the Milky Way and its image as the umbilical cord from which divine sustenance reaches man, who is the offspring of the gods.

Several constellations recognized in Old World astronomy were also known in Mesoamerica, albeit with different mythical names or images (see Illustration 16). Among those recognized were the Pleiades, Orion, and Gemini (Beyer 1965:266–284). The culmination of the Pleiades marked the New Fire rituals every fifty-two years. The whole southern section of the nocturnal sky was with its stars a collection of gods known as the Four Hundred (a synonym for the multitude) gods. Huitzilopochtli, the sun, in one of the myths of his birth, had been born of Coatlicue, the earth mother, after she swallowed hummingbird feathers, to save her from the Four Hundred gods of the southern stars, who were also her children and whom he battled. This image of the myth, in which the hummingbird god (light, the sun) is born of Coatlicue (the earth), is a poetic mythic metaphor for the sunrise. His winning the battle over the Four Hundred gods is the image of the sun's emergence dispelling the forces of darkness = the night with its stars. The battle is the alternation of daytime and nighttime, the struggle of both to rule over the earth. In the same myth, the sister of both southern god (sun) and Four Hundred gods (stars), Coyolxauhqui, the moon-fire, takes an ambivalent role, at times an enemy of the sun, at times neutral between them. Obviously, the moon which is sometimes lighted like a minor sun, at other times absent, leaving the sky to be ruled only by the stars, fitted this metaphor with great economy and beauty (for clarification see Chart 4).

All apparent celestial movements, periodic revolutions of planets, and sequential passages of stars were mythologically assigned adventures, persona, stages of growth, sex, and so forth.

The changing of the position of the celestial pole, due to the equinoctial precession that changes the pole star and the planetary orbitings, was expressed in the complicated myths of Tezcatlipoca's transformations. The sequential cosmic mythical eras in which the god changed from one Tezcatlipoca form into another (or was replaced by another divine form) were named after the different "suns" that ruled and illuminated the earth, and also the different "stars" that ruled the pole at night (the stars of the northern circumpolar region).

The mythical texts describing these sacred transformations are extremely detailed, and if we knew each of the correct star symbols, the calendric counts associated with them would provide us with a series of prehispanic astronomical counts of dated events in the equinoctial precession. Although we do not have the total picture, pieces of it were preserved by the sixteenth-century native and Spanish scholars who recorded these sacred myths for posterity.

Tezcatilpoca, the multifaceted god of all these events combined, appears described as such in the myths. Specifically, his divine "movement" or "change" (that is, the change of position of the northern polar center from one star to another) was recorded in written form in the *Historia de los Mexicanos por sus Pinturas*, in the sixteenth century. For example, the movement of the celestial northern pole from a previous position to that of Alpha Ursae Minoris is symbolically stated in this text as the "change of Tezcatlipoca into Quetzalcoatl." "Another" Tezcatlipoca is also Ursa Major in the primary colonial texts. In the mythic text of the *Historia*, Quetzalcoatl tumbles down (kicks) the previous celestial polestar, making it "fall" (change position) into the celestial ocean (the lower sky). And thus Ursa Major = Tezcatlipoca "appears in the sky, because they say that the Ursa Major descends into the water and it is there in his memory" (*ibid.*, p. 213, my translation). The water is the mythic celestial ocean = the sky below the equator. The god "descends" (disappears), of course, because Ursa Major is then at the "side" of the circumpolar sky of the autumnal equinox point (west); this is the only period of the year in which that constellation is not completely visible in southern central Mexico, and west is the side where the sun also descends! Whenever a celestial object disappears from the sky it is said, in the myth, that it descends in the west. We must remember that spring and summer were the ascending period (= east and south) and fall and winter the descending period (= west and north).

When these myths are analyzed and combined, they all give four eras, suns, or changing polestars for the northern sky. The fifth polestar era is the present one. This analysis suggests, of course, that astronomical observations had recorded at least four previous changed positions of the "north polar star," but the number of years assigned to these precessional changes varies from myth to myth. Therefore we cannot be sure which specific stars were observed and assigned as polar stars for each of the cosmic "eras." Moreover, the picture is complicated because the myths of the unfolding of Tezcatlipoca also deal with the conjuctions of planets' orbits with zodiacal constellations. For example, in the myth in which the northerly located Tezcatlipoca changes into Mixcoatl, to make light and fire with the Fire Sticks (the Gemini constellation), the plot appears to refer to an astronomical event indicating some conjunction of Mars's (and/or Jupiter's) orbit in relation to the Gemini star cluster, or perhaps to the time period of the summer solstice, since this is the conjunction that comes closest to this solstitial point.

The Visible Spectrum

The spectrum was deified as the great rainbow snake, also a celestial visual phenomenon. Prehispanic peoples knew pigments of many colors, and named many of them. For religious and sacred purposes, however, five colors were dominant: black, white, red, yellow and blue-green (turquoise). Other colors appearing in the codices are symbolic variants of these five (for example, purplish instead of black). Colors played a part in the transformational game at all levels; that is, they were associated with all the other transformational codes in incredibly complex ways. The variation of color assignments is not yet understood. I believe that the reason for 'confusion arises from previous scholars' attempts to reduce the many transformational color combinations to a single one, when in fact the mythical color taxonomy was constantly being rearranged, in different contexts (see, for example, Thompson 1934).

The fact that only five colors are of major religious significance and the extreme complexity of arbitrary color transformations strongly suggest that the sacred colors appeared early in the transformational taxonomy of the light spectrum since these five colors were the first to appear in the first four stages (of a possible total of eight) in the evolution of language terms for color (Berlin 1970:8). If it is true that ritual color assignments are old, they have had ample time to evolve into a mythical subsystem which has "exhausted all its codings." I believe that with this new view of the mythical color taxonomy, it may be possible to unravel the meanings of the color transformations in the codices, which up to the present time are not well understood. The taxonomy of colors among present-day Indians (Wauchope, vols. 7 and 8), which is also unclear, can be better studied if the multiplicity of color contexts is taken as a starting point, rather than if a single unitary classification is assumed.

Huitzilopochtli's dominant colors were usually two: blue and yellowish white. The god's image was often painted blue, with blue paraphernalia. He was the blue Tezcatlipoca in correspondence with the spring and summer sun. But as the god dominant in the summer sky, the southern one, the color associated with him was white (white was often the color assigned to the south in the codices—and to the hawk and the hummingbird in the Zinacantecan poem). His priestesses ("his sisters") were dressed in white. For a discussion of white images in Zinacantan, see below, pp. 235–237.

Minerals

Minerals that possessed cultural, social, or economic significance were attached to the gods' planetary or celestial images. For example, flint, a symbol of knives, was a day sign, and it usually indicated north (whence come the cold "cutting" winds). Flint was also a marker of yearly calendar sections.

Salt, an important item of diet and trade among prehispanic peoples, had its own goddesses, who were associated with the water-moon deities, a logical connection if we remember that: (*a*) most salt in Mesoamerica is produced by water evaporation from saline rivers and from deposits near bodies of water; (*b*) the moon and salt are white; and (*c*) the moon goddesses were also water deities. Salt was an important trade item in prehispanic Zinacantan, and remains one today. Its goddess is now the Virgin of the Rosary.

Precious metals (such as gold) belonged to Xipe (Mars), who was also the god of jewelers. This god's association with precious metals is based on metaphors of skin and color. Xipe's name meant "the flayed one," and he wore a loose human skin for clothing. He was the god of the precious vegetation or "skin" ornamenting the earth's surface. He literally wore a precious skin as an ornament. He was thus also god of the ornaments of the human body. The symbolic equation reads: human skin = earth skin = vegetation = earth ornament = body ornaments = jewelry. But gold = reddish yellow = the color of Xipe, which is the planet Mars!

Turquoise represented the light of the sky and water among other things. Many of the sculptured images of the gods were made of precious minerals: jadeite or "emeralds," pure colored gray or black obsidian, rock crystal, turquoise mosaic, and so on. Huitzilopochtli in the Texcoco temple was made of wood, but his face bands (see section on facial painting, p. 160) were made of gold and turquoise because yellow and blue-green are the colors of the daytime sky when the sun is present (Pomar 1941:11). Hence, the precious jewels of the sky, the stars and planets with their sacred colors, became solidified into the precious jewels of the earth, the metals and gems.

Contemporary Zinacantecans, poorer than their prehispanic forebears, have statues made of sculptured wood, many in the Spanish Baroque tradition. These images, however, are close to invisible, being covered by layers of sumptuous clothes and a myriad of mirror circles and precious coins hanging from long ribbons, and, often, elaborate crowns (see, for example, Vogt 1969, photos on pp. 356, 357, and 518).

On a spectrum of past and present, native and European, Zinacantecan saints look a lot more native and ancestral than European and contemporary. Moreover, although the relation of their clothing to symbolic attributes of their prehispanic counterparts is unclear, there is some evidence that the small symbols that cover the images are related to prehispanic symbolism throughout Mesoamerica. On household altars, for example, one can find archaeological obsidian nuclei, faceted rock crystals and jadeite beads of prehispanic origin adorning the images of Christian saints, or lying side by side with them, sharing in the worship.

As saints and prehispanic symbols today share in the worship, the whole of the religion is a new melody, composed of old and new notes together, in beautiful syncretic harmony. In later chapters we will return to this theme. Before that, however, we must explore further prehispanic antecedents, in the domain of man-made symbols: culture.

CHAPTER 5

Cultural Orders

Nature was not the only object of detailed taxonomical construction in prehispanic religion. All cultural domains were likewise invaded by the desire to order and make sense of reality, and cultural taxonomies were also embedded in the religious transformational system. A complete list of these categories is perhaps an impossbile task at this time. I will focus on the classes that were often used in the construction of divine images or ideological clusters of symbols (that is, the theological "sentence matrices").

Material Culture
Tools and Weapons

Implements of work and war were symbols of human activities that were attributed to the gods. They identified divine images with the professions and statuses, or were symbols of their other attributes (sex, rank and so on). Arrows, knives, and shields were common possessions for warrior gods; the tumpline symbolized the gods' burden of carrying time over space, a truly divine activity; brooms, pots, thread spindles, and other household tools identified female deities. Huitzilopochtli, a warrior god, had a shield characteristic of kings, with a quincunx of five tufts of eagle feathers. He also carried arrows and atlatl darts, all warring and hunting tools. Other specific and characteristic attributes included pectorals, nose plugs, leg bands, paper fans of different shapes, and staffs. Huitzilopochtli's staff, a blue snake, represented the light of day descending from the god's hand (see Illustration 20).

Household Equipment and Furniture

Household goods were also attached to the gods to indicate their sex, status, activity, and the domain of life they controlled. Married

20. Huitzilopochtli pictured in full regalia, with the hummingbird head and feathers serving as a cape-headdress. (A) As divine ruler of the New Fire rituals for the year 2 Reed, standing above the temple in the festival of "Raising the Banners." *Codex Borbonicus*, p. 34. (B) As one of the gods in a circular divine parade in front of the temple of the goddess Cihuacoatl. *Codex Borbonicus*, p. 36.

pairs of deities were pictorially represented seated on a woven marriage mat. Sometimes they appeared making love under a blanket, or even uncovered, as Tlaloc and his wife are pictured in the *Porfirio Diaz Codex*. Single gods were often depicted standing, walking, or seated on a bench, inside a house, temple, or palace. Huitzilopochtli, as a statue image, had a "blue wooden bench in the fashion of a litter. . . . This bench was sky blue indicating that Huitzilopochtli's abode was in the heavens" (Duran 1971:72), as was appropriate for the sun (see Illustration 6, where the god appears seated on his bench).

The attributes of the kitchen were deified as a set of goddesses in their own right. They were known as the three goddesses of sustenance, and were symbolized by the three stones over which the tortilla-grill and cooking pots were placed. Sometimes, as in the *Borgia Codex*, the "stones" were pictured as three skulls, in memory of an old myth in which Tezcatlipoca made them skulls as a punishment for misdeeds. These "skulls" = goddesses of three stones of the hearth are still very much alive in Cuicatec myth, but in Zinacantan, with a few exceptions (the chief being the Virgin of the Rosary, who rules salt and women), male gods dominate the divine landscape—as is "appropriate" in a patrilineal society! However, the major sacred mountain of Zinacantan, Muk'ta Vits (east of Zinacantan Center, called "senior large mountain") is also called *7oshyoket*, or "three hearth stones," suggesting that some associations of the old complex of female goddesses may still remain. (I am indebted to Nan Vogt for this suggestion.) The hypothesis derives some support from the Zinacantecan beliefs that within this mountain is the home of the ancestral deities, that every homestead has a hearth, and that the ancestral gods are married pairs of deities. It also ties in with the fact that the central east-west line represents the celestial equator, and the star constellation in this position is Orion's belt. Cuicatecs also believe the three goddesses to be, simultaneously, the three skulls, the cooking stones, and the three stars of Orion's belt. In the sky they are "watched" by a human family of three members (= Orion's sword). In Zinacantan Orion's belt is called "the trio of women" (*7osh7lot*) and Orion's sword is called "the three eavesdroppers"— *7osh-lotj7elek'* (Robert Laughlin, personal communication).

Clothing

Clothing had enormous social importance among prehispanic peoples. It was the major symbol in the presentation of the self as a social being, identifying age and sex status, social class, ethnic group, profession, and special privileges. The gods, being of the highest status, were always richly dressed, like noblemen and kings (see Illustration 20). Elaborate variations in clothing details (in the shape of pectorals, for example, and in greca designs on headdresses and mantles) formed a complex sartorial language of divine identifications. Huitzilopochtli, for example, had a blue-green mantle, blue sandals (the poor must normally have gone barefooted, as today's Indians do), and gold bracelets. His hair was eagle feathers, and his headdress was of blue feathers with a gold beak "as a simile of the head of a small bird which lives in this land, which is called hummingbird" (Pomar, 1941:11, my translation).

Bodo Spranz (1964) has written an elaborate comparison of the gods' iconography as found in the codices of the *Borgia* group, which includes their clothing, tools, headdresses and jewelry. (In addition, he discusses the face masks and face painting of a large number of gods, the subject of my next category.)

Some of the clothing markers of divine figures are still used in Zinacantan today by the ritual impersonators of sacred beings. Among these are jaguar skins, headdresses, and masks. The costumes of gods as well as of men have been modified by colonial and more recent fashions, but the same symbol arrangements persist, and many pieces of clothing are still made in the prehispanic fashion (for instance, sandals, single piece "jackets"). As with hummingbirds, men in Zinacantan are much more colorfully garbed than the women. Also, as Vogt has pointed out (1969:107), Zinacantecans "appear to attach an extraordinary amount of social significance" to clothing.

Face Painting and Masks

Prehispanic peoples used face painting or ornamentation to indicate their status, religious or secular, in the same manner in which they used clothing, and other societies use tattoos and scarification. All the gods had special colors and designs over their faces, which identified them with others having the same symbols. The god of wind had an elongated mouth mask, an imitation of a person blowing with distended lips. Sometimes this was a bird beak. Zinacantecans today give him a bird mask headdress with a huge beak, which may be a modification of the original distended lips (see Illustration 2a, b, and c). Huitzilopochtli's face was painted with a blue forehead, a blue band over the nose from ear to ear and an intermediate light yellow band, to represent the light of sun and day sky. In sculptural form, as I stated previously, these facial bands were covered with mosaic of turquoise and gold (Pomar 1941:11). Mask and facial painting as well as headdresses of complicated design and rich costumes with gold and mirrors are worn both by sacred figures (such as saints) and ritual impersonators in Zinacantan. It would be interesting to know whether the designs of saints' clothes and faces are identified in any way with autochthonous deities. Like Huitzilopochtli, the *Capitán* impersonators in Zina-cantan's Saint Lawrence rituals wear gold bands on their faces, a fact that we will consider later, in the section on the armature of con-temporary symbols at Zinacantan.

Social Structure and Stratification
Professions

Crisscrossing with other associations, in a multiplicity of jeux-d'esprit but also of sacred symbolisms, the gods were the tutelary guardians of prehispanic professions. Prehispanic peoples had devel-oped a complex division of labor and professional specializations, including an elaborate bureaucracy and many nonagrarian roles. These are illustrated in the *Florentine Codex*. Professional groups were identified as special groups of people, and professions were ranked but they were also criss-crossed by social class membership. Each had its tutelary deity, connected through an ideological trans-formation: for example, Camaxtli, the god of war, was also protector of the hunt and hunters. Midwives had tutelaries who were, fit-tingly, goddesses belonging to the "postlabor" age category. They were married and fertile (such as Teteoinnan, mother of gods). Huit-zilopochtli, as I have mentioned, ruled the warriors. Women who died in labor were considered dead warriors (see Illustration 21).

The gods mapped out the social order according to the division of labor in the society, combining to make a system that Durkheim would have found pleasing in terms of his theories. In Zinacantecan ritual a few of these identifications still appear to be meaningful, a subject that will be discussed in the final sections of this book. It should suffice to say here that the Zinacantecan saints and impersons-ators also represent human categories in the division of labor.

Food as Marker of Social Status

Since each god had his own place in the calendrical rituals, he also had his special food. These foods were cooked and eaten by the participants in specified rituals, as offerings to the deity. Divine foods were also eaten by priests and some worshippers as part of the

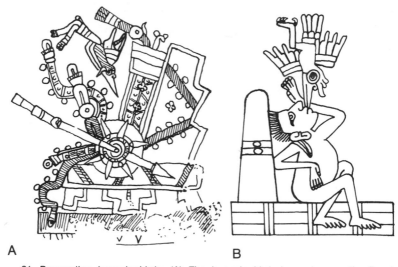

A   B

21. Descending hummingbirds. (A) The hummingbird descends over the Royal Throne of the Sun, symbolizing the death of the sun-king. In the codex picture to the left of this one, he is being killed by the Venus star god. *Cospi Codex*, p. 9, obverse. (B) The hummingbird descends over the lips of a pregnant woman, symbolizing her death in labor. She is one of the "western warrior women" who died in childbirth and later accompanied the sun from midday to sunset. In the codex to her right is the god of death, receiving her. *Codex Laud*, p. 6.

cult, on the appropriate dates. In general, they were foods unlikely to be eaten in the daily diet or by commoners. Some were luxury foods, such as deer meat, cacao, and sweet cakes. Others were seasonal foods which could be prepared for rituals only at a particular time of year. One of Huitzilopochtli's special foods was pulque dyed blue (*matlaloctli*—Sahagun 1969, 1:199).

Food metaphors appeared in astronomical symbolism, as the following riddle indicates: "What is a small blue gourd filled with popcorn?" "It's the sky with its stars" (Sahagun 1970, Part 7:237).

The categories of foods and statuses combine, in Durkheimian fashion, the divine presences and the social structure at the macrolevel, adding Lévi-Strauss's favorite image for culture: cooked food.

In contemporary Mexico (including Zinacantan), Indians have an elaborate schedule of cooked ritual foods. Each major holiday and holy day has a typical food that is eaten during the ritual period.

These vary from region to region, and from village to village, and include many items of European origin (such as wheat, bread, and rice). Cooked and salted foods are also sacred metaphors for "civilized" (see the Matlacihuatl myth, pp. 102–107).

Historical Culture Heroes: Mesoamerican Euhemerism

Many of the prehispanic deities had apparently been living human beings who were deified after their deaths. Others were historically real culture heroes who for some reason had become identified with an already existing deity (for example, because they were priests of that god).

Several major gods had such historical antecedents. The idea of Quetzalcoatl as a god may have been older than the period of Tula, but the priestly king of that city, also named Quetzalcoatl, had become one with the god by the time that the Spaniards arrived.

Gonzales (1967) has argued well that Huitzilopochtli had been in fact a historical personage among the Aztec, only later incorporated as a god into the pantheon (see above, p. 60, for the myth of Huitzilopochtli guiding the Aztec, peregrination). Zinacantecans believe that the sun-Jesus and Saint Sebastian, among other divinities, were local culture heroes.

Ethnic Groups

Because such historically real culture heroes had lived among the peoples of specific ethnic or language groups or city states, they became tutelary images of these same groups or cities, and were imagined as having a lawyer-client relation with their protégés (see Nicholson 1971:409).

Huitzilopochtli, hero of the Mexica, was also their supreme deity. Other gods, however, ruled over smaller, humbler groups: wards of towns, villages, or even small hamlets. They were also protectors of descent groups, of whom they were the mythical parents. These parental gods appear in Zinacantan as the ancestral pairs who founded the *municipio*. But this connection leads us to the next cultural transformational class.

Kinship

The gods, like man, had intricate genealogical relationships with each other. Also, like the Greek gods, they had had offspring by human beings. Apparently, at least as far as the extant accounts show, the theologians never worked out a complete divine genealogy (*ibid.*). It is probable in fact that a unitary genealogy could not be manufactured without discarding some of the mythological apparatus, since many myths held as sacred by the same ethnic groups had contradictory information about the genealogical relationships of the deities.

Some contradictions stemmed from the oppositional relations developed in myth, the dynamics of which created intricate foldings of genealogical space. Others existed because of the use of incest as a metaphor for nature (Lévi-Strauss 1949). Thus gods were simultaneously spouses and siblings, and when certain related myths are put together as a set, sometimes a particular god, like the man in the joke, ends up being his own father.

However, when the gods are taken in small mythical sets of two or three, they form genealogical constellations of primary lineal relatives. Huitzilopochtli, like the other gods, fitted into these microgenealogies, and was related to many gods in the pantheon. I will give some examples.

Huitzilopochtli was one of Tezcatlipoca's aspects; mythically he was his self-generated brother. Taking Tezcatlipoca as a quadripartite set, Huitzilopochtli was the "youngest brother" (= Teicauhtzin, one of his names) of the other three Tezcatlipocas (*HDLMPSP:* 209). In this mythical context Tezcatlipoca-Huitzilopochtli was a son of the primeval couple of *tona* gods. His placing thus indicated the planetary role of the sun as an object of religious-astronomical importance. In his second mythical birth (a mystery), Huitzilopochtli was son of the earth mother, Coatlicue. But since Coatlicue had been created by Tezcatlipoca, he was indirectly Tezcatlipoca's grandson. In the Coatlicue myth he also was the youngest brother, since he had been born last of Coatlicue's children, after the Centzon Huitzinahua, Four Hundred gods of the south, (the stars) and his elder sister and enemy, Coyolxauhqui (the moon-fire). The Four Hundred gods, stars of the southern sky, were half-siblings and oppositions of Huitzilopochtli, the southern sun. They "retreated" (disappeared from the sky) when he "arrived" (at sunrise). Paynal, the swift (probably Mercury), was an aspect of Huitzilopochtli "his messenger" or *his* younger sibling, replicating the unfolding of Tezcatlipoca and Huitzilopochtli, with inverted ages (see Chart 4). The young priests who served in Huitzilopochtli's temple, and feasted a whole year in his honor, were also called his "brothers."

Quetzalcoatl, another of Tezcatlipoca's aspects, was the solar god's sibling and partner, and in many ways also his opposition or counterpart. For example, the one was born in the year that the other died (2 Cane). The relation was a set of metaphors for the spring equinox, with the southern sun ascending and equinotial spring winds appearing simultaneously. But it is also a metaphor of the light of the sun "killing" the light of Venus as morning star.

Because of this relation, both were also siblings of Xipe Totec, the god of the renewal of the earth vegetation in spring, and they were kinsmen of Tlaloc, symbolizing the onset of the rainy season. That is, the kinship relations symbolized the conjunction of the climatic, planetary, and ecological conditions of spring and summer, or inversely, kinship relations based on generation and age rank were symbolized by ecological ones. In other myths Quetzalcoatl and Huitzilopochtli were siblings because both were sons of Coatlicue (the earth).

Huitzilopochtli's position as a younger sibling of many other gods corresponds with his factual historical arrival in the Mesoamerican pantheon. He was the last of the gods to be incorporated as a major deity, rising to theological ascendance with the meteoric social ascendance of his worshippers, the Mexica, who were newcomers (Nicholson 1971:426) in the Post-Classic Period. He, in fact, usurped the divine images of older solar deities deriving from other ethnic groups. Tlaloc was also associated with Huitzilopochtli in the rituals

Chart 5. Some meanings of the kinship associations of Huitzilopochtli

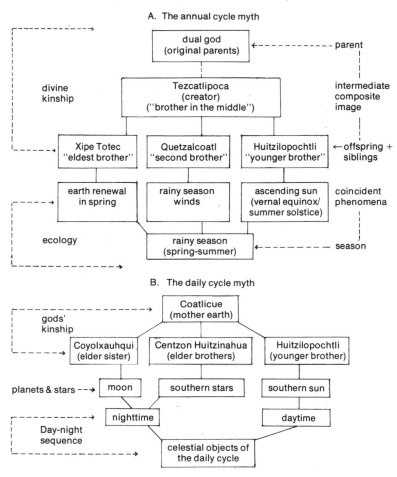

A. The annual cycle myth

B. The daily cycle myth

and the temple placement in Tenochtitlan. Thus the oldest and youngest gods, historically, shared in the cult.

The relation between Huitzilopochtli and the spring-summer period was also exemplified in his kinship to Macuilxochitl, a god of the joys of spring and summer.

In Zinacantan there is, apparently, no worked-out genealogy of the ancestral deities or saints, but the same primary relations of senior and junior sibling, husband and wife, or parent and child are utilized to relate images to each other in the context of prayer, myth, and ritual.

The other dimension of the gods' relations, in territoriality, is discussed later on in the context of sacred numerology.

Names and Language Transformations

> Words are seals of the mind, results—or, more correctly, stations—of an infinite series of experiences, which reach from an unimaginable distant past into the present, and which feel their way into an equally unimaginable distant future. They are "the audible that clings to the inaudible," the forms and potentialities of thought, which grow from that which is beyond thought.
>
> Lama Anagarika Govinda, *Foundations of Tibetan Mysticism*

Prehispanic Mesoamerican religion, based as it was in complex games of a mytho-poetic nature, reached one of its most developed forms in its imaginative, elegant, creative use of language. Hence it is not surprising that in the ideas about the divinity, plays on words, puns, homonymy, and homophony had a most important role, particularly in the cultural context of names. Ideas based on word or name manipulation were often used as transformations of the gods. This manipulation was enhanced by the use of personal calendrical names which associated the gods with day and year names, and with cardinal directions.

Huitzilopochtli is a prime example of a play on names. Literally, the name of the god has been glossed as "hummingbird-left," from *huitzil-* (of *huitzi(tzi)lin*) = hummingbird and *opochtli* = left. However, *huitzli* (thorn, south, as in *huitztlampa*: the land of thorns or the land of the south) was used, in a play on words, interchangeably with hummingbird. And *telpochtli* (Spanish: *mancebo, varón maduro joven*; English: youthful male, bachelor) and *oquichtli* (brave or valiant male, warrior) were also combined with *opochtli* to make a sacred pun (Garibay 1961).

Thus the name of the god was a complex mythical pun meaning:

The left-handed hummingbird
The warrior hummingbird

The youthful male hummingbird
The valiant male hummingbird
The valiant male (of the) south
The warrior (of the) south
The youthful male (of the) south
The thorny warrior
The southern left-handed (one)
The brave hummingbird

Moreover, *huitz-* means to come, and *huetzi* means "to come down, to throw oneself, falling." The god is thus the one who "comes down or throws himself from the left or the south." This is, of course, an appropriate sacred pun, because the sun of spring and summer moves from left to right, that is, from south to north over the ecliptic. He is described in our poem with this imagery of "coming out and down." In a veiled reference, sound plays on words for cooking (*huicci*, to cook oneself, and *huicxitli*, a dialectal form meaning "to put to cook"), are again, symbolically linked, because in the myth of origin the humanoid being who became the sun did so by throwing himself into the divine fire and cooking himself. In the *Borgia Codex* he appears, in fact, inside a cooking pot atop the mythic fire, being cooked (see *ibid.*, p. 345).

Incredible as it may seem, the god himself, by transformational logic, represented all these ideas simultaneously. Added to these, since hummingbirds are often iridescent blue-green, the color of the sky in the daytime, the god became the blue southern sun of the daytime, that is, the sun's light of day and its fire in spring and summer (see also Chart 6). The name could also mean "the precious left" because hummingbirds and quetzals with their beautiful feathers were used metaphorically to mean "precious" or "jewel."

The association of left and south is also explicit in pictorial form, in some of the *Divine Calendar Books* (the *Count of the Days* or *Prophecy Books*). There the east is painted at the top of the page, with south to its left (see for example, Duran 1971:359, Plate 35), in contrast to our maps, where north is at the top. There was "method in this madness." South had to be at the left of the page because west is the direction in which the sun "dies" every day (at sunset). Therefore,

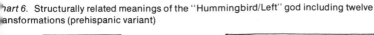

Chart 6. Structurally related meanings of the "Hummingbird/Left" god including twelve transformations (prehispanic variant)

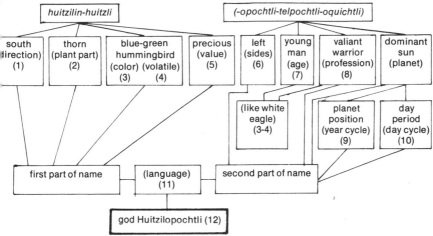

west = dying = going to the underworld = going below = bottom of the page. If west is to be at the bottom, east has to be on top and south = left side (of the page)! There is also a linked explanation, mentioned before, if one imagines the sun as a person walking face forward from east to west, his left hand will be south, his right hand north. This example shows the multivalence of iconographic symbols, or, as Turner would say, iconographic multivocality.

Zinacantecans today place great emphasis in their rituals on the right-left distinction, which they connect with the birth and death of the sun at sunrise and sunset. Vogt (1976) has glossed these directions as "rising heat (of the sun)" and "waning heat (of the sun)." Also, as in the prehispanic rituals of Huitzilopochtli's path which followed a counterclockwise direction, Zinacantecans follow in their ritual a counterclockwise route, moving "in the sun's direction" (Duran, 1971:87; Vogt 1976), that is, the direction of his daily path.

Ethos

Durkheim's discovery that man abstracts and idealizes his social map in his conception of the divine order is paralleled by Freud's discovery that man projects his psychic attitudes in his conception of the same divine order. The world of the deities is not only a cognitive map of the social structure, but is also an expressive map of man's psychic experience: his infantile feelings about parents, his youthful ambivalences, his adult hopes and fears. Gods, like a child's parents, or like the other adults who populate a child's emotional landscape, are in most cultures and for most men ambivalent figures, both nurturant and punitive, simultaneously protective and authoritative. The Mesoamerican peoples of the past mapped out, in their conceptions of the gods, their ambivalences about the social, moral, and psychic domains. Their descendants still do this today. None of the deities were without ambivalent images, none of them were pure metaphors for good or bad, wholly beneficial or destructive. The earth was both nurturant mother and cannibalistic monster. The sun was a nurturant warm father as well as the destructive fire of the sky. The gods who reflected sexuality were also ambivalent images. The goddess of love, Tlazolteotl, was simultaneously, the goddess of sin, the "filth eater."

The ambivalent qualities of the gods were expressed in mythical and pictorial symbolism by opposed dualities, the "unfoldings" of a god into positive and negative images. These were presented as metaphors of mood, value, or moral character. For example, the god Tlaloc could be beneficial rain : male fertility : *friendly* god, or damaging storm : male destructiveness : *angry* god. The sun, in parallel fashion, could be warming light : hummingbird : *gentle* god, or destructive fire : eagle : *fierce* god.

Ambivalence was built in, integral to all levels of the pantheon. All attempts to exalt the deities singly or collectively as representing purely good or evil, spirituality or materiality, body or soul, in either the prehispanic pantheon or the contemporary one, lead to distortion. Séjourné (1957), for example, who has some interesting insights on prehispanic religion, fails completely when she attempts to identify Quetzalcoatl as the dominant image of the pure spirituality or divinity of man, as pure light, pure soul or spirit. To sustain that theory and her ideas about the "spirituality" of the Mesoamerican doctrines, she is forced to argue against ambiguity and goes through contortions of analysis in dealing with specific individual symbols of the deities; as, for example, when she must take the position that Quetzalcoatl's twin, Xolotl, represents only materiality and darkness, impurity of soul, though he is nonetheless the evening star! This dual, twin nature is a defining element of the whole pantheon. As Venus is both the evening and the morning star, humanity and animality, Quetzalcoatl and Xolotl, so other deities unfold in pairs representing alternate poles of an ethical, emotional, or orectic material continuum.

The deities of contemporary Zinacantan are equally ambivalent figures. Neither what Vogt calls the ancient gods nor the syncretic Roman Catholic divine figures are seen as purely good or bad, nurturant or punitive. The marginal identification of the devil with many of the ancient gods in Mesoamerica seems to be a result of the influence of Catholic priests. For the living Indians, as for their ancestors, the gods are above human moral judgment or human emotional need. To obtain their favor requires constant cajoling and gifts. They simultaneously bind burdens of sickness and fear upon man and feed him with precious corn.

CHAPTER 6

Mathematical Orders

Prehispanic peoples used mathematics in accounting and astronomy, and for 'other practical needs; they also raised it to the status of an esoteric art. Numerological transformations in a sophisticated civilization are usually associated with the calendar, and with horoscope prediction for individuals and the scheduling of planting (as in China or India). Both activities are culturally relevant in a society with a peasant base which cultivates according to seasonal cycles. The many social activities of the bureaucratized state were ordered in calendrical cycles, involving a complicated numerology. These cyclical schedules were necessary to organize the complex division of labor and coordinate the multiple tasks of the different social groups. The importance of the subsistence base, farming, was ritually signified by the dominance of water, vegetation, and earth gods, and by the fertility rituals that dotted the annual calendar. Rituals for the gods of water and vegetative fertility alone represented over a third of the total (Nicholson 1971:434).

Numerology as a religious development in Mesoamerica was in my opinion an offshoot of the growth of an agrarian calendar, and later was overlayed with more esoteric astronomical models, religious ideas, and the scheduling of other social activities.

The long calendar of a 52-year "century" was a complex transformational system in its own right. The core was a system of calculation using the 365-day solar year. But superimposed on this was a complex cycle of 260 days. The cycle included a system of 20 day signs, with 20 patron gods, 13 day numbers, 4 year signs, and 13 "accompanying" volatiles, 13 "carrier" gods which supported time, 4 patron gods of yearly divisions, and a divination system that combined the meanings of the other transformational classes to make predictions about individuals' lives, statecraft, success in harvests, and so on.

I will not attempt to develop a complete account of the calendric transformations here, for several reasons. First, they have been studied and elaborately reported on by specialists far more competent than I (for instance, Satterthwaite 1965; Caso 1967, 1968). Second, their relevance for a study based on the god Huitzilopochtli and the hummingbird tale of Zinacantan is tenuous. The hummingbird god had very few associations with the long formal calendar structure used for divination. In all probability this was so because he was a newcomer to the pantheon. Elder gods had been introduced (according to archaeological evidence) while the transformational structure of the divinatory calendar was acquiring coherence and complexity over time. Hypothetically we could assume that if the Spanish conquest had not taken place, prehispanic religion would have continued to evolve, and in the process, Huitzilopochtli would have made a place for himself in the most important ritual divinatory calendar, as long as he was god of a powerful political group. However, the Mexica had not invented the calendar for ritual and divination, and their culture hero did not belong to any of the standard formal groupings: neither to the twenty day-sign series, the thirteen god series, the nine god series, nor to accompanying deities, nor any others. His only claim to membership in the most esoteric of orders derived from his usurpation of the images of other gods with which he had partially merged—for example, the other sun gods, such as Tonatiuh, or the fire god whose bird was a blue hummingbird (see Table 3).

His rituals, however, had been integrated into the annual agrarian-solar calendar at least in the great city of Tenochtitlan. Also he had day, month, and year dates associated with him. Before these matters can be discussed, I will briefly indicate the transformational orders present in the calendar.

To simplify matters, I present in Table 3 a list of the deities with their Nahuatl names, according to their patronage of the principal numerical cycles, to show how gods and cycles corresponded.

Table 3. Some divine patrons of the major divinatory cycles

Divine patron	The twenty day signs in sequence	The thirteen numerals in order	The twenty periods of thirteen days	Accompanying volatile order	The night rulers order	The year rulers order
Tonacatecuhtli (and Tonacacihuatl)	Earth monster, 1st		1st, 1 Earth monster 1–13th day			
Quetzalcoatl	Wind, 2nd	9	2nd, 1 Jaguar 14–26th day	9th, turkey		year House, direction west, animal snake
Tepeyollotl	*House*, 3rd		3rd, 1 Deer 27–39th day		8th	
Huehuecoyotl (and Ixnextli)	Lizard, 4th		4th, 1 Flower 40–52nd day			
Chalchihuitlicue	Snake, 5th	3	5th, 1 Cane 53–65th day	3rd, falcon	6th	
Tecciztecatl	Death, 6th		6th, 1 Death 66–78th day			
Tlaloc	Deer, 7th	8	7th, 1 Rain 79–91st day	8th, a kind of eagle? (*Codex Laud*: seagull?)	9th	
Mayahuel	*Rabbit*, 8th		8th, 1 Straw 92–104th day			
Xiuhtecuhtli	Water, 9th	1	20th, 1 Rabbit 248–260th day	1st, blue hummingbird	1st	
Mictlantecuhtli	Dog, 10th	6	10th, 1 Flint 118–130th day	6th, screech owl	5th	
Xochipilli (and Centeotl)	Monkey, 11th	7	same as Mayahuel	7th, butterfly	4th	
Patecatl	Straw, 12th		11th, 1 Monkey 131–143rd day			
(Iztlacoliuhqui) *Tezcatlipoca*	*Cane*, 13th	10	12th, 1 Lizard 144–156th day	10th, horned owl	2nd	year Flint, direction north, animal jaguar

Tlazolteotl	Jaguar, 14th	5	13th, Undulant movement 157–169th day	5th, eagle	7th	year Cane, direction east, animal eagle
Xipe Totec	Eagle, 15th		14th, 1 Dog 170–182nd day			
Itzpapalotl	Buzzard, 16th		15th, 1 House 183–195th day			
Xolotl	Undulant movement, 17th		16th, 1 Buzzard 196–208th day			
Chalchiuhtotolin	*Flint*, 18th		17th, 1 Water 209–221st day			
Chantico (and *Tonatiuh*)	Rain, 19th	4	18th, 1 Wind 222–224th day	4th, quail		year Rabbit, direction south, animal rabbit
Xochiquetzal	Flower, 20th		19th, 1 Eagle 235–247th day			
Tlaltecuhtli (= aspect of earth, Mictlantecuhtli)		2		2nd, green hummingbird?		
Tlahuizcalpantecuhtli (= aspect of Quetzalcoatl)		12	9th, 1 Snake 105–117th day	12th, quetzal		
Ilamatecuhtli (= old age aspect of Tlazolteotl)		13		13th, parrot		
Piltzintecuhtli (= young aspect of Tonatiuh)					3rd	
Yoaltecuhtli (= aspect of night, Mictlantecuhtli)		11		11th, macaw		

Note: The divine patrons whose names are in italic were the five cosmogonic suns. Tonatiuh, the present sun, was also named blue Tezcatlipoca, Huitzilopochtli and 4 Olin (his calendrical name). The day signs in italic were the four year signs almost all over Mesoamerica.

The Maya calendar versions and other Highland versions known to us, either historically or in the contemporary record, *are identical in armature* to the example I give here. However, there was some code variation from one locale to another. The major variants included, first, a different set of four year-bearer signs, usually one that used the day sign immediately above these in the Nahuatl list in Table 3. The Cuicatec at the time of the conquest, and in earlier times some of the Lowland Maya, had used the signs Wind, Deer, Straw, and Undulant Movement (or their equivalent named positions), to name the years. This variation implies that the calendar year-bearer names were corrected by a change of one day at the start of the year. The correction took place sometime *before* the Aztec adopted the Mesoamerican calendar. It was accepted practically all over the highland core region of Mesoamerica, but the Cuicatec held to the older year bearers, being, on many counts, highly conservative vis-à-vis other Mesoamerican cultures even to the present day.

Second, different ethnic groups in Mesoamerica may have started the year at different times. In most calendars it seems apparent that the start coincided more or less with the beginning of corn planting, near the spring equinox. However, there is some weak evidence that for some groups the year started at the winter solstice, while for others it began at the summer solstice. The evidence for its beginning at the winter solstice is better than that for the summer, but no definite answer can yet be given to the problem of a universal starting date for the year.

Third, the day names, month names and the names of the patron deities show local variation throughout Mesoamerica. What is House in one calendar becomes Cave in another and, by symbolic drift, Darkness in a third. This connection makes sense if we remember that Indian houses, like caves, have no windows and are very dark indeed compared with our houses. It also relates to the metaphor for the interior of the earth (the night southern pole), which was the house of darkness, or the cave, the tomb. Moreover, for some of the local calendars, even early colonial ones, our information on bearer gods, companions and patrons is incomplete. There is no doubt, however, from the information we do have, that the structure of the calendar was pan-Mesoamerican, and therefore, the Nahuatl example I have provided should suffice for an understanding of variants.

Directions

Prehispanic peoples conceived of the cosmos as having a number of dimensions and directions which corresponded with several alternate models, all of which are basic mathematical-topological constructs.

The simplest model conceived the earth's plane as floating in a spatial continuum, which was a plane made up of water, comprising both the ocean below and the sky above. "The word for the universe in Nahuatl 'that surrounded by water' clearly expresses this notion" (Nicholson 1971:403). In this model, the sky-ocean water was both a plane above and below and a one-sided topological construct, like a Moebius strip, a Kleinian bottle, or a three-dimensional torus. The earth plane between them was shaped as a quincunx, with four sides and a center point (see Illustration 26 for a contemporary approximation).

However, prehispanic peoples also conceived of several other models. According to one, the earth's surface was a horizontal plane with four sides, the directions here being visualized as sides. The northern side was the northernmost passage of the sun, the tropical line. The southern side was the tropical line of the most southerly passage of the sun. These are what Zinacantecans call "the sides of the sky" (Vogt 1969:304). The eastern and western sides were the varying positions of sunrise and sunset, each point being the sun's appearance and disappearance during the course of a year. When the center of the earth was added, the plane was conceived as a quincunx, the four intercardinal points NE, NW, SW, and SE being columns, trees, or divinities which supported the world above them, and apparently were also constellations identified as gods. The twist in the Moebius strip, as a topological quality of the universe, was expressed in the cosmic myths in which the four gods, four aspects of Tezcatlipoca, and his assistants, *had dug passages into the earth, to lift the sky up from underneath* (*HDLMPSP* 1941:214). That is, up and down, below and above, were the same side, overlapped. When the four cardinal directions and the up and down directions were combined, the world was said to have six points of support. This gave a Moebius strip with plane boundaries (see Courant and Robbins 1941:259–264).

Another model perceived the earth and the sky as two separate planes, one above or involving the other. In this model there were eight earth and sky supporters (bearers or columns), as in the model prevailing today in Zinacantan, where the Vashakmen (Tezcatlipoca) is "eight" and "four" simultaneously (Vogt 1969:303–304). These two planes tilt in opposite directions during the year. When earth = north, sky = south; that is why the summer sun is "southern." The idea of an alternating tilt perhaps explains why in the *Borgia Codex* the four supporters of the sky and the four columns of the earth are paired in opposites—an eastern sky bearer with a western earth column, a northern sky supporter with a southern earth one.

In an even more complex model, earth, sky, and underworld were conceived as three separate planes, tied together by the path of the sun around them. This model has twenty or twenty-one points of support depending on whether the center of the earth is counted as one of them.

The numbers that were of ritual significance in prehispanic religion could emerge indirectly from these models, but they had other multivocal referents. Five, for example, which was written as a horizontal bar, had apparently been derived from the number of fingers on one hand. In fact, in early stone calendrics, the five bar is represented by a finger, complete with fingernail. Twenty was a most important number, since in many Mesoamerican languages twenty is used as the unit of counting (the radix), as we use ten—a common practice in societies speaking languages in which fingers and toes are not linguistically distinct. That the numeral 20 is body-related is attested by the fact that in several Mesoamerican lan-

guages, including Tzotzil, the language of Zinacantan, "twenty" is a
homonym of "man."

The Space-Time Continuum, or What Time Is This Place?

The cardinal directions were markers not simply of space, but also
of time. By a simple transformational arrangement, winter was
equated with north, summer with south and therefore spring with
east and fall with west. Furthermore, the directions marked shorter
and longer time periods as well; weeks, months, years, and year
clusters had "directions" too. The reason for this transformational

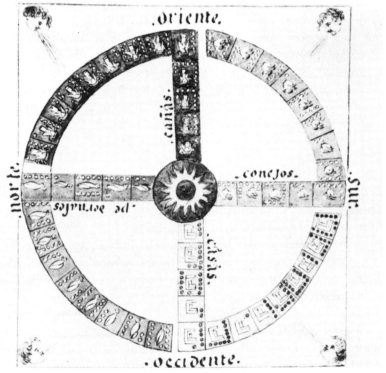

22. Year calendar with the directions and their associations. Plate 35 from *Book of the
Gods and Rites and the Ancient Calendar*, by Fray Diego Duran. Copyright 1971 by the
University of Oklahoma Press.

overlap has not been well understood, but I have been able to obtain relevant ethnographic information from Cuicatec Indians, which, in my opinion, simultaneously solves two mysteries of the prehispanic space-time continuum model. One is the link of the directions with time periods. The other is the origin of the division of the calendar by thirteen and of the multiple cycles of thirteen that were used in it. Both will be explained in a paper now in preparation, but a brief summary is given in the section on contemporary survivals, pp. 206–209, below.

The relation space-time determined the location of ritual events. Thus fall events took place in temples in the western direction, winter in northerly ritual locations, and so on. In consequence, deities which had a dominant time period also had a dominant direction as a symbolic meaning. This symbolism was actually carried over into architecture in that the deity's temples were built in an appropriate direction with respect to the center of a city or to a temple complex. The relevance of this connection for contemporary Zinacantan will be seen later, in the development of my argument about Saint Sebastian and his mythic-ritual locations.

Geometric Designs

Stereotyped geometric shapes with a religious symbolic value—circles, eye shapes, undulant lines, squares, and many other figures—abound in prehispanic architecture, painting and writing. Each one served to identify a more complex idea connected with astronomical images, calendric counts, or divinity signs.

A number of the most complex ideas represented by simple geometric shapes were symbols of the space-time continuum itself. The most characteristic is the symbol *olin*.

Since their notions of the space-time continuum were basically topological models, highly abstracted, prehispanic peoples had no more success than modern mathematicians in presenting these models in graphic form. Topologists today may use perspective drawing, but often have to resort to purely mathematico-logical formulae, because of difficulties in transferring all the dimensions of their ideas onto paper in other ways. In the same fashion, prehispanic graphic representations by themselves could not do justice to their complex models. Furthermore, since prehispanic peoples did not know the conventions of perspective invented in Europe during the Renaissance, their difficulties were compounded. (Even given our technique of perspective, representing such models is a clumsy task.)

The solution chosen by prehispanic painters was to take only one aspect of a total concept at a time, that is, to simplify, for artistic religious purposes, a cosmological-astronomical model. They communicated ideas with the pictures by allusion to traditional motifs, producing a visual arrangement of the symbols of these simplified concepts. Nicholson (1971:403) has pointed out one such artistic attempt at coping with topological simplification in the design of the *Codex Borbonicus* (after Seler 1963:2:270, fig. 270).

The same arduous problem of design was faced when the prehispanic artist had to represent the idea of the quincunx, the space-time continuum. Sometimes the solution was a highly elaborate one, as on pp. 49–53 of *Borgia* or p. 1 of *Fejervary-Mayer*. Sometimes it was a simple, elegant symbol which contained the basic ideas in kernel. The symbol used was *olin*, which is both "undulant movement" and the name of the sun. Like its homophone *olli*, which means rubber (and rubber ball), it could be topologically changed in shape, stretched, and bounced between space and time; it could indicate the four-cornered value of the cardinal dimensions, day and night, the passage of the seasons, the cyclical nature of the daily solar movement, and the year's journey over the ecliptic. But although it alluded to the complexity involved it did not solve the problem of transforming the multidimensional concept into a two-dimensional one or a dynamic concept into a fixed one. Such a complex, topological-visual metaphor could not, of course, be explored all at once in the same design without creating a messy, unartistic product. Thus each artist chose to simplify by selection. A painting of *olin* appears in the Cuicatec codices (Illustration 23a) which focuses on the metaphors of (*a*) day/night and dry season/rainy season, represented in

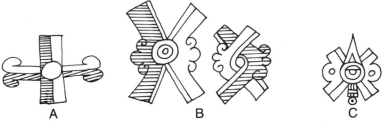

23. The space-time continuum—variants of the symbol for undulant movement. (A) Cuicatec version. *Codex Porfirio Diaz*, p. G. (B) Mixteco-Poblana region versions. *Borgia Codex*, pp. 10 and 25. (C) Version from the valley of Mexico, an area of Nahuatl speakers. Drawn from a stone monument.

the vertical, two-colored design for the sky, and (*b*) above/below, the above earth/below earth, represented in the traditional symbol used for the earth's surface doubled in a mirror image. (This earth's surface symbol also appears in toponymics or place names, forming the bottom of the design, which represents the earth in many codices.) In the Nahuatl version (Illustration 23c) the artist struggled to include more allusions. Thus the four-cornered design includes at the top the motif for the sun's ray moving over the surface of the earth, in the sky, and it also includes at the bottom the symbol for *chalchihuitl* (green precious stone), which represents the celestial water below. The semicircular sides, I believe, may indicate the curvature of the earth. The circles are, perhaps, entrances to the underworld. In the *Borgia Codex*, however (Illustration 23b), the artist chose to focus on the idea of *olin* as the cyclical interlacing of solar space-time by drawing the duality both in juxtaposition and curled around itself.

The *olin* symbol, which is one of the day signs, was also the name of the present era of the universe and its sun. That is, the sun's complete name was "four undulant movement." Four alludes to the four cardinal sides (the eye in the center of *olin* is then the sun or the navel = cardinal center), as well as to the myth that there were four previous eras before the present one, which were destroyed. The fifth and present one had a sun too. This preliminary exploration of one relatively simple visual symbol indicates the problems of the symbolic analysis of this complex macrocosmology. It also points up the intrinsic impossibility that the prehispanic artist faced in trying to present the associated symbols in their intricate topological totality. Only abstract mathematical conceptions could cope with the total vision. The artist was limited, then, to drawing from this total vision only those bits and pieces that appeared to have poetico-mythical value in the context in which they were placed.

Since the earth, the sun, and other cosmic elements are part and parcel of the space-time continuum, they can all be represented by variants of the quincunx. The commonest forms occur for the earth, sun, and Venus, but the quincunx also appears as a marker of cosmic fire, of the rains of the four directions, and other element-deities.

Many of these geometric designs developed over time into the combined forms of writing—hieroglyphic, logographic, rebus, syllabic, and phonemic—of prehispanic Mesoamerica. During the early colonial period some symbols became an incipient syllabary (Dibble 1971; Thompson 1965a). Among the Maya, glyphs and syllables used in writing also stood for complex religious images. For example, the moon-earth deity was personified in the glyph of the day named *Kaban*. The symbol "day" was "flower" as well as "sun." Among the highland plateau peoples, the face of the god Tlaloc represented the day sign rain. Thompson believes that in fact the day signs and writing glyphs *were* the gods, in total identification (1965a:644), and he is of the opinion that such "mystical associations" cannot be fully understood and "will never serve as material to feed into a computing machine; one can no more treat Maya mysticism in that way than one can reduce El Greco's Burial of the Count of Orgaz to a mathematical formula." In the same article, however, Thompson clearly illustrates that with patience and ingenuity many of the glyphs' obscure meanings can be unraveled. Recent work by Knorozov (1965) and others suggest that the questions on Maya writing may be answerable in the near future (see also Rendón and Specha 1965).

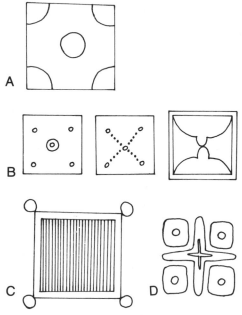

24. Other simple geometric images of the directional space-time quincunx. (A) Base of the statue of the goddess of the earth, Coatlicue. Museo Nacional de Antropología, Mexico. (B) Three Mayan glyphs, nos. 585, 727, and 527 of Thompson's (1962) classification. (C) Design of the "Mantle of Five Roses." *Codex Magliabecchiano*, pp. 8 and 9. (D) Quincunx of Venus-Lamat, glyph no. 510 of Thompson's (1962) classification.

Numerology and Signs

In brief outline, the number symbols were derived from the following calendric series:

The Solar Year

This unit was made up of two parts: a series of 360 days with a number and sign attached to each, and a series of 5 "uncounted" days that followed the 360-day sequence. In Nahuatl the two were called the *xihuitl* and *nemonteni* days. The latter were called *uayeb* among the Maya. They were also known as *xmakaba* (nameless days) and in Tzotzil they are known as *ch' ay k' in* (lost days). Thus a year was composed of 365 days (Caso 1967:77). The year was graphically symbolized in different ways depending on the area of Mesoamerica. In the central plateau one of the symbols was that for "turquoise" or "sky." The Mixtec used an "A" and "O" intertwined: 🔯 The old solar calendar was used until recently in Zinacantan, and in the adjacent *municipio* of Chamula it is still in use by the shamans.

The solar year provided the closed frame or armature for the scheduling of all major rituals, which were fitted into the agricultural and hunting cycle. The rituals were also timed in monthly periods, each major one located in the last days of a month. Other schedules for ritual as well as secular events followed named days of the ritual periods discussed below. The link between the solar year and the ritual period also served to schedule all kinds of other socially relevant activities.

The Month

The 360-day sequence was divided into 18 months of 20 days each. Another month series based on the phases of the moon (the *meztlapohualli*) also existed, and apparently was quite important among the Maya, for whom month and moon were homonyms. The term *meztlapohualli* also applied to the 20-day months of the solar year. Caso (*ibid.*, pp. 79–85) has tried to clarify the relationship of the two series on the basis of presently understood data, but the question of the fit of the lunar months is still poorly researched, and scholars do not agree about it (see Satterthwaite 1965:620–626).

The solar months were named after rituals with which they ended or other events which took place within them. At first glance the naming appears arbitrary, but it was in fact an accurate reflection of scheduled behaviors, which coincided with (*a*) agrarian activities, (*b*) domestic schedules, (*c*) professional activities, (*d*) astronomical events such as equinoxes and solstices, (*e*) a progression of symbols from those of infancy to those of old age, and (*f*) a series of public religious rituals for specific deities which fitted into the other transformational levels, giving them meaning in terms of focused collective action.

For example, at the end of the rainy season, when the irrigation canals were opened, the major god celebrated was Tlaloc, as god of water, and the month's name was "the water comes down." The following month, the year's penultimate one, was dedicated to celebrations of all the gods, but particularly of elderly ones. Ritual games were performed in which old women were harassed, goddesses connected with surface water were worshipped (this was a dry period when irrigation was necessary), and the month was called "wrinkled," referring to the wrinkles of old people, or symbolically, to the old age of the year. Gary Gossen (1974) provides a detailed discussion of the month names for Chamula, which should be compared with Caso's (1967) master lists. Many contemporary variants of the month sequences, year cycles and other cycles of the prehispanic calendar have survived, incomplete, among contemporary Indians, particularly in the Highland Maya area of Mexico and Guatemala. Susan Miles (1952) provides a brief comparison of survivals, while Steward Lincoln (1942) gives the most detailed account of a surviving system, that of the Ixil of Guatemala.

Two things become obvious when these surviving systems are compared. They are all derived from the single system prevalent throughout Mesoamerica in pre-Columbian times, and they have arbitrarily lost some cycles and kept others, primarily and obviously because of historical accident and symbolic free play. In most of Mesoamerica, as I shall demonstrate later, the underlying armature of the prehispanic calendar has continued to provide a frame for the rituals of the "Christian" calendar, but the actual calendric cycles and their names have been forgotten, or transformed beyond recognition. The increased cantonalization and isolation of different language regions throughout the colonial period reinforced the pattern of local deviation and variation.

The Ritual Divinatory Cycle

This section deals with extremely complex materials, and the discussion must be taken as a brief summary of a long subject. For clarification, see Table 3.

The ritual divinatory cycle was a period of 260 days. This period was internally divided. First, there were 20 day signs (these are listed in Table 3 in the second column). Second, there were 13 day numerals (third column). Every day had a name consisting of a numeral and a sign. Third, there were 20 major periods of 13 days each ("weeks"). These periods (fourth column of the table) started on days which were marked by the numeral 1. The system assigned names to the days of the "month," and numbers to the days of the "week," the reverse of our nomenclature. The gods were directly connected with the 260-day cycle because they were patrons, regents, or rulers of all aspects of the cyclic calendar. First, each one of the 13 day numerals had a patron god (according to Seler and Nicholson these were 13 "hours" of the day, but Caso does not agree). The patron gods of all the cycles are listed in the first column of the table. Second, each of the 20 day signs had a patron god. Third, each of the 20 periods of 13 days ("weeks"), which started with a day numeral 1, also had a patron god. Moreover, each 13-day cycle was accompanied by a sacred volatile. Again, each one of the 13 volatiles had a patron god, because these fliers were theriomorphic aspects (theophanies) of the gods. Moreover, the 260-day cycle had a list of 9 deities of the night, which were also patrons of 9 of the day periods.

One would expect that a real bricolage, a fantastically large number of gods, ruled over divinatory calculations. If we add together 20 divine patrons of the days, plus 13 patrons of the numerals, plus 13 patrons of the fliers, plus 20 patrons of the 13 day periods, plus the 9 night patrons, we have a minimum of 75 possible patrons. However, there were not that many, because the *same* gods appeared in *different* arrangements of sequences for each one of the cycles. As can be ascertained from the first column in the table, there were only 29 recognizable major deities governing the principal cycles.

Because of the pantheistic axioms of the religion, one could argue that these were all aspects of the same deity, and all were multiple and infinite. However, by the time this cycle was worked out, the subdivided images of the gods had become culturally stable. There were now (*a*) a number of major gods, (*b*) their major aspects which corresponded with the time periods and cardinal directions, (*c*) their secondary aspects, some of which were innovations in the context of specific sacred texts (for instance, when two major deities and their attributes were combined), and (*d*) a large roster of synonyms, which included the name of a deity's calendrical birthday, its personal name, and the name based on its most salient transformational attributes.

I have compared my table of 29 major calendrical deities with two other recent lists. Caso (1971) provides us with a large list that includes the gods he has been able to identify himself plus those identified by the great scholar Seler. His largest number of readings gives 46 deities. Nicholson (1971) provides his own list with the largest number of readings at 33. However, most of these are alternative names, being various true synonyms of one single aspect of a deity. I reduced them by a simple set of rules. First, if a deity appeared twice in the same cycle under different names or major aspects, both names were kept. Second, if different sex-aspects of the same deity (for example Tonacatecuhtli and Tonacacihuatl) appeared, both were kept. Third, if a deity's aspect appeared in codex pictures as distinct from its "parent" deity, it was also kept. For example, Tezcatlipoca in his "precious turkey" theophany was counted separately from his other aspects. However, a deity appearing in two different lists or cycles under two parts of its name (that is, under its calendrical and under its personal name) was counted only once. A deity appearing in two lists or cycles under variants of the same personal name (for example, "Obsidian Blade Tezcatlipoca" and "Curved Obsidian Blade Tezcatlipoca") was also counted once.

I also considered that 23 deities appear at least twice in Caso's lists. And of those appearing only once, only 6 were clearly neither synonyms nor calendrical alternatives of a deity's personal name. Of the 23 deities which appeared more than once, 10 appeared more than five times each. If quantity is equal to importance, these obviously were the most important calendrical deities. Their names are Tlazolteotl, Xiuhtecuhtli, Quetzalcoatl, Chalchihuitlicue, her "husband" Tlaloc, Tonatiuh, Mictlantecuhtli, Centeotl, Xochipilli, and Tezcatlipoca.

As can be seen in the chart, my final list does not reduce major aspects of any deity. For instance, Centeotl was patron of corn, and

Xochipilli was patron of plants and flowers. Ixnextli was a very special aspect of Tlazolteotl—the "crying abandoned mistress." In some contexts these gods were interchangeable. Tlahuizcalpante-cuhtli, the "dawn star" (Venus), was an alternate of Quetzalcoatl. I have kept them all, since they contrast in the cycles. Moreover, I have tried to follow the primary sources and not force identifications that were not made in all contexts.

Adding all the alternative readings but reducing by my rules, we are left with a smaller number than 75—that is, 29. The minimum possible would be 20, because the 20-day cycle is the longest of the single short cycles. In Table 3, I have listed all the cycles in vertical columns. The patrons are listed in the first column. Each position within a cycle is placed in the same horizontal row as the name of the deity that was its patron. For example, Xipe Totec was the god who governed the day sign Eagle, which was the fifteenth day sign. He did not rule over the 13 numerals, and therefore that space is empty. Of the 20 thirteen-day periods, he governed the fourteenth, which started with the day 1 Dog. Dog was the tenth day sign, but because of the arrangement of the sequence of 13 numerals, the combination numeral-1 and sign-Dog appeared in the 170th day and concluded its period of dominance in the 182nd day. Xipe Totec did not rule over the night (9-day) cycle, and therefore that space is empty.

A second example should suffice to make the series under-standable as they appear on the chart. The ruling goddess Chalchi-huitlicue is the fifth from the top in the first column. She was an old deity and had worked herself into the whole series of cycles. Read-ing across the row, we find that she governed the day sign Snake, which was the fifth sign of the twenty. She also governed the nu-meral 3. Of the 20 thirteen-day periods, she was patron of the fifth, 1 Cane. Cane was the thirteenth day sign, but following the same pattern of sequences, in this position the deity ruled from the 53rd to the 65th day of the 260-day period. Her accompanying bird was the falcon, which occupied the third position in the sequence of vol-atiles. Chalchihuitlicue was also a patron of the night. In this se-quence she occupied the sixth position of the 9 possible ones.

These combinations do not exhaust the influence of the deities on the calendar. Each deity had a day name that was its calendrical birthday, and each had a day name that marked its death. Each also had a year name, the year of either its birth or its death. There were other calendrical points over which the deities had some influence, for example, those that marked the date of some important event in their mythic lives, or days in the solar month in which their rituals were celebrated. All these dates were patronized in some way by the deity to which they "belonged." The "luck" or "destiny" of any particular point in time was thus predetermined by the cluster of deities which *together* governed over it.

The ritual divinatory cycle of 260 days was further divided into complex numerical cycles. I have listed in the pages that follow some of the clearer ones mentioned in the literature. Others (for instance, the birthdays of the deities) appear in Caso's work (1967). From the researches of many scholars, it has become clear that these cycles are not mere superstitious games of divination. In fact, as Seler, Teeple, and other authors have amply demonstrated, they were correlated with complicated astronomical calculations of the synodical periods of planets, the occurrence of eclipses, and other celestial events.

The Day Signs and Numerals

The twenty day signs were derived from the other transformational taxonomies and referred to abbreviated sign-images of the gods, constellations, animals, and so on. The thirteen numbers were derived from conceptions of the space-time continuum which are not well understood, but I believe that some contemporary ethnographic evidence may be relevant to this issue (see below, p. 207). The day signs represented different levels of abstraction and derived from different taxonomies, but were linked in their sequence so that each had at least one attribute in common with the signs that preceded it and the one that followed. All the calendars share certain features but they show some minor deviation of day and month signs and names (see Gossen 1974, for contemporary information on a town next to Zinacantan). In the Central Mexican calendar there were three "crawler" day signs: *Cipactli* (the earth monster), Lizard, and Snake; five "four-legged animals": Deer, Rabbit, Dog, Monkey, and Jaguar; two "volatiles": Eagle and Buzzard; three "vegetable or plant parts": Straw, Cane, and Flower; four "elements": Wind, Water, Rain, and Flint; and three unique ones which are "earth" symbols: House (which is an earth symbol of the underworld), Death (a skull, another earth symbol of the underworld, sign of the god of death), and the symbol of the space-time continuum, *Olin* or undulant movement. (*Olin* is also a solar symbol.) This made twenty in all. It is possible, of course, to classify these symbols in different ways by linking together their other connotations. For example, deer, jaguar, house, and *cipactli* are earth symbols, while eagle, buzzard, *olin*, and wind are sky symbols. The point is that the ordering of the day signs followed an internal logic of allusion and connotations, which was ambiguously structured to allow for intuition in the divinatory horoscope arts, but which also reflected the mysteries of the gods' multiple identities and of astronomical configurations, since most of these day signs symbolized either planets or constellations. For example: the days Dog and Monkey were constellations, while Wind, the sign of the god Quetzalcoatl, was also the planet Venus (Beyer 1965).

The sequence itself had some importance as a system of concatenated ideas used in marking time and "luck," and it is difficult to determine to what extent a conscious effort had been made to adjust its structure over time, to increase the overall efficiency of its meaning. At the time of the conquest, it appeared already formed and fully mature. But archaeological evidence suggests that the system grew by the accretion of substructures, although efforts had obviously been made to develop the sequence into a symbolic chain.

Variations of day signs between Mesoamerican calendar lists show the same type of symbolic linkages, using conversions, transpositions or meaningful replacements of symbols. For example, we have already mentioned that the day sign Eagle is replaced in some calendars (such as the Meztitlan) by Hawk. The hawk is an equivalent symbol because of the similarities between the two birds. Other examples follow similar logic. The Mixe call the ninth day "River" instead of Water. Motolinía (1969) gives "Flint Knife" the name "Stone for Sacrificing," which is one of the uses of the flint knife. The same sign in Momostenango is named "Cutting and Bleeding." Rose occasionally replaces Flower as a sign. Air replaces Wind (Caso 1967: Comparative calendar chart facing p. 84). The variants cover synonyms, sequentially related ideas, particular forms of a general category, or two particular variants of a more inclusive class.

The Thirteen Cycle Series

The numbers 1 to 13 were used to number the days of the divinatory "week." Each day possessed not only one of these consecutive numbers but also one of the 20 consecutive day signs. As the beginnings of the two series coincided only at the start of the cycle, every one of the 260 days had a different identity. Since the year had 365 days and the divinatory cycle only 260, they began on the same day only once every 52 years.

$$365 \text{ (days)} \times 52 \text{ (years)} = 18{,}980 \text{ (days)}$$
$$= 260 \text{ (days)} \times 73 \text{ (cycles)}$$

The 13-cycle is complex because it was a dominant organizing symbol of the calendar, and it was used as follows.

A. The cycle of 260 named days was called *tonalpohualli* in Nahuatl (meaning the count of days) and has been named *tzolkin* (day count) by Mayanist scholars. The count of days was recorded in complex ritual calendrical books used for horoscopes and for historical and astronomical reckoning. These books were called *tonalamatl* (meaning "the book of the days") in Nahuatl and *Chilam Balam* in certain Mayan texts. Some of them have been preserved practically complete, and these are one of the major sources of data on Mesoamerican religion (for example, the *Tonalamatl* of the Aubin collection, and the *Codex Borbonicus*.

B. There was also a series of "13 lords of the day." These were gods who "carried the burden of the day" and were identified or associated with the day names. Since there were 13 of them, like the "week" numerals, rather than 20, they modified the meaning of the day's luck. All these day lords were major gods. Five of them were "cosmogonic suns," that is, they had governed previous eras of the universe.

C. A series of 13 volatiles accompanied the day lord series, linked to it not only because they occurred simultaneously, but also because the lords and volatiles were transformational symbols of each other. The logic of some of these transformations is quite obvious. For instance, the first lord, the god of fire, is linked to the blue hummingbird, for both are symbols of the sun's light. But other associations are quite obscure from our point of view (that is, we do not have the data to explain them). For example, the reason why the volatile "macaw" was linked to the eleventh lord, the god of death, is not known to me. It is possible, however, that they were related because they were stars in a constellation of the same name. Seler (1901) believed these sequences also represented the daylight hours, but Caso (1971) is not convinced.

D. A series of 13 years, called *tlalpilli* in Nahuatl, was also reckoned. Four of these series made up the Mesoamerican "century" of 52 years (see below). I do not know how this unit was significant for the society in terms of scheduled secular activities.

E. Each 13-day group or "week" which began with the number 1 had a patron deity of its own, which, according to both Seler and Caso, duplicated the series of deities who were the patrons or lords of the day series, except for the eleventh place, which was filled by a different god; the rest followed in the same sequence, until the last two places. The god omitted, Xochipilli, was then placed in another slot (with Mayahuel; see Table 3). This rearrangement may have been produced in part by the logistics of fitting the deities with their many aspects into a 20-day series. But the change may have been a later structural elaboration· of the cycle that added "mysteries" to horoscope counts, or an astronomical adjustment made for reasons at present undetermined. Burland (1967) has also imaginatively explored the symbolic connections or transformations between the day, the week, and the patron deities. As with the series of day lords and 13 volatiles, some transformations are obvious, and others are still obscure to us. For example, the day 1 Rain, which started the seventh week, had Tlaloc, god of rain, as patron. But why was the ninth day, Water, under the patronage of the fire god? Is this a play on the symbol of "burning water," which some contemporary scholars so love? (Séjourné 1957). Or why was the week starting with 1 Water ruled by the turkey theriophany of Tezcatlipoca?

F. The heavens (the upper sky, above the celestial equator) had 13 layers with associated transformational values. Different sources give different lists, but at least we know that there were (*a*) a series of 13 deities, one for each layer, (*b*) a series of 13 celestial volatiles, and (*c*) a series of astronomic "inhabitants" of each layer, which included stars, planets, and winds. The 13 celestial volatiles overlap in all but two cases with the 13 volatiles accompanying the series of the days. The two exceptions are the raven, which is eagle in the day series, and the dove, which is in place of the hawk. The switch, dove = hawk, also appears in the "Hummingbird" poem, but the symbolic link is not clear to me, except as an inversion of peaceful to warlike, which in the poem's context does not make much sense, unless it is an obscure reference to the transformation of the hummingbird into two other aspects—one a predator, one a victim—a duality of opposites. This argument is quite contrived, however, and I have not been able to find any other significant interpretation.

G. The first day of each 13-day period was ritually dedicated to the period's ruling deity. Also, five of the periods of 13 days were dedicated to the west directional deities (female) the *cihuatlpipil*, who "descended" to earth during those times and required propitiatory rituals (Nicholson 1971:435).

The Nine Cycle

A. Nine was the number associated with witchcraft, the night, the underworld, and the lower sky (that is, the sky below the celestial equator). Unlike the other major numbers, it does not fit perfectly into the 260 cycle.

B. Seler believed that this cycle marked the nighttime hours, which suggests that the Mesoamerican peoples may have divided the day into 22 "hours," 13 for the daytime, and 9 for the nighttime.

C. The underworld and lower sky had 9 layers, which, like the 13 heavens, had associated symbols.

D. There was also a cycle of 9 deities which ran concurrently with the 13 day lords, and were "night lords," each assigned to a day in the 260-day sequence. Since the series is shorter, it linked in with the day series in different arrangements, modifying the overall "luck" or "meaning" of the day. The series was called "the accompanying ones," to distinguish it from the day series of "carriers of the burden" (of the day).

E. It appears that cycles of 9 were used for "underworld" activities such as witchcraft rites.

The Four Cycle

A. Four indicated the sides of the universe and the 4 cardinal directions, and simultaneously the 4 seasons of the year, each with a ruling deity associated with it.

B. There were 4 year signs. Each had a patron deity, from the same list in Table 3.

C. The 20-day cycle was divided by 4 into sequences of 5 days each. These were used for scheduling market days, which took place every 5 days, that is, 4 times per month.

D. Four groups of 13 years each made up a "century" of 52 years, called in Nahuatl the *xuihmolpilli* ("bundle" or "bouquet" of years, also translatable as "the binding of the years"). At this point the solar year and the 260-day cycle coincided, giving a unique sign-number combination for each of the 52 years, each year name being made up of 4 year signs plus a numeral from the 1 to 13 cycle in sequence. That is, "the years were named after sequences of days which were separated by 365 in two or three successive tonalpohuallis" (Caso 1967:41). The year names of the Aztec were Cane, Flint, House and Rabbit, and were determined by the overlap of the solar year-*tonalpo-*

hualli cycle. Some other ethnic groups in Mesoamerica, the Cuicatec among them, used 4 different year signs.

E. The prehispanic peoples reckoned that the universe had lasted 4 "eras" or cosmogonic suns, each of which had ended in a celestial catastrophe, and each of which had had a type of man of a lower animal order than the present humanity. Each of these 4 eras had a ruling deity. Probably, these "eras" represented 4 historic periods of political development or the prehispanic people view of the evolution of their society marked into 4 distinct astronomical epochs.

F. Many of the important gods were divided or unfolded into 4 manifestations, one for each of the cardinal directions or 4 different time periods. Tezcatlipoca-Itzam Na and Tlaloc-Chac are the most commonly divided in this way.

G. Combined with the 4 manifestations, some gods were represented as dualities, which gave them a set of 8 aspects, moods, attributes, and so on. These were mythically gods who supported the earth and sky, the bearers, which are still important deities in Zinacantan. Eight was also related to the numerical calculations of the Venus cycles. Moreover, a special ritual performance took place every 8 years.

H. The 260-day cycle was divided into 4 periods of 65 days, which gave 4 ritual quarters, which the Zapotec named *cocijos*. These corresponded with the 4 "growth" quarters of the "annual" ritual calendar: infancy, youth, adulthood, and old age.

I. The number 4 (often in combination with an additional 1) was symbolically utilized in arranging all sorts of secular affairs. In fact, together with the number 2, the duality of senior-junior, it defined a very large number of aspects of the social organization. The Aztec king (the center of the political realm), for example, had 4 royal advisers (*ayos*) and 2 "houses of parliament" (*tlacxitlan* and *teccalco*) made up of noblemen. There were also 4 councils: the chiefs' house, the nobles' house, the principals' house and the warriors' house. There were 4 kinds of children of noblemen: the king's sons, the chiefs' sons, the legitimate sons and the house's sons (a euphemism for children of royal concubines). There were 4 priestly age-grades through which the sacerdotal class had to pass. In many major city states there were 4 divisions of the capital, for example in Tenochtitlan, in Cholula, and in Rabinal, among the Quiche in Guatemala. These associations of 4 combined with the senior-junior official duality which is still important in Zinacantan today. In prehispanic Mesoamerica this duality ran the whole gamut of the social roles. For instance, among the peoples of the valley of Mexico there were two kinds of school, a senior one for noble children and a junior one for commoners. There were also two high courts, two major army officer titles, two merchant officer titles, two major titles for hunters, two different kinds of honorific titles for brave warriors (different from officerships), and many other senior-junior relationships.

Schedules for some activities were also run according to the 4 cycle. Many citizens' duties were performed by 4 groups in rotation, in 4 periods of time. Cotton tribute was paid in a cycle with 4 divisions. These arrangements have persisted in local societies throughout Mesoamerica when political posts, officerships in the Church, age grades, rotation of political duty between town wards, and similar assignments are made.

The Five Cycle

A. The symbol of the 5 sequence was the quincunx, the space-time continuum indicating the 4 directions and the center. In numerical writing, 5 was often represented as a bar, unlike smaller units, which were indicated by dots. The quincunx symbol has been replaced all over Mesoamerica by the Cross, which is not only the dominant symbol of Christianity, but in Zinacantan, as Vogt points out, may mean a variety of ideas from "entrance" to "pine bough" to a "meeting place for the ancestral deities."

B. Five was used to divide other cycles including a division of the month into periods of 4 days, a division of the year into sequences of 73 days, and a division of the *tonalpohualli* (of 260 days) into periods of 52 days (52 also being the cycle of a century).

C. The gods which represented luck or chance, feasting and

youthful pleasure were named by combining the number 5 in their calendrical names. The commonest name of the deity of chance is "five flower," but his calendrical names were several, all with the number 5 or the name flower. The 5 directions of space-time signified chance or luck in other contexts. Five grains of corn or other divinatory tools were used, thrown against a mantle or mat surface, for casting horoscopes or for divining illness. There are some amusing illustrations of this symbolic usage in one of the codices collected and published by Zelia Nuttal. Cuicatec Indians still keep up this practice.

D. The quincunx was used in many symbolic contexts, to ornament divine or sacred paraphernalia: for example, on mantles of "five flowers," or as the five feather tufts that ornamented the god Huitzilopochtli's shield. The quincunx was also a common spatial arrangement in the codex pages where the 4 aspects of the deities are represented. Each quarter of the page represented one aspect. At the center sat the defining, total god.

E. Five was the number of "uncounted" days at the end of the solar year of 360 days. These were "bad luck" days.

F. There were 5 major class divisions in the society: nobles by birth, nobles by achievement, commoners, serfs, and slaves.

G. Markets were held every fifth day.

The Twenty Cycle

Mesoamerican counting was normally vigesimal, with 20 as the radix. Twenty was the number of days in the month. It was also the number of deities which were patrons of the days, and the number of divisions of the *tonalpohualli* into periods of 13. Each of these 20 divisions also had a patron.[1]

---

1. The Mayan Katun, a period of 20 years of 360 days (the *tun*) is also a combination of an approximate observation of the solar year and cycles in languages that count with 20 as the radix. Other vigesimal computations follow this numerology, which has been called the calendric "long count." The *baktun* = 400 *tuns*, the *piktun* = 8,000 *tuns*, the *kalabtun* = 160,000 *tuns* and the *kilchiltun* = 3,200,000 *tuns*.

The Twenty-Six Cycle

This number was apparently unimportant in most of Mesoamerica, but Cuicatecs divided the century into two "generations" of 26 years each (Hunt 1972). This division was a mnemonic device, used to count the generations of ruling kings of mankind. A 26-year period was equal to one ruler's life within a dynasty. Thus, ten generations = 260 = the number of the divinatory cycle. This gave approximate, fixed, mechanical numbers to apply to the oral memorization of secular historical events, which were then dated by fixed periods, marked by the different ruling kings.

In some of the divinatory books 26 is also used as a cycle.

The Fifty-Two Cycle

As indicated, there were cycles of 52 days and of 52 years (the century), and a few others of lesser importance. The cycle of 52 years, which contained 18,980 differently named days, was apparently related to lunar computations, but scholars are not in total agreement on this issue (see Caso 1967:81). The most significant astronomical fact about the 52-year cycle is that it fits 500 times into the complete cycle of the precession of the equinoxes (26,000 years). Among the Aztec 52 was the age at which a man retired from his secular duties.

Other Cycles

Other longer and shorter cycles were used in Mesoamerica, some of them, like the Cuicatec "generation," of apparently only local importance. In the codices these cycles were marked by painting footsteps at their beginning or end. Major cycles of longer durations were calculated for determining eclipses, the orbital movements of some planets, and other astronomical events. Among the most important cycles in the calendric ritual books are Venus calculations, particularly in the *Borgia Codex*, and Mars revolutions. For example, the *tonalpohualli* repeated three times gave the equivalent of one synodical revolution of Mars.

A cycle named by the Aztec *"Huehuetiliztli"* was considered the most perfect cyclical number period because "it included the tonalpohualli, the year, and the synodical revolution of Venus" (Caso 1971:348).

A cycle of 7 also appeared to be associated with Venus, at least in Seler's opinion. It was, in addition, associated with the cosmic directions, including the 4 sides, the center, and the points of sunrise and sunset, or, instead of east and west, the up and down direction. Seven is the relative distance of Venus according to Bode's law.[2]

All these numbers were used not only for scientific purposes, but

2. I suggested in the section on planets that some of the important numbers that occur in the calendric counts are the same as those derived from Bode's law of the relative distance of planets. This hypothesis, which appears at first sight somewhat far-fetched, requires discussion. According to Bode's law, "if a series of four be written down, and three be added to the second, six to the third, twelve to the fourth, and so on, each of the added numbers being double its predecessor, the sums of the first seven numbers are 4, 7, 10, 16, 28, 52 and 100. These numbers divided by 10 were found to give with a surprising closeness the relative distance of the planets as far as Saturn, except that no planet was known to revolve in the orbit corresponding to 28 between the orbits of Mars and Jupiter" (*Encyclopaedia Britannica* 1942, 17:998). This is the position of the asteroid planet, Ceres, invisible with the naked eye. These numbers thus correspond as follows: Mercury, 4; Venus, 7; Earth, 10; Mars, 16; Ceres, 28; Jupiter, 52; Saturn, 100..Taken at face value, the theory appears full of holes. What about 10, 16, and 28, which prehispanic peoples did not often treat as major sacred numbers? A moment of reflection, however, shows the following: first, the earth was not counted with the planets revolving around the sun because prehispanic astronomy was geocentric. This eliminates the importance of the number 10. Instead, 13, the number of points of the earth space-time continuum, was substituted. Second, Ceres was not known to prehispanic peoples or even to Westerners until 1801. This eliminates the importance of 28. Mars, a relatively unimportant planet in prehispanic calculations, occurs with the relatively unimportant ritual number 16. But the planets which were most vividly depicted in deified numerology and best understood by prehispanic astronomers had the most significant numbers attached to them. It is hard to believe that this is pure coincidence.

In other words, I am saying that the initial conception of the prehispanic 260–365 combination cycle must have been derived from (1) a 4-sided model of the earth plane with a fifth point as a center; (2) a 13-sided model of the time-space continuum made up of the 4-sided plane intersected by a plane formed by the points of the sun's path in the day-year cycle; (3) a calculation of the solar year of 365 days; (4) a system of vigesimal counting; and (5) some mathematic notions about planetary-associated numbers, perhaps equivalent to Bode's law.

At this stage, obviously this is no more than a hypothesis. Much further work is needed to corroborate that sacred numerology was, in fact, derived from astronomical laws. Possibly, however, prehispanic astronomers had calculated the relative distance of these planets by other mathematical means which gave equivalent results.

also for embellishing divine images and elaborating the artistic, multivocal, and decorative elements of the pictorial, sculptural, and architectural arts.

Some numbers, however, appear more frequently than others. The most important numerical nodal symbols are those that can divide the 260 cycle perfectly: 2, 4, 5, 13, 20, and 52. For example, 2 represented the divine sexual duality, and thus was found in the names of many of the gods (for example, Ometeotl ["two god"], Tezcatlipoca in his unfolding as Omacatl ["two cane"], and "two rabbit," one of the rabbit gods which represented maguey beer and fertility).

Other numbers of importance, which do not divide the *tonalpo-hualli*, apparently correspond not to lunar or solar cycles, but to other planetary cycles which were juxtaposed to the cycles previously listed. The most frequent of these, are 7, which named a corn deity; 9 (the associations of which have already been discussed) and 400, which was a synonym for "multitude." All the deities which came as a multitude or crowd received this number within their name.

All the numbers and signs for the day, month, year and other time spans, plus their associated symbols and deities, were used for horoscope prediction. For divinatory purposes, each cluster of signs and numbers was given a "luck" value, a prognosticatory value. Since bearer gods, numbers, accompanying gods, nine gods, volatiles, and so on, all had their own luck values, the calculating of horoscopes and destinies, the recording of histories, the meaning of the planetary movements, and other aspects of divination were tied into a system that required great knowledge and specialized skill for its understanding and interpretation. To facilitate these esoteric, highly skilled religious activities, prehispanic peoples wrote their calculations, astronomical visions, and deified calendric myths in the "book of the days" (see above, p. 192). Caso writes that at least five different criteria concerning the numbers, the signs, and the deity patrons were necessary to produce an appropriate horoscope or prophesy (1967:26). I believe, however, that prediction was even more complicated than that. To know the particular luck of a specific day, one had to know (*a*) which deity ruled the day sign, (*b*) which deity ruled the day numeral, (*c*) which deity ruled the period of thirteen days in which the particular day was included, (*d*) which night ruler belonged to that day, (*e*) which accompanying flier was assigned to that time period, (*f*) which deity ruled the day name, that is, the specific sign-number combination, (*g*) which deity ruled the year name in which the specific day was included, (*h*) which mythic divine events were assigned to the specific day, (*i*) which single aspect of the many of a deity ruler was actually listed in the sacred books of the period investigated, (*j*) the combined value of the sets of deities coinciding in the day, (*k*) the luck of each of these criteria, and (*l*) the rules by which one luck value and another could be combined to give an average overall value. There may even have been other criteria which are not recorded in the early sources. One of our problems with this topic is that the chroniclers tried to simplify the system because they could not make sense of what their informants said. Just like some bad modern anthropologists, they chose to hide their ignorance behind definite statements. But one can observe them falling into contradictions (again just like the moderns) and here and there revealing scraps of the complicated truth.

Clearly, sign and number names as well as other esoteric combinations were transformationally derived from all the taxonomic or-

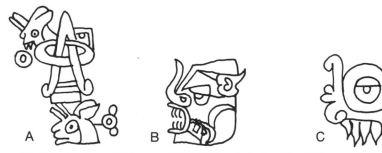

25. Calendar signs. (A) The year "Rabbit." *Borgia Codex* style. (B) The month "Bat" (*zotz*, a Mayan glyph). (C) The day sign "Rain" as the face of the god Tlaloc. *Borgia Codex* style.

ders combined: natural, cultural, divine, and logical-mathematical. Therefore, the possibilities of playing with the system were well-nigh inexhaustible. Much of the system became fixed, however, because of the efforts of theologians to regularize dogma and the stabilization which accompanies written records, which are less manipulable than oral traditions. Hence, all the *tonalpohualli* books that have been preserved for posterity vary in detail, but not in overall meaning or structure (Caso 1968; Kirchhoff 1968). We can safely assume that any "survivals" present in Mesoamerican Indian villages today are heirs of the shared prehispanic structure and have preserved its partial meanings in culturally relevant ways.

Human Settlements and Numerology

The numerology of the space-time directions had a practical application in the planning of prehispanic cities and towns, and certainly in the arrangement of temples and other public places.

First, there is some evidence that the layout of major thoroughfares and public buildings was oriented according to the cardinal directions and in relation to the stars. The measurements seem to have varied with the choice of star markers. For example, it appears that Tula is 17 degrees off from true north, and Teotihuacan over 15 degrees off. Santillana and Dechend, however, have pointed out that since astronomical alignments change with the precession of the equinoxes, the divergences may be due not to inaccurate measures but to changes in the relation between the observed point on earth and the angle of the line toward a particular star (Santillana and Dechend 1969; Millon 1974; Pina Chan 1966).

In a recent paper (1974) Vogt has attempted to relate the position of contemporary town markers, particularly the orientation of churches, to markers of solar points. I believe, however, that for the prehispanic peoples, who could measure angles quite accurately, it was the nighttime sky that provided the orientations and not the sun, although the east-west axis is obviously sun-derived.

These alignments of nighttime-daytime angles were the basis for the ideal ground plan of prehispanic settlements. Even today in

Mesoamerica, villages utilize natural and man-made markers (such as crosses and waterholes) as if they were arranged in a quadrilateral structure modeled on the sky. As I have already pointed out, the quadrilateral shape may not be an exactly regular one, in that all the angles may not be identical, but in the relative location of the markers as an armature set the "cognized model" can be seen. Moreover, contemporary Mesoamerican peasants have neither the equipment (for instance, accurate compasses) nor the knowledge of the night-time sky necessary to produce accurate alignments. Furthermore, natural features are set there "by the hands of the gods," and not by human design, so that the architectural model is only a "vision," an approximation of abstracted armatures, a compromise between the real position on the earth's surface of natural markers such as mountains, solar or astronomical markers, and man-made or imagined markers (see the section on waterholes and mythical patterns of mountains among the Cuicatec, pp. 97–98).

For purposes of myth and ritual the symbols of the human model and the cosmic model are seen as isomorphic. The major cities of prehispanic times were laid out with a quadrilateral ground plan in mind, so that Teotihuacan, for example, is clearly aligned with the "street of the Dead" approximately north-south, and a double street set east-west (Millon 1974:335–362). Tenochtitlan, again, was said to have been designed so that the siting of the different localized clans and neighborhoods followed a four-sided model, with the temple of Huitzilopochtli-Tlaloc, the main temple, at the dead center. This design was illustrated in the myths and also in the iconography, for example, in the *Mendocino Codex* p. 1 (Lombardo de Ruiz 1973). The same arrangement was followed for the other sacred numbers, so that moieties and quadrants were internally divided in overlapping sections, to mark further divisions into six, seven, nine, ten, twelve, or thirteen units, or other sacred divisions.

The same sort of compromise between sociopolitical units, territorial units, and sacred numerology seems to have existed for Cholula (Carrasco p. 1971b). That is, the cosmic model served as an instrument for urban planning, at the same time that the social order served as a set of symbols of the cosmic sacredness of the landscape.

Both are models for and models of each other, more or less congruent.

Furthermore, roads, imagined as umbilical lines, rivers, tree trunks, or flow passages between the cities and towns of man, are equivalent to the roads, directions, angles, and position of the cosmic unit—symbols of the nighttime sky, the stars and planets. Thus the gods went up and down upon these roads (for example, the *axis mundi*, the Milky Way) as men move on the connecting paths between settlements. Often, whatever the actual number of paths entering or leaving a village, four of these are "cognized" as major entrances and exits, and named accordingly as major streets (*calle mayor*), or royal roads (*caminos reales*). Joyce Marcus, in a recent paper (1973), argues quite convincingly with good data that not only did the internal layout of cities follow from the sacred quincunx arrangements and other sacred number models, but that among the Maya the relations between cities and subordinate settlements, and between different major centers were also conceived on the basis of a quadripartite model with numerical subdivisions.

For those readers who are suspicious of such "fancy" models as being nothing more than the investigators' imagination projected onto the past, it is necessary to indicate once more that the assumption that such models "force" reality, or should be "exact" in relation to evidence found on the ground, is a misunderstanding of the function of symbolic models. Cultural armatures do not alone determine why or how man does anything, from building cities to imagining the gods. Cultural symbolics only provide a fluid map, an arrangement of social or cultural man-made features. Culture is not a factory template which "obligates" man, nor does it actually change the location of mountains, caves, waterholes, or streets! What it does do, is to provide an ordered arrangement for thinking *about* and in sympathy *with* social reality. In this sense, numerological symbolism and models based on the cardinal directions, are, again, models of and models for the perception and ordering of the real world. They are not frozen realities or jails for thought and action.

It is in this fluid sense that contemporary Zinacantecans perceive and treat natural and man-made markers—waterholes, mountain caves, arrangements of crosses within the central settlement, or roads between churches. The east-west road, marking the entrances and exits to the town, is only approximately a straight line, since it must obviously follow accidents of the terrain; the placing of the two major churches in Zinacantan Center, directly north and south of each other, again represents a compromise between the symbolic armature and the real landscape, but the arrangement of crosses clearly displays a quadrilateral geometric form that demarcates the village's central space and geometrically replicates the order seen in the quadrilateral space of the mountains and their gods which "encircle" Zinacantan.

Contemporary "Survivals" and Ancestors

Prehispanic numerology must appear arbitrary and phantasmal if the origin of the permutations, particularly the 13 and 260 cycle, cannot be determined. (The 365 day is obviously the solar year and is so described in the sources.) Archaeologists and calendar experts have argued about the possible origin of these numerological cycle transformations, without as yet finding a satisfactory answer.

Prem (1971) is of the opinion that "contemporary ethnographic data cannot possibly be available" to interpret the prehispanic 260-day calendar. This is, I believe, untrue and is an opinion based on negative evidence (that is, up to the time he wrote no one had attempted to gather the relevant ethnographic information). My work among the Cuicatec Indians has led me to believe that the apparently arbitrary numerals of the prehispanic "week," "month," and 260-day cycle, the notions about bearer gods, about the layers of heaven and the underworld, and so on, were directly derived from a simple, elegant, primeval conception, that is, from the mathematical-astronomical knowledge of the space-time continuum.[3]

Cuicatecs today (as prehispanic peoples did) conceive of time and space as a single continuum. This is also true in contemporary Chamula (Gossen 1974) and apparently in Zinacantan as well (Vogt

3. This argument will be presented in detail in a work now in preparation.

1969:604, from Bricker 1966). The interlocking of time and space is produced by observations of the sun's movements during the year, and the presence and absence of the sun, and the position of the planets in the daytime and the nighttime, all set in the earth-sky planes and in relation to stars.

Cuicatecs have a cognitive map or model of first, the earth, and second, the sky/underworld, as two intersecting four-sided planes (see Illustration 26). As at Zinacantan, the northern side of the horizontal plane of the earth is the passage of the sun over the tropic line in summer. The southern side is the passage of the sun over the tropic line in winter. The top of the second, "vertical" plane is the sky, the bottom is the underworld, but the center of the top is also the zenith point and northern celestial pole and the bottom the nadir. When the two planes are visualized with the sun present (daytime), the points for east and west (sunrise and sunset) are added. When these concur, the crossing sunrise-sunset (east/west) with the zenith-nadir (up/down) gives the exact point of the earth center. This produces an image of the space-time continuum (in the daytime and during the longer planetary cycle) which has thirteen points, as follows:

A. Daytime "planes"

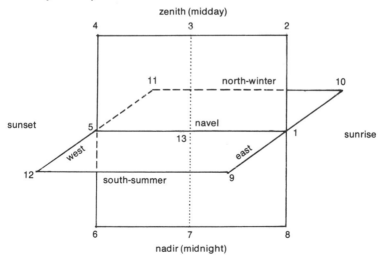

B. Nighttime "planes"

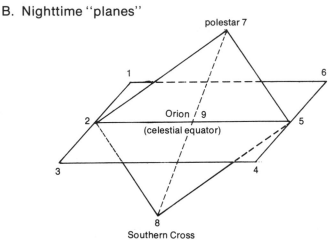

26. The space-time continuum—symbol for undulant movement—visualized as intersecting planes. (A) Daytime "planes." (B) Nighttime "planes."

The "tilting" of these two planes in a double pendular motion, during the solar year cycle, gives the changes in the seasons, from summer to winter and back.

When the sun is absent (during the night), the points of its path are eliminated, and an image of nine points obtains. These are star constellations which Cuicatecs recognize, such as Polaris, Orion's belt in his house (the four major stars of Orion), and the Southern Cross, which mark the three layers of planes of heaven, earth and underworld (or north = polestar, center = sky equator = Orion, south = Southern Cross). These beliefs, extant among the Cuicatec, are identical with prehispanic numerology in which the heavens have thirteen reference points or "layers" and the underworld nine "layers."

The Cuicatec affirm that there are nine "layers," but actually I was able to obtain names and descriptions for only five of them. The coincidence with the prehispanic layers is striking:

Prehispanic layers	Contemporary Cuicatec description
On the Earth	(1) The Earth—where we are—one enters through a cave opening.
Water Passage or Nine River	(2) The nine rivers, a place where one passes a hanging bridge and there is a dog guardian, over a river in an abyss. It takes nine days to cross this place.
Obsidian Knife Hill or the Eight Hills	(3) A forest of rubber trees and road in the mountains.
Where someone is shot with arrows or where someone's heart is eaten	(4) A dangerous place where one can get killed or charmers steal the soul.
The Place of the Dead, where the streets are on the left	(5) The place where dead souls live. The Big City of the Gods, where the houses are on the right and the streets on the left. The (Milky Way) railroad in which the sun travels at night is located on this level.

In Chiapas, this model of the cosmos as composed of thirteen layers above and nine below is still extant in Larrainzar, but not in Zinacantan (Holland 1964; Vogt 1969:600–603).

Zinacantecans still use in their ritual numerology 1, 2, 3, 4, 5, 6, 7, 8, 13, and 52, particularly in connection with double officerships, divinatory rituals, and year renewal ceremonies, and with ritual waterholes (Vogt 1976). We know also that at least until 1688, the solar month calendar was still in use (Juan Rodax, quoted in Vogt 1969:603). At present they use the Roman Catholic year but the rituals that punctuate it are still embedded, to a large extent, in prehispanic symbolism (see below p. 219). The Indians of Chamula still use the old Maya calendar of 18 months of 20 days each (Pozas 1959:77–78).

Another Zinacantecan "survival" is connected to the series of 13. As the reader may recall, the day symbols were accompanied by *two* other series of symbols called "the accompanying ones" and the "carriers of burdens," which modified the meaning or "luck" of the day symbols. One set were volatiles, the other god images. The

Zinacantecans have preserved the idea of "burdens" in the naming of officerships (Bricker 1966). But apparently it is possible that these two sets of symbols were, in Zinacantan, also identified with human souls born on the day to which they were attached, because in Zinacantan nowadays people are believed to have thirteen soul parts, and the spirit companions of man are believed to be cared for by mythical divine officers called "the Embracers" and "the Carriers," which may correspond to the original prehispanic notions of the two day-companion series (Vogt 1969:370–371). This is not as obtuse a hypothesis as it may seem initially, for in prehispanic times, in Chiapas as well as the rest of Mesoamerica, a person's name was a calendric day name, so that the "company" and "carrier" of a day may have also been the symbolic attributes of the soul of a person born on that date and named after it, and that these symbols were used for the preparation of a person's calendric horoscope (Baroco 1970). It is also interesting that the Zinacantan god Vashakmen ("eight mirror") also appeared to have a calendrical name, from an apparently "unclassified" day (ibid., p. 146). That is, it may have been an alternate or synonymous name of one of the regular cycle days named after the god. Such a variation is possible because the names of days themselves were multivocal images which signified the deities or the phenomena the deities stood for, in terms of the calendar cycles. Thus, in the Mayan glyphs, the "day" glyph also means the sun (god), time, festival, and flower.

The patterns of color and design and placing of number cycles (or numerological patterns) in the codices were used by prehispanic peoples in divination. Today Zinacantecan shamans cast colored corn seeds in different numerical arrangements as part of the diagnostic curing rituals, with exactly this purpose (Vogt 1976). Again, in the Cuicatec area where I worked, these numerical arrangements are utilized for curative divination by associating numbers with body parts and associating the number and position of corn kernels used in divination with space and time locations in the local landscape. For example, a set of corn seeds in a group of three in the left side of the divinatory mantle with two near the center may indicate: (*a*) that the person has a sickness in the left side of his body, (*b*) that the sickness caught him during the rainy season (left = rainy season; right = dry season), and (*c*) that the place where the sickness struck him is in the direction SE from where the divination is taking place, for example, in the SE waterhole of the village (south plus east = left, north plus west = right).

The original cosmic rationale behind the structural transformation of sign + number + direction = body part = time + space has been lost both in Zinacantan and in the Cuicatec region. It is apparent, however, that these original transformations became part of the cult when the prehispanic codex painters started to experiment with the arrangement of the astronomical-calendric symbols for the twenty-day series and other calendric cycles, by overlapping them onto the body parts of gods that they were painting in the sacred books, or by overlapping them on top of other sacred symbols that were being simultaneously displayed on the same page. The example I have given before of the Tezcatlipoca image with the day symbols signifying body parts is one of the most obvious ones (see Illustration 8, p. 113). But there were others which linked the space-time signs with other *numerical* patterned phenomena, such as geographic directions, seasons, and celestial events. The ingenuity of arrangements of the number signs was the result of esoteric, sacred mathematical games, played by the artist-scientist-theologians. The only comparable expression in Western art seems to be the Glass Bead Game invented by Herman Hesse (1949) and played by the characters in his novel of the same name who were mathematicians, theologians, and musicians combined. (But see below, p. 214 for astronomical numerology in the history of Europe. Similar systems exist elsewhere: for example, Chinese geomancy.)

A couple of examples from pages in the *Borgia Codex* ought to clarify this argument. On p. 72, four feathered snakes, each associated with a cardinal direction, appear in the painting. Each snake is of a different color and material. The southern snake is yellow and made of bone and grass; the western snake is made apparently of dart throwers and air, and is colored bluish. The northern snake is multicolor and made of blood-earth, and the eastern snake is made of green water. Inside each coiled snake is a different deity (for example, logically, the god of wind in the western snake, the god of water in the eastern one). But on top of these multivocal, multivalent arrangements, the artist chose to complicate the picture still more by distributing the twenty day signs in the four quarters of the painting, five in each quarter. The arrangement, moreover, is not a simple one, such as the assignment of the first five symbols to the east, the next five to the north, the next five to the west, and so on. Instead, the artist painted the day signs in sequential order following the circle, so that the first sign falls in the east (first = east = spring = beginning of day = beginning of year), the second falls in the north, the third in the west, the fourth in the south, the fifth again in the east, and so on, counterclockwise. We must remember that the planets (and sun) appear to move in a counterclockwise direction. This gives an arrangement as follows:

days: 4–8–12–16–20   days: 3–7–11–15–19
(south)   (west)

days: 1–5–9–13–17   days: 2–6–10–14–18
(east)   (north)

On the following page of *Borgia*, p. 73, the life-death gods are depicted (see Illustration 11, p. 128). Here the day signs are allocated to different parts of the bodies of the gods. Again the arrangement is not a simple one. The signs are arranged as follows: the first with the life god, the next three with the death god, the next three with the life god again; the next sign is in the middle between the two gods, overlapped with the line which joins their bodies, the next two with the death god, the next three with the life god; then, again, there is one in the middle, and the two following go with the death god; then one with the life god; and the last three with the death god. The formal arrangement of the twenty days follows what appears at first to be an arbitrary clustering of symbols:

(left side of page) Life god	Center line	(right side of page) Death god
1st-Earth monster		2nd-Wind 3rd-House 4th-Lizard
5th-Snake 6th-Death 7th-Deer	8th-Rabbit	
		9th-Water 10th-Dog
11th-Monkey 12th-Straw 13th-Cane	14th-Jaguar	
		15th-Eagle 16th-Buzzard
17th-Undulant movement		18th-Flint 19th-Rain 20th-Flower

It would probably be vain to try to unravel all the meanings of the association between the names of the signs and their positions, for we do not have the evidence necessary to interpret them. However, the arrangement of the numbers is not accidental, and in fact there is a distinct pattern or clustering as follows:

Twenty day signs	God of life	Middle	God of death
First four	1	—	3
Next six	3	1	2
Next six	3	1	2
Last four	1	—	3

These two examples show clearly and sufficiently that the divinatory system involved complex numerical-mathematical transmutations, and that the present system of divination of Zinacantecans and other Mexican Indians is but a pale reflection of its ancestral form. The loss of motivation for the structure has occurred because a major element of the system, the sacred count of days of the 260-day cycle which gave it unified meanings, has been lost; that is, the number-ordered calendar sequences (of 13, of 20, of 52, and so on) from which the numbers and their internal arrangements could be tied to personal destinies, as in horoscopes and the divining of cures for sickness, have been forgotten by Zinacantecan peasants.

Again, the same appears to have happened with the 13-day number cycle since Zinacantecans still arrange symbols in groups of 13, but they do not to my knowledge attach them to day sequences.

Those readers who may be prone to interpret these numerical-astronomical arrangements as the arbitrary thinking of primitive peoples should remember that equivalent manipulations of ideas gave rise to the major conceptions of mathematics in our own culture, and historically, these early mathematical-astronomical discoveries were intimately connected with religious ideas and cults. We tend to think of Pythagoras as "that man with the theorem," often forgetting that he was also a founder of an Orphic religious sect which dominated much intellectual-cult activity throughout the Mediterranean, and which was based on the associations of planetary movements, numbers, musical harmonics (that is, the music of the spheres), human life, and the ideological-moral values of numbers. For the Pythagoreans, the arithmetical ratios of musical intervals, the orbits of the planets, moral principles, and man's health, mood and destiny were all embedded in the mystery of numbers. Numbers represented space and time. "One" represented the odd, the limit, the point; "two" represented "even" and "unlimited," the line. But they also represented right and left, male and female, rest and motion, dark and light, good and evil. Five represented marriage because it is the union of the first masculine and feminine numbers (3 + 2); four was justice because it is the first square of a number, the product of equals; ten was perfection. The numbers also gave the basic geometric figures: some numbers were triangular, some oblong, some square. Many of the doctrines that these numerologies produced died with the practitioners of the religions, but the numerical theories, particularly the contributions to geometry, have persisted.

Moreover, we need not go back as far as Pythagoras to find examples of the uses of astronomy and numerology in combination with religion as well as science. Kepler was not only a great astronomer, but also an astrologer of fame. Both Galileo and Copernicus studied medicine because they believed that the numerological ratios were derived from the planetary orbits and that the planets' angular positions gave clues for medical treatment, because the human body was affected, like the celestial bodies, by cosmic configurations. Newton himself was a mystic, and although we remember that he succeeded in discovering the law of gravity, we often forget that he failed, although he tried, to interpret Biblical texts with numerological correlates. In our own day, the deep secular religiosity of Einstein was reaffirmed by the cosmic mysteries he was able to give humanity as a gift, and the metaphoric language still employed by astronomers who speak, for example, of the life and death of stars, twin stars, and cannibal stars, is deeply embedded both in mathematical aesthetics and in anthropomorphic language.

Today in the field of ideas we tend to discriminate between the parts of an author's work that have become accepted as "science" and the parts that have become obsolete. We speak of the former as truths or "laws," of the latter as beliefs or superstitions. But in these works the two parts are never so simply divorced from each other. Kepler's lunar geography, for example, is not only a theoretical treatise on the moon, but also an esoteric-mythic paradigm, much of it mystical and scientifically "naive," of Kepler's own life, his ideas about the nature of insight, the Muses and Genie, witchcraft, his own mother, biological adaptation in animal species, the geography of the Atlantic Ocean, and many other things (Thiel 1957; Caspar 1959; Lear 1965).

When we look at the work of prehispanic mathematicians, or even at the simplified numerical games played by Zincantan shamans, we call them beliefs. But with equal justice, and less ethnocentrism, we could call them scientific theories. That we may consider them incorrect, or anachronistic, does not make them any less scientific in the context of the traditions of their particular cultures. After all, Pythagoras's ideas about the invisible counterearth, which were a joking matter for Renaissance astronomers and physicists, are no longer so absurd in the light of modern theories about antimatter.

In summary, prehispanic religious thought included a complex astronomical divinatory numerology based on notions about the time-space continuum, the full meaning of which has been eroded so that the total structure, at the moment, is not completely under-stood. But the numbers themselves have preserved their ritual sacred value all over Indian Mesoamerica, although not all prehis-panic numbers are extant in every Indian community.

Among contemporary Cuicatecs the dominant symbol as a reli-gious number is that of the quincunx earth plane (5), which is used in ritual contexts, myths, curing rituals, funerary rituals, body direc-tionality, mountain locations and many other transformational classes. But 13 has been abandoned for ritual (the *tonalpohualli* is no longer in use), whereas in Zinacantan, souls, *7anheletik*, and some other symbols are known in groups of thirteen. If Lévi-Strauss's theory of the decay of structural logic over time is remembered, it becomes clear that some Mesoamerican villages preserved one part of the system while others preserved different parts. In Zinacantan the numeral 13 held on. Among the Cuicatec, it has lost some significance although some of the other numerals have lasted.

One of the mistakes of previous analyses has been in trying to develop a single unitary model to explain the symbolic-calendric structure. It is clear that Cuicatecs, Zinacantecans, and other Meso-american peoples have several partial, alternate topological models which they use in context according to their orthodox practice, but they do not have a single model. Nor did prehispanic peoples, the evidence established (cf. Nicholson 1971). The combinations of gods in the prehispanic past, as well as their numerology and calendar, I believe, were based on the same sort of alternative models.

The solar months, myths, and rituals, and solar symbol "num-bers" have apparently survived more widely than the numbers and calculations associated with planets and nighttime celestial objects. Some villages in Guatemala, among the Ixil, have preserved both. Perhaps the explanation lies in the use to which these calendars were put. The solar calendar, of great importance for the agricultural cycle, has been at least partially preserved, or replaced, by the Roman Catholic calendar, which serves the same purpose. The astro-nomical nighttime calendar and the divinatory calendar, which were based on purely scientific speculations—the astronomy games of specialists versed in the mysteries of the ecliptic and zodiacal world—did not have the same immediate value for the peasant masses. In addition, the Christian church was much more interested in eradicating the "heathen" divinatory ritual calendar than the agrarian calendar, which it viewed as having more neutral religious associations, and it made positive moves to suppress the former. The combination of these forces led to the dislocation of the structure. Bits and pieces of it, however, survived in the less obvious symbolism to which the Christian priests had no immediate access (that is, shamanistic rituals).

One has to understand the original sociological value of the complicated calendrical cycles to see why they have not often survived in contemporary Indian villages. Their social value in scheduling the complexity of events in an urbanized, bureaucratized agrarian society ceased to exist when the prehispanic state was decapitated. The scheduling of contemporary peasant life, with its simple division of labor, neither requires nor can accommodate such finely divided measurements of time. The Christian solar calendar provides for all the cadences of secular work, ritual, and leisure. For the same reasons, Indians of the southwestern United States, who have the same quadripartite, "quincunx" arrangement of symbols and calendar, did not borrow the rest of the *tonalpohualli* from Mesoamerica (see Ortiz 1969). Their society was never complex enough to require its use (I am indebted to my student, Felix Aquino, for pointing this out to me in an unpublished paper).

Huitzilopochtli's role in the ecological solar annual calendar was quite significant, particularly in the valley of Mexico. Since he was identified with other solar deities and with the sun itself, ecological periods based on the sun's equinoxes and solstices, or ecliptic values, were attributed to him. These attributions appear in disguised, parable form in "The Hummingbird."

His position in the long calculations of the *tonalpohualli*, however, was quite humble, as I have pointed out. A few dates are of significance, and were used for mythico-poetic transformations. For example: the year 1 Flint was the date he started the Aztec peregrination southwards. It was also his calendrical day name. Therefore, the day of that name was propitious for his rituals. The day 2 Cane was likewise propitious because it was the birth date of Tezcatlipoca, from which Huitzilopochtli unfolded. Four months of the annual calendar, one in each quarter, were dedicated to Huitzilopochtli's rituals. The year 2 Cane was the date of his birth as well as the date of Quetzalcoatl's death, which made these two gods oppositional partners in one more of their multiple associations. Two Cane was also the date of the creation of fire by Tezcatlipoca, which, since the hummingbird god was sun = celestial fire, was of importance to him.

It is probable that some of these dates reflect historical events dated by the calendar, in cases when these gods had been living persons who were later deified. At the boundary between myth and history, the calendar played a key role. It is possible also that some dates refer to astronomical events that were historically recorded (for example, "Tezcatlipoca making himself into Mixcoatl, with his seat at the North Pole, making fire" may refer obscurely to astronomical events involving a planet and the pole star or the "fire drill constellation," which took place in the year 2 Cane). Again, at the boundary between science and myth the calendar stood unchallenged. However, it is also most likely that some of these dates were themselves symbols of purely religious transformational games played by the theologians. (For example, it is my opinion that the goddess of maguey and pulque was said to have been born on the day 1 Rabbit because of the symbolic links between pulque, rabbits, and fertility that I explained earlier.) We may never know which explanation is correct in many cases, but partial answers may be forthcoming. It is unfortunate that no analysis of the significance of these dates has yet been produced. We have, however, Caso's (1967) useful list to start this particular research journey.

CHAPTER 7

Contemporary Correlates
of the Structure
of "The Hummingbird"

What factors in the native life of Zinacantan today preserved the beauty of "The Hummingbird" until it was recorded? One could argue that its very aesthetic beauty ensured its survival, that Zinacantecans sometimes enjoy poetic obscurity simply for its own sake just as we do. Robert Browning was once scolded by his future wife, Elizabeth Barrett. She complained that there was a particular line in one of his poems that she could not understand, and she asked him to explain it. Browning with characteristic flair admitted that "at the time of writing, God and Robert Browning knew the meaning of the line, but now only God knows it." Thus we *could* argue that the poetic text of "The Hummingbird" has a message not manifestly understood today by Zinacantecans; they, like us, can enjoy a poem without understanding it. I firmly believe that this is possible. However, in a more pedestrian anthropological context, since we frown on the idea of meaningless survivals, an explanation is required.

First, as I have shown in many examples, much of Zinacantan's symbolism and ritual life is of prehispanic authocthonous origin, not Christian, and has survived quite intact. Again, as I have shown, much of this symbolism relates to the analysis of "The Hummingbird." Furthermore, there is much in Zinacantan's native intellectual and religious life that supports my opinion that this mythological poem is still meaningful at many levels. Zinacantecans still cultivate, as their ancestors did, by the slash and burn method. At the very end of the dry season, they burn the fields to get rid of the stubble of previous crops, to kill weeds, and to fertilize the soil with ashes. The fires begin around March. Then, "smoke from thousands of small Indian fields fills the Chiapas atmosphere. The smoke persists until the rains arrive in May and signal the time for planting" (Vogt 1969:45). No wonder that when Zinacantecans "were burning bean pods" (line 4 of the poem, p. 29, above) "the fire could be seen well" (line 5); small wonder that the spring hummingbird "saw the fire" (line 9), that "its eyes were snuffed out by the smoke" (line 10) or that, less metaphorically, the spring sky is filled with smoke and the ascending sun cannot look down or be seen!

The planting season in Zinacantan follows ceremonies connected with water and the increase of rain to fertilize the crops (K'in Krus, Skantelail Chobtik), and its beginnings coincide with the resuscitation of God at Easter. K'in Krus also may take place at the end of the rainy season in October. Like the hummingbird god, who was used by the colonial priests to explain the resurrection, Jesus (Hmanvaneh) is resurrected at Easter's Holy Week. He "comes back" from the dead, "comes out" after the death that was to pay for man's sins. The movable fast period of Lent begins on Ash Wednesday and extends into March and April. Easter itself ends on Glory Saturday, but the Easter season concludes on Corpus Christi and Sacred Heart, well into the rainy season at the end of spring. The god of the ascending sun, of the resurrected rain and spring, the hummingbird of yesteryear, or Jesus Christ of today *are*, by syncretic merging, one and the same god. Moreover, the identification of the Holy Week Jesus with the sunlight of the daytime also appears metaphorically in a Zinacantecan myth, which states that Hmanvaneh made the sky blue (*ibid.*, p. 360). There is no mystery in this coincidence. Roman Catholicism on the one hand, with its calendar derived from the Judaic and Greco-Roman traditions in content as well as in the allocation of sacred dates, and prehispanic religion on the other, have happily and easily merged their rituals and symbols. This is not surprising. Both were official religions of agrarian states, with astronomical and agricultural overtones that make sense in the Northern Hemisphere.

Jesus's identification with the sun is prevalent, as Huitzilopochtli's was in the prehispanic days, all over Mesoamerica (for example, in the Cuicatec area where I worked). In Chamula, the next village to Zinacantan, the sun god (*htotik*, our father), is also the Jesus of present-day religion (Vogt 1973:101). In Zinacantan, the moon, divine mother, is the Virgin Mary (*ibid.*). Also in Zinacantan the spring rains are believed to be directly controlled by the Lord of the Earth and the father-mother gods (*totilme'il*) which appear in the text of "The Hummingbird." These are probably modern versions of *Teteo innan Teteo inta* (literally: "gods—their mother, gods—their father") which Nicholson believes were fire deities (1971: Table 3). According to Vogt (1969:456, 367) they are apparently distinguished from the sun although that is disputable since the Zinacantan "sun" is called the "father" also (Vogt 1973). He is also said in Zinacantan not merely to be the one who made the sky blue, but the clearest identification of the divinity: "God himself." In any case, even if the two (that is, mother-father gods and father sun) are not perceived in Zinacantan as totally identified, the hummingbird and hawk are said to be their messengers and incarnations, or *nahual* (see prior discussions, pp. 58–59, and Vogt 1969:299 for the mother-father god as hawk; see Laughlin, 1969:117; also Guiteras-Holmes 1961; Blaffer 1972). Hence, the mythical transformation is no less explicit now than it was in the prehispanic past, or than it is in other contemporary Mayan myths where the hummingbird is one of the images of the sun (Thompson 1970:166, 202, 235, 313, 358 ff.).

It is significant, moreover, that the major rain ceremonies are performed on the top of a mountain, preceded by a peregrination in a south-southeast direction from Zinacantan Center. *Thus the association of rains and the rainy season with the easterly and southerly directions and with the mountains still exists.* But another even more revealing association has persisted in the contemporary context. The mountain in question is called "younger brother mountain" (Vogt 1969:473). The elder ancestral gods live in "senior brother mountain." If we remember that Huitzilopochtli was younger brother of the elder ancestral gods, it seems highly possible that this mountain's name was or is an epithet of the god Huitzilopochtli. That is, senior ancestral gods : senior brother mountain : : hummingbird god : junior brother mountain. Put another way, senior god : hummingbird : : senior brother mountain : junior brother mountain. This finding suggests that at the top of "younger brother mountain," where there are major archaeological ruins (*ibid.*, 386, 473), there may have been a prehispanic temple or sacred precincts dedicated to Huitzilopochtli, or to one of the gods of the season of the spring and summer sun and rain, a season which corresponds with the east and south. Archaeological research ought to be able to test this hypothesis.

Thus, all the gods that bring rain in the spring—the Christian

Chart 7. The hummingbird of Zinacantan: kinship, seasons and directional associations in 14 transformational classes

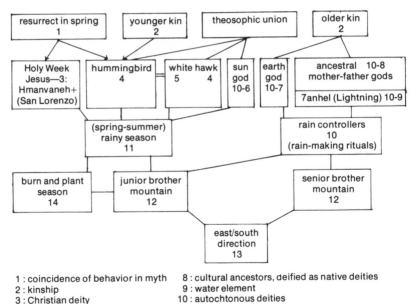

1 : coincidence of behavior in myth
2 : kinship
3 : Christian deity
4 : volatiles
5 : colors
6 : planet sun
7 : earth element

8 : cultural ancestors, deified as native deities
9 : water element
10 : autochtonous deities
11 : ecology-climate-seasons
12 : features of the landscape
13 : cardinal directions
14 : agrarian cycle

Jesus of Holy Week and Easter, the autochthonous mother-father gods, and the junior, humble sun-hummingbird—are associated with the east and south. If this interpretation is correct, it should follow that the celebrations of other Catholic saints and Christian personages should also have time periods and directional associations corresponding to those of their prehispanic predecessors who are still "alive." That is, not only should the Christian counterparts of the spring-summer autochthonous deities or the native deities themselves fall into place vis-à-vis the old space-time continuum, but in addition, the deities and saints connected with the dry season ought to belong to the fall-winter period and have westerly and northerly associations. It is one of the joys of structural analysis that when a valid symbolic key is found, the ethnographic evidence to confirm it pours out in torrents, but if the key is not the right one the ethnographic evidence quickly destroys the hypothesis. (For a discussion of prediction of error in structural analysis, see Yalman 1971:5.)

The first evidence concerning these associations deals with the two major calendrical rituals of Zinacantan, the fiestas of San Lorenzo (Saint Lawrence) and San Sebastian. They occur approximately six months apart. San Lorenzo takes place in August between the 7th and the 11th. San Sebastian is performed in January between the 18th and 23rd. The two churches or chapels which house these saints and in which the major rituals take place are, *according to prediction*, precisely south and north of each other: Saint Lawrence, the summer saint, in the south; Saint Sebastian, the winter saint, in the north. The two churches are "connected by a straight trail resembling an ancient causeway" (Vogt 1969:137). Moreover, the rituals and the myths of the saints confirm that they were originally and still are solar celebrations. Saint Lawrence is an old Christian symbol of the fire of the summer sun. His sign is the gridiron, because the saint was "roasted to death" in the summer. In the midst of his martyrdom he told his tormentors: "I am roasted enough on this side, turn me around and eat." The meteorites which appear annually near the middle of August are known in Spain and Latin America as Saint Lawrence's tears.

The ritual horse races of these two major fiestas also appear to be an equivalent of the prehispanic ritual "race" of the sun's solstice which was celebrated in honor of Huitzilopochtli and was called "The Fleet Path of Huitzilopochtli." Like their prehispanic counterpart, the modern rituals are not really races (no one wins or loses) but the rapid running of a circle in a counterclockwise direction. The prehispanic version was run in fact from the major temple of Huitzilopochtli in Tenochtitlan to Chapultepec Hill (west), to Tacubaya (southwest) from there to Coyoacan (south), and back to the city's center (north) (see Illustration 27). The Zinacantan version is run in the central church plaza from east to west back and forth to the same point (Duran 1971:87). In Chamula, similar "races" are run on foot over a fire path (lighted straw which represents the sun's path), or on horseback (Pozas 1959:166, 176). The dates of the fiesta of Saint Lawrence coincide with the point at which the sun is straight overhead in the latitude of Zinacantan (Vogt, personal communication).

[Professor Vogt has pointed out to me in a personal communication that the major ritual impersonators of this fiesta may represent the "one-legged hummingbird," the image of the summer sun] I believe that this interpretation is correct, and that minimal empirical probing in the field would demonstrate it. These impersonators are called *Capitanes* (captains, soldiers), and are "the most characteristic feature of the fiesta" (Vogt 1969:560). Like Hummingbird, they are warriors, soldiers. Their clothing is obviously a mixture of historically blended symbols, like that of other ritual impersonators. Out of the historic stream of Zinacantecan experience, Spanish conquistadors, prehispanic warriors, and Mexican military men called *Capitanes* become one and the same. But the hummingbird is still there, hidden in the modernized, hybrid clothing of the sacred impersonators (see Bricker 1974, for a detailed discussion of the historic merging of costumes and symbols). Moreover, the behavior of the impersonators during the ritual is directly connected with the symbol of the hummingbird and of "one-leg," the name under which he appears in the poem.

Much of the costume of the *Capitanes* is blue-green (scarf and breeches). They also use touches of red (leggings, a turban). Over it, they wear black coats, which seem to be the modern equivalent of the "nettle leaf cape, which was painted black" and was placed on the image of Huitzilopochtli for the celebration of Toxcatl, one of

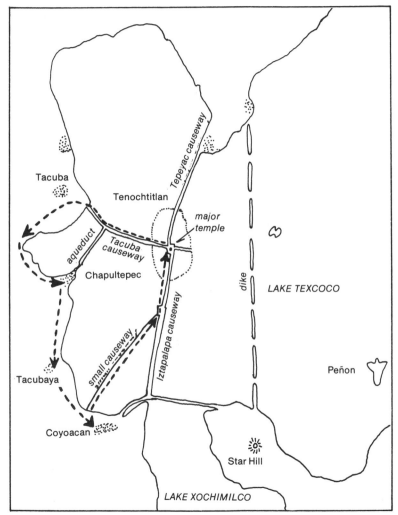

27. Ritual of the Fleet Path of Huitzilopochtli. Arrows show direction of "race" according to Duran.

the rituals of the prehispanic calendrical quarter of summer (cf. Leon-Portilla 1962:72). Moreover, like the mask of Huitzilopochtli, their faces are painted with gold streaks.

The clinching argument, in my opinion, is that the ritual impersonators' characteristic behavior, their function during the ritual, is to dance on one leg (the name of the hummingbird in the poem), hopping, at the end of the procession of the saint's images which are brought together for the fiesta of Saint Lawrence.

Since we know that in prehispanic rituals the impersonators symbolized the god they were celebrating, the transformational equation now reads, in my opinion, summer sun : Saint Lawrence : *Capitanes* who dance on one leg : hummingbird god. Just as Jesus-Hmanaveh is the Easter (spring) image of the sun, so Saint Lawrence is the summer image, and Sebastian the winter image. But let us consider further evidence. In the course of the enquiry, we may discover why "one leg" is the hummingbird's name.

A complete analysis of all the directional associations of the Zinacantan rituals connected with the calendar cannot be covered in this work, but the published evidence for these connections is overwhelming. The Zinacantan calendar appears to be arranged like the prehispanic one in roughly four sections (see Table 9). Holidays which may be assigned to the west-north directions fall also in the fall-winter period.

Most important of all, Saint Sebastian, of the winter holy days, has been syncretized with the prehispanic "dark, northern sun," the "defeated sun" of the winter solstice, the black Tezcatlipoca; and the images of the old, dark sun god have been transferred to Saint Sebastian in the myths. The chapel of the saint is directly to the north of Zinacantan Center. According to the myth, the Vashakmen, bearer god(s) of the four directions, built this chapel in ancestral times, long before the lifetime of presently living Zinacantecans. When the chapel was built, "it became dark, there was no day, no night, just darkness on the land" (Vogt 1969:326), which is the prehispanic metaphor for the winter solstice, an image that makes more sense if we remember that Tezcatlipoca created daylight from darkness. However, this is also a metaphor for the mythic times before the birth of the present cosmic sun. The dark Tezcatlipoca created the new world from cosmic darkness. Thus the sun of the winter solstice (the dark part of the year) repeats the event in eternal cyclic fashion. Further support comes from the Saint Sebastian myths, because the saint's chapel was built at a time when the stones moved themselves, "came by themselves . . . worked by themselves" (Vogt 1969:326–330, the myth of Saint Sebastian). The world bearers (Vashakmen) ordered them to do so. Prehispanic peoples had the same idea, because the people of the contact period believed that their own cities of the Classic period had been built by the gods in the time of darkness, before the present solar era, and at that time the stones moved into place by themselves without human help. For the decadent post-Classic Maya, only a magic time could have produced such architectural wonders. Apparently they could not conceive of the mastery and organization of human labor that went into their building.

The saint of the chapel, Saint Sebastian, is called the Martyr. He is "the defeated saint, shot with arrows," persecuted, according to the myth, by the forces of darkness (for example, "jaguars in the forest"). Even though he was killed, he "returned just the same," just as the sun returns after he has "died" in the darkness of the winter

Table 4. Transformation of the calendric oppositions of Zinacantan

Cardinal direction	north	south
Season	winter	summer
Date of fiesta	January 18–23	August 7–11
Symbol of the saint in the iconography	saint shot with arrows	saint burned or roasted
"Planet" position	winter solstice, weak sun, defeated sun	(sun at zenith) summer solstice, strong hot sun
Color	dark, black, red (death luck)	white, light, blue (good luck)
Day length	long nights	long days
Associated ritual impersonators and mythic symbols	"Blackmen" (bats, buzzards), Moss Men jaguars, plumed serpents who are ravens	white hawks, white hummingbirds which appear in August, Capitanes who dance on one leg

solstice. The martyr saint, in his escape and mythical wanderings, *moves always in the northern quarter*. He takes refuge in a cave, north of Zinacantan center, in a rock (*bolom ton*), also north, his waterhole (*nio'*) rituals are located in the north of the town, and black mythical creatures of darkness appear in his ritual—plumed serpents which are ravens, Moss Men (moss is a symbol of the interior of the forest and wildness, and Moss Men are sexually wild and aggressive), and Blackmen who are evil bats or buzzards (Vogt 1969:329, 356–8, 482, 542, 545, *passim*), and are the contemporary form of the mythic *zaqui coxol*, little black men of the forest of the Maya creation myths of the Quiche (Thompson 1965b:17). The ritual impersonators use many red pieces of clothing. The link here is red = death. A person's "red hour" or "red luck" is his time of death. The opposite, birth and good luck, is the "blue-green hour"—another example of the complexity of color associations.

The western-fall rituals also correspond. Those concerning All Souls Day occur at the end of October and on November 1, associated with west. In this holy period, the souls of ancestral Zinacantecans come out of their graves to visit their living kin. The cemetery from which they come and to which Zinacantecans go to leave offerings is west of Zinacantan Center, in the direction of the hamlet of Salinas (Vogt 1969:220–221 and Map 5 in the same work). The ritual of the goddess of salt and patroness of women, the Virgin of the Rosary, takes place in a western hamlet the first Friday before October 7 (*ibid.*, p. 481 and Map 5 in the same work).

Practices in Zinacantan exhibit some discrepancies and variants vis-à-vis the central valley's historical ritual calendar. These could reflect actual differences between ancestral Zinacantan rituals and those of the highland valleys. But most likely the dates do not synchronize perfectly, in some cases, because Zinacantecans have had to compromise between their ideas about what was ritually proper and the Roman Catholic calendar, over which they had very limited (if any) control. What Zinacantecans have done, like many other Indians of Mesoamerica, is to choose the closest analogue between a prehispanic deity and a Christian personage or saint, at the nearest possible calendar date. These compromises have produced variations and apparent "arbitrariness." For example, the goddess of salt, within the present structure, is congruent with west-fall; among the Aztec in prehispanic times she was celebrated at approximately July 19 (dates according to Duran [1971] Correlation). The Virgin of the Rosary who syncretically replaced her in Zinacantan is celebrated in the first week of October, which means that this ritual may have been moved from the south-summer quarter to the west-fall quarter, a difference of approximately seventy-three days. But what is important to notice is that the direction/month correspondence has been preserved. When the day of the ritual was moved from summer to fall, the direction may also have been moved from south to west, unless the prehispanic Zinacantecans placed July 19 in the west quarter. However, in the prehispanic fourfold arrangements of direction and time, west was the direction connected with goddesses. They accompanied the sun on the journey into sunset (day), fall (year), that is, into death. Therefore, the Virgin of the Rosary is simply carrying on a long tradition of symbolic linkages.[1]

An additional source of arbitrariness can be found in recent Christian innovations which do not fit into the overall space-time armature of the calendric structure. For example, a new ritual has developed in the hamlet of Navenchauk, as a nativistic response to protestant missionary activity. This ritual occurs in a chapel, built about fifteen years ago, and does not fit the space-time correlation. The old rituals, which are also the most important ones, are all clearly congruent, however. If we take it as given that four saints are chosen, one in each of four different calendar quarters of a year, the statistical probability that they will correlate with four directions by chance alone, rather than by design, is 4 in 100, above the minimum accepted significance level in the social sciences. If we consider that only the choice of any four saint celebrations is given, the probability that they will correspond both with four yearly quarters and

---

1. To complete this analysis we should discover what animals are transformations of west-fall. We know the association with woman and salt (Virgin of the Rosary), probably with moon too. But which are its colors and volatiles?

four calendar directions, by chance alone, is 17 in 10,000. Furthermore, the probability that four saints (out of a minimum of 365 saint-days in the year), fitting four calendar quarters and *also* corresponding with four cardinal directions, will be chosen by chance alone, is equal to 18 in 1,000,000! I believe that nothing further is needed to prove that this correlation is not accidental.

Thus, not only have prehispanic symbolism and deities survived in the shape of contemporary theophanic forms as animals and season/color/direction transformations, sometimes even with their original prehispanic names, but they have also merged and become congruent with Christian personages, saints, and their rituals and myths.

The matching of prehispanic images with present-day "ancestral gods" and Christian personages creates a duplicate symbol structure. I have no way of knowing whether the ancestral gods and saints are directly and consistently identified throughout the whole symbol system. I would not expect consistency because my theory suggests that the divine symbols are not discrete but are dynamic images of a pantheistic god, constantly reinterpreted. Single identifications are obvious, such as Jesus and the sun, Mary and the moon, and the *Pukuh* (devil) and Blackmen, gods of the underworld (the god of death, *Ah Puch*, and the God *Ycal Ahau*, "thirteen death" or "black lord") with Christian devils. Vogt and his co-workers have made these identifications. Moreover, the two groups of symbols for the "deities" seem to form isomorphic matched sets. Over the years Zinacantecans have replicated the symbolic structure of the ancestral autochthonous deities which they still maintain, in the parallel overlapping structure of Christian images that they inherited from their conquerors. Probably because of persecution by colonial church officials, but also because the old sacred images were not allowed within the precincts of the new temples (the Christian churches), the divine images took a new lease on life. Half of them continued to be attached to their transformational symbols in the landscape and cosmos (such as mountains). The other half now live happily inside the chapels of Zinacantan, *and* wander in mythic time among the same sacred markers of the religious landscape.

A tentative list of possible matchings would include the sun god as Jesus, for spring, Saint Lawrence for summer, and Saint Sebastian for winter. Perhaps Sebastian himself or his "younger brother" Saint Fabian may symbolize the fall quarter. The female deity, moon, is the Virgin Mary, but obviously all goddesses are linked together in the western-fall quarter of the year, symbolized primarily by the Virgin of the Rosary, as they were in prehispanic times when the west was called "the region of women." Her negative images are the Charcoal Crunchers, as the negative images of the sun of the dark winter and of death are the Blackmen and the Pukuhetik (demons). While Saint Sebastian is the good side of Tezcatlipoca, the winter sun, the Blackmen and Pukuh are his bad side, identified with the Christian devil, lord of darkness and the underworld. Pukuh is particularly interesting, because he connects with the Mayan prehispanic lord of the underworld, the god of death (Ah Puch). Moreover, the ritual dominance of Saint Sebastian and the impersonators of his negative image, together with the name of Zinacantan ("place of bats"), suggests that the prehispanic town was dedicated to a winter-period god, one of the winter aspects of Tezcatlipoca-Itzam Na. Tezcatlipoca-Itzam Na as "oneness," the unifying divine principle, is now Yahval Balamil, the Lord of the World and of Rain and Earth. Inside the Church, however, he may be God the Father. His generic name is Kahvaltik in Tzotzil, and he includes the sun, Christ, the mother-father gods, and the Lord of the World (Robert Laughlin, personal communication). The word Kahvaltik comes from the root *7ohov* = *ahau* = Lord, as in Yahaval (classic spelling) or Yahval (modern spelling) Balamil.

The duality of mother-father gods is the *totilme'iletik*, but is also Jesus and Mary, and other paired "couple" saints. Some of these are in the chapels; for example, Sebastian and Saint Catherine symbolize the northern pair. Others are in the mountains; for example, Saint Cecilia and Saint Christopher symbolize the southern pair, with their feasts on appropriately June 9 and July 25. Tezcatlipoca-Itzam Na as a quadripartite deity complex appears in several related images. First and foremost, he is the Vashakmen. But he is also a series of certain Christian symbols, which form sets of four and are intermingled with sacred mountains, which are also in sets of four. The sets are often listed together in prayer and myth. For example, in the prayers for the waterhole rituals that I discussed above (Vogt 1976), the deities and mountains are listed in a series of invocations, in the following sequence: (1) oneness: Jesus Christ, (2) duality: father-mother gods in general, (3) the fourfold group of Holy Kalvario, Saint Kristobal, divine Maria Cecilia, and divine Maria Mushul. These are the four most important nearby mountains visited by Zinacantecans on ritual pilgrimages. They are located south and southeast of Zinacantan Center and form a quadrilateral pattern in space. But they also correspond, respectively, with the sacred site at which Christ was crucified, Saint Christopher, and two female saints, Saint Cecilia and Maria Mushul. Both female saints are called Maria—that is, they are transformational apparitions of the Virgin Mary—but I do not know the Spanish (or English) equivalent of Mushul. All these sacred images listed are invoked as the "*four* holy fathers and mothers*"* in the lines of the prayer that follow. The prayer proceeds to list them again, by their synonym names, as holy fathers and mothers, as holy great and ancient mountains and holy "yellow" ones. (In Tzotzil yellow is a homonym of old, mature, or ripe.) The major mountain (east of Zinacantan) where all the sets of ancestral divine figures live together is then invoked. A pair of mountains to the northwest of Zinacantan, *Lac cikin* and *Nakleb 7ok*, are then listed in sequence and called holy father and mother, followed immediately by the salt well of the Virgin of the Rosary (west) invoked as such and by the names "holy woman of the sky" and "divine lady of the sky." *Lac cikin* is a mountain belonging to Saint Sebastian (northwest) where he left his mythic sacred drum (Vogt 1969:359). *Nakleb 7ok* is its "entrance" or junior twin mountain. Another pair of mountains to the southwest of Zinacantan is then invoked, one senior, one junior, and then both are invoked again as "holy stones" and "mothers and fathers." Finally, the prayer, which has moved in textual-geographic space counterclockwise, from southern mountains, to the east, to northwest, to west, to southwest, goes to the center of Zinacantan, the sacred core of the church. Here the text lists *four* Christian sacred images: Saint Lawrence, the Virgin of the Rosary, Saint Dominic, and an image of Jesus called Señor Esquipulas.

It seems then that all these symbols are ancestral father and mother "deities," because all are divine beings ancestral to Zinacantecans. They appear in different guises, sometimes as a unity, sometimes as a pair or trio, sometimes as a quadripartite set. The final lines of the prayer clearly indicate the overlap of all these symbolic dimensions, because they are said to "in divine unison, in divine accord, . . . protect . . . the center of the sky . . . the center of divine glory." As if this were not sufficient identification, the "saintly divine Vashakmen," the four world bearers, are then invoked, as a single "lord" sitting "in the middle of the holy sky," being also the holy mother and father. All these images of the deity are then asked to "take the trouble, observe us here forever, encircle us here forever"—"encircle us" because they are the mountains encircling Zinacantan, and because they are the unitary divinity which embraces man from all four cardinal quarters and the center, in all time.

If my interpretation is correct, the "father-mother gods" are not a separate set of divinities, but simply the general name of the divine oneness of the parental divine duality, and of the quadripartite divinity, which is elaborated into multiple images of prehispanic as well as of European origin. It is simply the textual sequence in the prayer and the logistics of anthropological reporting that make these divine images appear *as if* they were separate discrete entities, unblended. In a pantheistic religion in which God is one, two, and four simultaneously, in which he divides and transforms himself into infinite images, he is both one and all of the sacred symbols that have been invoked. But the Zinacantecan symbolic pantheon is ordered, like all symbolic structures, to make sense out of the bewildering reality of the universe. First, it moves counterclockwise like the sun. Second, it encompasses space and time in cosmic oneness. Third, it is duality (rainy and dry seasons, for example, or male and female). Simultaneously it is the four quarters, that is, the four cardinal directions, the four holy mothers and fathers of the prayer quoted, the four ritual periods of the year's sacred calendar. God can divide and transform himself even further. He can be the six ancestral divine couples who founded the town of Zinacantan, or the same six male and six female ancestors who now live in the twelve mountains around Zinacantan Center. He can be thirteen if one adds to these mountains the "navel of the world" in Zinacantan's center. Ultimately, he can be infinite and unaccountable. In this cyclic dual-quadripartite-six- or twelve-pointed oneness, autochthonous ancestral gods and Christian divine personages are one and many, one and the same. Syncretism, in this context, is simply the technical name of a process already inherent in the nature of the pantheon before the influence of Christianity was ever felt.

It should be pointed out that Evon Vogt and his students and colleagues who worked in Zinacantan have interpreted the rituals of Saint Lawrence and Saint Sebastian somewhat differently, focusing on other multivocal elements of the rituals and myths. My interpretation of blue and white Tezcatlipoca = Hmanvaneh plus Saint Lawrence = wet season, and spring and summer period, or Hmanvaneh = east = spring period, does not contradict previous analyses. On the contarary, it reinforces them by supplying one more codified dimension to the syntagmatic-paradigmatic structure that forms the ordered invariant armature of Zinacantecan symbolism. The new equation in fact suggests strongly that the system of ordering that previous researchers discovered has even deeper implications and ramifications. Bricker (1973), for example, has extensively analyzed the ritual symbolism of joking as it relates to the performance of sex roles, differences between ethnic groups (Ladino and Indian), and Christian as well as animal imagery in historical perspective. What I suggest here is that the armature is exhibited, redundantly, in many codes simultaneously—some are verbal (myth); some are behavioral (ritual peregrinations). I am simply adding one more set of codes (space-time, solar-astronomical, seasonal-ecological) to those discussed by previous authors. It seems clear to me that adding, for example, an astronomical code may serve to explain some of the hitherto unexplained up/down symbolism of Zinacantecan rituals, such as the climbing of the Jaguar Tree by ritual impersonators (Vogt 1969:547) and the reversed and forward marches of dancers, of officers being initiated, and of other ritual actors (*ibid.*, pp. 477–567).

The same structure of cosmic solar directionality/time will explain why Zinacantecans place the strong (hot) side of any object or ritual event at the east, and the weak (colder) side at the west. In this patrilineal society, the strong side is male (the sun) and the weak side female (the moon, his companion). Thus the strong period of the sun (spring and summer, the rainy season) is transformed into east-south, into male "gods,"while its weak period (fall and winter, the dry season) is transformed into the north-west directions, which are half female, the moon, and half defeated male, the sun (Virgin of the Rosary, Saint Sebastian).

Hence, at one level, the rituals and myths bear a message of nuclear families, descent rules, social hierarchy, normative behavior, historic events, and Rabelaisian humor. At another level, the symbols tell a message of cosmic dramas, planetary reversals, solstices and equinoxes, up and down, right and left, calendric cycles of annual and daily periodicity. All the codes together create, sustain, and flesh out a single armature, supporting the whole complex symbolic life of the Zinacantecans.

It is because previous analysis had led the way that I have been able in this book to suggest additions and alternatives to, or reinterpretations of the orchestration of Zinacantan symbols. Symbolic analysis, because of the nature of mythic structures, particularly in a society with a pantheistic view of the world, cannot lead to single solutions. In fact, the more intensive the research, the larger the number of legitimate meanings that can be uncovered. Like the symbolic structures of dreams, religious symbolic structures have a bottomless series of levels.

We have a few more questions to answer about hummingbird one-leg. Why should "white," the image of triumphant spring becoming summer, still be meaningful today for Zinacantecans? Could it be a metaphor for rain? In his description of a rain-making ceremony for

Table 5. Some calendrical rituals with associated symbols in Zinacantan*

Associational class	The year			
	1st quarter	2nd quarter	3rd quarter	4th quarter
Falling water Direction	rain begins east (Lok'eb K'ak'al: "rising heat")	full rain south (Shokon Vinahel: "side of heaven")	rains ending west (Maleb K'ak'al: "waning heat")	dry north (Shokon Vinahel: "side of heaven")
"Christian" rituals	Lent/Easter period, ending at Sacred Heart	1st major fiesta; Saint Lawrence ritual period	All Souls—Virgin of the Rosary period	2nd major fiesta; Saint Sebastian ritual period
Sun position	spring equinox (sun ascends)	summer solstice (sun victorious)	autumnal equinox (sun descends)	winter solstice (sun defeated) "shot with arrows"
Agricultural activity	fields prepared by burning and planting	finish planting; corn growing; work on fields, 2nd weeding	finish cultivating; harvesting	corn stocks dry and empty in fields; rest; corn sale, transportation, dividing harvest
Volatiles	blue-green hummingbird	hawk, white hummingbird	? yellow?	raven, crow ("plumed" serpent), bat, black men (red)
"Native" rituals	rain & planting ceremonies. 1st K'in Krus	2nd rain & mid-year ceremonies. One-leg Capitanes dances	ceremonies for dead ancestors in homes & cemeteries	New Year ceremonies, dances of impersonators of forces of the winter solstice

*See footnote 1, Chap. 7.

the corn field, Jack Stauder (in Vogt 1969:458) gives us a clue. Several Zinacantecan men decided to have a second, extra ceremony to ask for rain, in July, because the milpa was drying for lack of water. As the ceremony progressed, the gods, apparently pleased, sent rain. At last the rain became so heavy that the ritual was interrupted. Then as Stauder observed:

They just wait(ed) for the rain to stop, making jokes and smoking and drinking. The glass is not used now: the bottle is passed straight from man to man, and to the little boys too, all of them holding onto the slick mountain-side, waiting for the rum liquor to warm their limbs and for the rain to be called away. The air is turned *watery white*, obscuring the corn fields below in a turbulent mist, leaves and ears of corn roaring with the torrents of wind and rain. [Emphasis mine.]

Is it not likely that an ancestral Zinacantecan, who created the original version of the hummingbird from his storage of mythical knowledge, also had personal experience of such *white summer rain?*

CHAPTER 8

Interpretations
and Conclusions

The text of "The Hummingbird" is loaded with symbolic conversions and with multivocal references to the mythical ecology of Mesoamerica, exemplified by the solar agrarian routine of Zinacantan, in which "poetic knowledge transformed into absolute knowledge is magical knowledge" (Maritain 1953:144).

So far, our analysis states that the latent content meaning of the poem is:

hummingbird	: hawk (or dove)
: : smallest bird	: large bird
: : blue-green	: white
: : spring	: summer
: : vernal equinox	: summer solstice
: : end of dry season	: rainy season
: : burning fire to prepare fields	: planting

Interpreting the text's mythical paradoxes, one could state the message in less poetic but more intelligible language. The hummingbird, which is a small bird that flies low, becomes a hawk, a large bird that flies high, changing as mysteriously as spring changes into summer. This metaphor is supported by the parallel, related metaphors of (1) a field of burning bean pod and stubble being prepared for planting, resembling the hot country, which becomes a colder field with a newly planted crop; (2) the ascending sun of the vernal equinox, which appears to come flying in the sky, and changes into the higher sun of the summer solstice; (3) the rising tall fire, resembling the heat of the dry season, which changes into the coolness of the white descending rain of the wet season; (4) the blue-green color of the spring sky, which gives place to the white color of a rainy sky in summer; (5) the young child, small like a humming-bird, who becomes an adult, a parent, larger and stronger, like a hawk or like the father-mother gods—obviously the image of the hummingbird as a messenger or incarnation of the father-mother gods is paralleled in our metaphor of "the child is father of the man." All these metaphors or poetic mythical transformations hidden in the text allude to the mythical structure that I have shown to be still extant in Zinacantan.

The lost key, however, is contained in the last line, the most perplexing of all the poem's enigmas. Before we tackle this last problem, we must discuss the lines of the text still unexplained: 19 to 23. All these lines deal with the same question.

Why had no one seen the hummingbird, why could no one recognize it (lines 19–21)? Because all the gods are "generally considered invisible, although theophanic manifestations could occur in dreams, in visions, and at other special times," such as in moments of poetic insight (Nicholson 1971:408). This is obviously as true today in Zinacantan as it was in the Mesoamerica of yesteryear. In line 22, an animal or bird is expressed onomatopoetically as "Ch'un Ch'un." It sounds so "in the evening," because this is the time when the hummingbird comes out to drink nectar from the flowers. Most Zinacantecans know who it is who says "ts'un ts'un" (or "ch'un ch'un" in Vogt's text): the hummingbird in Tzotzil is called *ch'unun* or *C'sunun* or *T'sunun* (sources have different spellings). "Ts'un ts'un" is a good imitation of the little bird's sound. In fact, in Cuban Spanish and other Central American dialects the name of the hummingbird is *zum-zum* or *chun-chun*.[1] In some ways, I would be glad if there were any mystery left!

1. I believe the translation here to be probably incorrect, on related grounds. In the published text the hummingbird is said to "say" *ch'un ch'un*. In a new unpublished translation which Laughlin provided me with after this book was written, the hummingbird is said to "sing" *t'sun t'sun*. However, this is the sound not of the bird's voice but of his wings. *T'sun t'sun* is the Tzotzil equivalent of *hum*—in English "to hum," "humming," and "hummingbird," and of *zum*, the name of the bird in Cuban Spanish. It is the onamatopoetic sound of the bird's wings in flight. (See discussion under "Hummingbird," *Encyclopaedia Britannica*.) This noise is not a sung or vocal sound.

However, the purpose of this lengthy analysis has been to divest the poem of its obscurity. We can now say that the message is about the changing of spring into summer, the onset of the rainy season, the first labors of the agricultural cycle and other linked metaphors, as well as about mystifying hummingbirds who are large, white hawks. The secret is revealed (thereby losing some of its charm), when we remember that in Mesoamerica hummingbirds "come out" and can be seen in the period of the renewal and revitalization of the earth, the period of rain, growth, the burning and planting of fields, of long days when the sun is high in the sky, ascending in the ecliptic path, and that all these events occur at the same time of the year.

Given the space-time ritual arrangements of the Zinacantecan calendar, in which spring-summer equal east-south and north equals winter, and the fact that winter equals darkness, blackness, dark animals or animals of the night such as bats, and the "redness" of death, it is also possible to say that the whole Zinacantan calendar is arranged in space-time quarters along with the color transformations, in which:

Winter : black (red) : north : : spring : blue-green : east : : summer : white : south : : autumn : ? : west

and also that:

Spring : hummingbirds : : summer : hawks : : winter : bats, ravens,

as well as:

Winter : north : black : "dark sun" of winter solstice : black northern Tezcatlipoca : Saint Sebastian : :
Summer : south : white : sun: (blue sky) of the summer solstice : blue-green Tezcatlipoca (i.e., Huitzilopochtli) : Saint Lawrence (and/or Hmanaveh).

So we finally confront the last line. Why is the hummingbird called "one leg"? *The hummingbird god is called the one leg in the poem because Huitzilopochtli was one of the four aspects of Tezcatlipoca.* The reader may remember that I mentioned that Tezcatlipoca was deformed. *This god's most noticeable physical characteristic in his "human" persona was that he was lame or "one-legged."* In one of the myths one of

28. The Emperor Tizoc dressed as Huitzilopochtli—the blue Tezcatlipoca—with whom he identified because of his clubfoot. Detail from the "Tizoc Stone," a bas-relief carving in circular shape depicting events from the life of the Emperor Tizoc. Museo Nacional de Antropología, Mexico.

his feet was eaten by the earth monster. In paintings he was often represented with one foot or leg missing, or with a deformed or club foot covered by a mirror (Seler 1963:107. See Illustrations 28–30). Why was Tezcatlipoca envisaged in this way? To understand this sacred riddle we must remember that Tezcatlipoca was in his protean nature god of all space and time, god of the hurricane, the cyclonic eastern winds which sweep Mexico, and of tornadoes, waterspouts, and whirlwinds, but that he also symbolically sat at the polar center, a point in the sky from which he could see "all things" with his mirror and permanently open eyes. His mirror symbol indicated "that Tezcatlipoca could see all that took place in the world" (Duran 1971:99). His name "smoking mirror" was the symbol of the dark spot, the celestial ecliptic pole, the center of the "wheel of the north," which the "middle, black-colored Tezcatlipoca" impersonated. His missing foot was the symbol of things that coil around themselves in a spiral motion like the circumpolar constellations, whirlwinds, and hurricanes. In fact, in the Mayan version of Mesoamerican mythology presented in the *Popol Vuh*, Tezcatlipoca's name is Hurakan, from *hum* (one), *ra* (third person possessive), and *kan* (leg). In Nahuatl also, one of his names means "he has only one leg" : *cee iicci.* [2]

Why do hurricanes, tornadoes, whirlwinds, and waterspouts have one leg? The image is not arbitrary but a perfect poetic conundrum. It does not require much imagination to see these helicoidal forms in terms of a gigantic divine leg coming down from the sky, the upper thigh and body covered by the clouds, the single foot walking over water or land (Ortiz 1947, chap. 7).

Thus, if "hummingbird" is "hurricane," and "hurricane" is one-legged, hummingbird is one-legged.

But there is even a more profound mythical truth involved here. The hummingbird god is an unfolding of Tezcatlipoca, because in the last analysis, Huitzilopochtli is the sun, one of the markers of the passage of time, and Tezcatlipoca is the combined image of all the forms of the passage of time, the total essence of the ecliptic world, all the planetary orbital motions, all the changing seasons, expressed by all kinds of symbols from animal to one-legged human, from planet to ecliptic pole. That is, the sun-hummingbird is an unfolding symbol of the passage of time. In the final line of poetic outburst, the hummingbird is telling us that all things, from the small, childlike, fierce hummingbird, to the fiery, hawklike sun, contribute to keep time, to give man the cyclical balance necessary in his peasant life.

2. In a footnote to his translation of the *Popul Vuh*, Edmonson states that there is no evidence that Hurakan was hurricane-Tezcatlipoca. I had the opportunity to speak to him about this point at a seminar in 1974. He argued that Huracan does not mean hurricane, but "one leg." When I pointed out to him that Tezcatlipoca had only one leg and Seler had identified them as the same, not just that Hurakan and hurricane are homonyms, he stated that this was a convincing argument, and he accepted my identification. That Hurakan = Tezcatlipoca can also be seen in his epithets in the *Popol Vuh* text, where he is " . . . Him who is the Heart of Heaven, One Leg by name." He is also the Heart of Earth, that is, the centers of both sky and earth planes simultaneously.

29. *Cipactli*, the earth monster, with Tezcatlipoca's leg in its mouth. Codex Fejervary-Mayer, p. 18 obverse, top-right section.

Zinacantecan men toiling in the fields learn this truth, "see it," "recognize" and "discover it" every year, when they begin their agrarian cyclical routine once more.

In summary, translated into flat prose, into explicit statements derived from information found in metaphor and myth, which have taken their code of similes from ecology, astronomy, the animal kingdom and the colors—the text of "The Hummingbird" is as follows: When Zinacantecan men, at the end of the hot dry season, prepare the fields for planting by burning the dry stubble and the dry empty bean pods left behind in a harvested field, they make big fires from which tall smoke rises, obscuring the sky (lines 3, 4, 5, 10). At the same time, the sun is on its upward journey in the ecliptic, passing the point of the vernal equinox, and crossing toward the north point of the summer solstice (lines 7, 8, 9). At this time also, the first rains come down, and the rainy season begins (lines 11, 12). The hummingbird, which is a positive symbol of the sun and the incarnation and messenger of the gods that control rain, is also the sacred symbolic image of the conjunction of these events (line 1). However, just as the planting season changes into the weeding season, just as the sun of the vernal equinox becomes the sun of the summer solstice, just as the hot dry season becomes the wet rainy season, the hummingbird becomes a white hawk—which is another solar incarnation. That is, a little blue-green sacred bird becomes a large white sacred hawk. The blue-green represents the renewal of vegetation in spring. The white represents the color of the white summer rain and the bright light of the summer sun. The small bird

30. The Mexican gods migrate to New England. The symbolism of prehispanic gods has persisted not only in Indian villages such as Zinacantan, but also in the culture of the national elite of Mexico. This mural by the Mexican painter Orozco adorns the walls of the library at Dartmouth College, Hanover, New Hampshire. The gods are, from left to right: Xipe, Tezcatlipoca, Quetzalcoatl, Tlaloc, Michtlantecuhtli, Huitzilopochtli, and Xiuhtecuhtli.[3] Photo, "Coming of Quetzalcoatl," fourth panel, from the *Orozco Frescos*, courtesy of Hopkins Center Art Galleries, Dartmouth College.

3. There has been much speculation and some degree of heated discussion about which of the prehispanic gods was the most important one. Probably every city state had a different "most important" local deity, and each researcher has his own favorite god for the position. My view is that the "oneness" god occupied the top of a pyramidal symbolic arrangement, but this positioning does not imply, necessarily, symbolic "superiority." In the twentieth century, many scholars and important Mexican public figures have argued for the dominance of Quetzalcoatl. There is no evidence, however, that Quetzalcoatl was a dominant god either ideologically or sociologically speaking, on a pan-Mesoamerican basis. He undoubtedly appears in the symbolism from Teotihuacan times. He appears to have been a historical figure during the late periods of Tula, and his influence, stylistic and social, appears in the Tula-influenced Maya city of Chichen Itza. At the time of the conquest he was worshipped in the major temple at Cholula, in the valley of Puebla, and he was a major deity in Guatemala. But otherwise there is no definite evidence of his cult being significantly dominant over those of other major gods such as Tlaloc or Xipe. The curious thing is that Quetzalcoatl became, *after the conquest*, a major symbol of Mexican identity, of the fusion of prehispanic and European life streams. Because he was mythically imagined as connected with the Gulf of Mexico, and he was said to be light-skinned and "blonde," prehispanic roots and the impact of Spanish racial and cultural influences have been merged in his image. He is, one could say, the first

represents the equinoctial sun, the big bird the sun of the solstice (lines 1, 2, 13, 14, 15, 16, 17, 18, 24, 25). Zinacantecans did not know what this little bird was like, because the deities are usually invisible (lines 20, 21, 23). But in the toils of the agrarian year, every spring and summer, Zinacantecans recognize this sacred truth (lines 19, 24). However, this little-large, bird-planet-season deity is directly linked to the other major ancestral gods as their spring-volatile theriophanic form and their summer-volatile theriophanic form (line 26). Its onomatopoeic sound is "ch'un" or "Ch'un" or "t'sun t'sun" (line 22), and that is why his name is *t'sunun*. However, spring and summer are only two of the four seasons of the year. Zinacantecans call the hummingbird "one leg," because he is one season of two (dry and wet), one aspect of a dual-quadripartite year, which is represented all together by the ancestral mother-father gods, the one-legged god, "the oneness," as prehispanic peoples called Tezcatlipoca, or the "one leg." Hence, hummingbird and hawk are two of the four volatile theophanic forms of the One, the one-legged God, who is as well the four seasons of the yearly cycle of the farmers (lines 26, 27).

Mestizo god. The Mexican elite has exploited his image ideologically, for its own purposes. He is now the symbol of the merging of cultures, of racial mixture, a pre-Christian image of Jesus and a posthispanic image of the high civilization and cultivation of the precolonial past.

He was said to have rejected human sacrifices, and thus represents the human virtues and sensitivities of the prehispanic intellectual classes at their best and most civilized. Since he was blonde and light-skinned, he is a racial antecedent of the process of "whitening" or racial crossing that created the Mexican Mestizo. Because he was associated with the Gulf and the eastern ocean, he is a premonition of the coming of the Spanish and the clash of cultures. Often in the colonial period he was imagined to be Jesus who, having arrived at the New World in disguise, was ruling over Tula. The myths in which he was defeated by Tezcatlipoca became images of the struggle of Jesus and the devil, the devil winning temporarily until the arrival of new Christian enlightenment.

Thus he became a mysterious oracle of things to come. He is a realization of the antagonisms, contradictions, innovations, and creativity of the new Mestizo man who rules Mexico. He is both indigenous and immigrant, white-skinned and Indian, civilized culture hero, humanistic light and simultaneously dark root of the ancestral common man.

For this combination of reasons, he appears in a dominant position in Orozco's mural at Dartmouth. However, his present symbolic power should not be projected backward. He was a mighty divine ruler, no doubt, but he did not rule alone.

I must admit that I greatly prefer the Zinacantecan poetic version to this crudely explicit, prosy one. It seems evident to me that symbolist literature and mythic thought will survive any historical crisis, simply because in the last resort art is aesthetically superior to science as an expression of man's analytic capacities.

It is only in a culture like ours, that of Western urban man, where we live by electric light, where birds are killed by our insecticide technology, where the sun and stars can be seen only through the fumes of gasoline that cloud the sky, where rain means the nuisance of having to take plastic raincoats and umbrellas, where our children know corn mostly in cans and our professors see the world from behind office desks; in a culture which has forgotten the natural rhythms of life, where growing old is shameful, where sex equals advertising, childbirth means hospital, food is a matter of frozen packages, calories, and dieting, and sickness entails loneliness; a culture where the past is a rejected encumbrance, God is dead, and hummingbirds are always unknown, that anyone could maintain that myths think themselves and that mythical symbolism has no reason and no history.

It has been a long journey, moving from a lovely poetic text of twenty-seven lines through a lengthy and dry analysis using a great many facts. It can now be seen that the journey was not without purpose, that there was method in my madness, an objective to be reached. Along the route we have witnessed some interesting sights. I also hope I have proved to the reader's satisfaction that the use of a documented historical perspective has true heuristic value for the structural analysis of contemporary culture. I think Sir Francis Bacon knew it all along. We should remember his words, those with which this book opened and also his wise observation that "parables serve as well to instruct and to illustrate as to wrap up and envelop" ("Preface to the Wisdom of the Ancients").

CHAPTER **9**

A Theoretical Epilogue

—And as for you, you with no eyes, no ears,
No senses, you the most superstitious
Of all—(for what greater superstition
Is there than the mumbo-jumbo of believing
In reality?)—you should be swallowed whole by Time
In the way that you swallow appearances.
Horns, what a waste of effort it has been
To give you Creation's vast and exquisite
Dilemma! Where altercation thrums
In every granule of the Milky Way,
Persisting still in the dead-sleep of the moon,
And heckling itself hoarse in that hot-head
The sun. And as for here, each acorn drops
Arguing to earth, and pollen's all polemic.—
We have given you a world as contradictory
As a female, as cabbalistic as the male,
A conscienceless hermaphrodite who plays
Heaven off against hell, hell off against heaven,
Revolving in the ballroom of the skies
Glittering with conflict as with diamonds:
We have wasted paradox and mystery on you
When all you ask us for, is cause and effect!

Christopher Fry, *The Lady's Not For Burning* [1]

When I gave the first draft of this book to two colleagues to read, one responded with a comment about the incredible lack of change in Zinacantecan symbolic structures, the other with a comment about how major were the changes and transformations that had taken place. One saw the design of Zinacantecan symbolism as an integrated, homeostatic structure fixed in time and space, beyond historical change. The other saw it as a patchwork, an unstable structure, fluid in time and space, the victim of every historical accident. When I told them both that they had spoken the truth (but not the whole truth), I was being neither hypocritical nor timid. The fact is that Zinacantecan symbolism has both changed profoundly and remained much the same, depending on the perspective.

1. From Act II. Used by permission of Oxford University Press.

The symbolic structure has not changed (the structure is still there), and paradoxically it has changed (it became "buried"). To clarify this paradoxical statement we must remember that the structure of a myth has three components: its armature, its code(s) and its message(s). The configuration is the gestalt, the combined structure of all three (Lévi-Strauss 1969:199).

The basic armature device of Zinacantecan myth that affects "The Hummingbird" and much of the rest of Zinacantecan's world view has continued to be a quadripartite, yearly, agrarian, solar calendric cycle. However, the esoteric code of the astronomical cycles of the nighttime sky has been lost, and in this sense the structure has lost motivation. For example, the Zinacantecans no longer can remember why 13 and 52 are sacred numbers in astronomy. The codes of religious expression have been modified also, because the patterns and functions of some of the deities have been reinterpreted to fit Christian iconographic clusters. The astronomical kinship code, for example, which in prehispanic myth read sun : moon : : senior brother : junior brother, or : : brother : sister, is a simple structural transformation that now reads sun : moon : : Jesus : Mary (husband : wife or son : mother). But the Trinity of "oneness" of God the Father, God the Son, and God the Holy Ghost is not equivalent in code function or armature to the *quadripartite* cluster of "oneness" of the prehispanic deity. Nor is it equivalent to the possible fivefold unity of Holy Ghost (media of impregnation), God the Father (genitor), Saint Joseph (pater), Mary (mother), and Jesus (son). The prehispanic Tezcatlipoca deities were four male siblings; and Zinacantecans, like other Mexican Indians, "garbled" the Christian codes by making the father = son and changing mother and son into husband and wife, even introducing incest by this change, and causing mutually exclusive pairs to merge into each other, thus increasing "arbitrariness."

There has also been a fundamental distortion of both Christian and prehispanic moral codes. The dichotomy of good and evil has been partially forced upon native deities which were originally neutral, or ambivalent, neither good nor bad but both. On the other hand, the dual evil/good aspect of the prehispanic gods has been transferred to the Christian symbols. Ultimately, a different combination of substructural properties has emerged that has not remained totally invariant, that is, the actual structure has been modified.

The most striking change, however, has been in the messages themselves, both in terms of the signifiers and what is signified. The messages of Zinacantecan myths have been expanded enormously at some levels and well-nigh extinguished at others.

First, Christian elements have slowly replaced aboriginal ones. Of course, many of these were adapted to the overall armature of the calendar, so that only the symbol messages "changed." Second, basic social changes, particularly the formation of two distinct ethnic clusters (Indian and Ladino, "native" versus "Christian") have been incorporated into the myth and ritual structure in elaborate form (see, for example, the detailed and high spirited analysis of Ladino/Indian humorous symbolism in Bricker 1973). Third, much of the complex mythic and ritual symbolism that pertained to a larger scale prehispanic society, with hierarchies of descent groups, multiple social statuses, many occupations, city states with complex temple hierarchies and bureaucracies, and so on, has been eroded or totally submerged, because Zinacantan has lost the framework of the original complex society from which it was born, and is now relegated to the status of a marginal rural enclave in Mexico. The Indians of Chiapas realized their loss of social position, and because of it they fought the rebellion of 1712 (Klein 1970). Significantly, these armed rebellions were viewed in religious terms as nativistic movements, and involved a clear attempt on the part of the Indians to reinterpret Christian symbolism to fit the needs of their ethnic group (*ibid.*).

Therefore, in a sequence of decreasing variation we move from message, to code, to armature. The armature has changed little, but the code and the symbol-units have changed greatly. The properties of the *symbolic sets as a system* (armature core) have remained nearly constant. These are deeply embedded in a root paradigm of ecology, agrarian schedules and invariant astronomical events. There are, however, myths in the background of Zinacantan, whose manifest symbolic values have been lost, and which now form part of schemata buried in the deep unconscious levels of its social history. I believe both these statements to be true. A new question can then be raised. When, and under what conditions, can we speak of total configurational change?

In the symbolism of Zinacantan, hummingbirds and hawks, the agrarian prehispanic state and an industrializing nation have been united. But the space-time continuum of their cultural and social life is the face of an old agrarian clock. Thus Zinacantecans organize the present by conceptualizing the past as one of its divine spatial-temporal phases. Both past and present, sun god and Jesus, are unified as symbol-vehicles in a space-time continuum in which "formerly connected things become disconnected and formerly disconnected things become connected" (V. Turner, personal communication). These old and new symbol vehicles become "encapsulated" in each other, as Vogt suggests, within the transitional systemics of their present religious-ideological structures (Vogt, 1969:chap. 24).

I would like to discuss this view of Zinacantecan religion in an historic-evolutionary processual perspective, taking as a starting point a seminal article by Earl Count (1960), and attempting to explore some of the implications of my discovery of the simultaneous permanence and change in Zinacantecan symbolism. What follows is not a final statement except in the overall order of this text. Rather, it is an argument, an opinion, open for further discussion.

Count, in his article on myth, posed some questions in general terms:

1. In the evolution of man, when and under what circumstances did the capacity to symbolize come into being?

2. What symbolopoetic ingredients produce whatever we define as "myth," or, what are the sources of myth?

3. What shall we settle upon as properly includable under myth?

4. What place has mythopoeia had in the building of cultural configuration?

5. As a cultural configuration is transformed (through elabora-

tion, transmutation, dissolution), what happens to its myths? (Count 1960:299).

The first question, as Count brilliantly explains, is the concern of neurophysiology and neuropsychology, comparative primatology, semiotics, and "archeological psychiatry." Some answers have already been supplied in the anthropological literature, and need not concern us here, since I am in no way proposing a theory of origins.

The second question has been partially answered both in this book and in many others: the poetic symbols that are the ingredients of myth are elements of man's varied experience, both natural and cultural, conscious and unconscious, manifest or repressed. Just as "dreams select their materials from any part of the dreamer's life" (Freud 1965:202), so myths select their materials from any part of the society's life.

This experience is filtered through the organism, which is not a *tabula rasa* or passive recipient, but is active in itself. "The organism meets it [the environment] in a very real way and to a very significant extent on the organism's own terms" (*ibid.*, p. 300). Secondarily, the experience is filtered through the cultural determinants of perception, which again are not passive elements but active modifiers of man's observational and symbolizing capacities. Perception, like thinking, is social. These determinants may belong to communication frames (language, rite, and so on), to the limitations of the social environment (for example, the nature of a society's social structure, in Radcliffe-Brown's sense of structure), and to a variety of other levels of phenomena which are suprasomatic, at least at the manifest level.

The reasons that a particular society selects some symbols as dominant rather than others are partly accidental, partly a matter of social projection, partly tied in with the self-generating quality of symbol structures, and partly linguistically induced. What functional load can be attributed to any one variable is an empirical question determined by the ethnographic situation studied, a question of the particular emphasis and import of the analysis, and a question of the theoretical model chosen. The ethnographic evidence

here and theories available in the literature do not allow us to conclude that there is any causal dominance of one variable over others.
Whether such prime movers may exist cannot be answered at this
stage. My own position has been that no single component of a
symbolic structure can be demonstrated to be the structure's sole
causative factor.

It seems possible, however, that some symbolic codes are more
refractory to arbitrary manipulation than others. Some cosmically
derived root paradigms based on astronomical codes appear to be
constant all over the world (for example, the images of the *axis
mundi*). This stability exists simply because the signified, the element which is selected from reality to be symbolically expressed, is
fixed within observable reality, showing only a limited number of
perceptible attributes to the naked eye. Other codes, color, for example, seem prone to rapid modification, great cultural variation,
and arbitrary selection. Probably these tendencies also have their
basis in the nature of observed reality, since the color spectrum is a
continuum, and its division into named segments is purely culture-
bound. One can choose to distinguish between blue and green and
incorporate the distinction into language or symbolism, or one can
continue calling them by the same name. But one cannot, except by
a great effort of symbolic distortion, imagine the pole star at the
celestial equator.

Question three, what is properly includable under myth, deals
with a typological issue, which could be regarded as extrinsic to a
discussion focused on symbols. However, I believe that to make
such a distinction is irrelevant at the moment. First, each society has
its own classification of oral traditions, many of which have been
disregarded or neglected by anthropologists (see Gossen 1974 on this
point). Unless we develop systematic accounts of oral symbol systems, well-grounded in ethnography, and show these taxonomic
questions to be of theoretical relevance, the issue remains pointless,
leading only to further complications in the vocabulary of the folklor-
ist and to the growth of a functionless metalanguage. Whether myth
and poetry are two distinct genres is an issue of Aristotelian classifi-

cation (Lévi-Strauss 1955), and the distinction is not necessarily an accurate one in the eyes of natives or of the anthropologist. The *Odyssey* combines both; so does "The Hummingbird." Again, if music is more like myth than painting is, why did Mesoamerican peoples expend so much effort in portraying their myth in plastic, tactile, and visual media? I prefer the position of Roland Barthes (1957, 1964), that any symbolic "text" can be seen as myth if so seeing it aids in interpreting the system. Other alternatives are either precious or sterile or both. Ultimately their function is to further the sophisticated dissection of the remains of dead culture rather than to enrich our understanding of living culture. Obviously, between the splitters and lumpers, I am a lumper. The choice is dictated by what we see as our task, and I do not choose to taxonomize in a vacuum.

However, Count's third question is of importance in relation to my work because I have dealt in this book with myth in the context of a poetic tale, and the question of the difference between poetry and myth becomes a crucial point of the analysis. Both Count and Boon (1972) take the view that mythic and poetic symbolism are in some way identical. Notwithstanding some of his statements, Lévi-Strauss's analysis of Baudelaire's "The Cats" seems to support this position. Without yet elaborating a definition, I have called "The Hummingbird" a mythic poem. To state my position clearly, it is necessary to spell out what I perceive the difference to be between poetry, myth, and mythic poems. The difference is not in the symbols themselves, or in their formal arrangements. The "texts" (Boon's term) or "tales, rituals, and monuments" (Count's terms) are structurally formed with identical material, using trope, metaphor, antonymy, synechdoche, *pars-pro-toto*, and so on. *The difference is in the effect upon the receiver, the perceptor.* In secular poetry the symbols are "as if" phenomena. Poetry is based on simile, received *as* simile. In part the pleasure of poetry exists in the receptor's ability to identify, aesthetically, humorously, emotionally, or intellectually, with the skill of the poet who creates the simile, and share with him his cleverness through identification. In myth the simile is transformed. The mythic symbols are not "as if" phenomena, but "is" phenomena. The signifier *is* the signified. The simile becomes an identity. This is what sacred transformational systems are all about. A mythic transformation means that the poetic truth is more than poetry, it is absolute truth.

In somewhat mystic but exquisite language, the Lama Anagarika Govinda (1973:18) states:

> The forms of divine life in the universe and in nature break forth from the seer as vision, from the singer as sound, and are there in the spell of vision and sound, pure and undisguised. Their existence is in the characteristic of the priestly power of the seer-poet. What sounds from his mouth is not the ordinary word, the *shabda*, of which speech is composed. It is *mantra*, the compulsion to create a mental image, power over that which *IS*, to be as it really is in its pure essence. Thus is knowledge. It is the truth of being, beyond right or wrong.

Hence, hummingbirds are not just *like* the sun. They *are* the sun. "The Hummingbird" is a poem in the sense of being built of figurative, formal language arrangements, such as double repetition of words, and trope. Its text uses formal stylistic devices such as parallel reiteration (for example in lines 7 and 8, "it came out, it came flying in the sky"). It uses ironic inversion, for example, the "hummingbird is big." It uses synechdoche, as in line 4, where "burning bean pods" stands for a field of dry, empty bean pods, and bean plant stubble being burned to make ready for planting. It uses synesthetic metaphor, for instance in line 10, where eyes are "snuffed out" by smoke, and the hummingbird is the sun in the whole poem. It uses metonymy, where "hummingbird" equals "one leg" in the last line, and hot country equals the season for burning the fields for planting in line 3. Moreover, it is a poem in a more general sense because it is a brief composition, designed to convey a vivid and imaginative sense of experience, using condensed language, and subtly suggested hidden meanings. The poetic devices listed above are semantic, but, as in much poetry the world over, the structure also utilizes sound devices that create rhythm, cadence and flow (see Appendix 3). The three most characteristic devices appearing in "The Hummingbird" are: (*a*) final consonance and assonance, usually of masculine rhymes, for example by using the terminal optional forms *7un* and *7une;* (*b*) internal consonance and assonance within lines, and between paired lines, for example in line 2,

> *ja7 yech'o la yech,*

in line 25,

> . . . *ko7ol schi7uk,/ko7ol smuk'ul schi7uk*

or in lines 23 and 24

> . . . *jna7tik k'u smuk'ul,*
> . . . *7iyilik ti k'u smuk'ule,*

and finally, (*c*) the use of homophones and quasi-synonyms, with alliteration as the tying device, which appears in the optional choice of specific pairs of words, for instance, . . . *xvinaj 7une* and *vinajel 7une* (in lines 5 and 8) or the words *chak* and *sak* in lines 15 and 16.

But "The Hummingbird" is mythic because the content of the poem refers to the mythic, sacred truth of identifications between metaphoric or metonymic elements, rather than to the secular ideas of similarity, contiguity, or opposition. "The Hummingbird" deals with a numinous world of sacred transformations, and not just with an instrumental-expressive world of secular aesthetics. The *Iliad* for contemporary Western man is a poem. For the Greek commoner who believed in a numinous world of gods, demigods and transformational relationships between gods, man, and nature, Homer's words were religious truths. We can assume that for orthodox Zinacantecans "The Hummingbird" is a truth in the mythico-religious sense, although for agnostic Zinacantecans it may be a thing of secular aesthetic value. What I have argued throughout this book is that in the whole of the Zinacantecans' world view as expressed in collective, ritual action, and in their common literary inheritance, "The Hummingbird" makes religious sense. It could be argued that it makes little secular sense, although I believe that it makes sense at the secular level too. To explore this position further we must consider the next question.

Count's questions four and five deal with the key problems that emerge from the present analysis. However, the questions are phrased somewhat ambiguously, because Count does not distinguish cultural from social configurations. In fact, he uses the concept of culture in the American tradition of Boas, rather than making the Parsonian distinction that "culture does not equal society," which I and some other younger anthropologists find more useful (see Geertz 1957).

Rephrasing Count's questions, then, I will ask what is the relationship between the social system—that is, the social configuration (the basic structure)—and the cultural system, or the cultural configuration (the superstructure)? Here I am using culture with the restricted meaning of cognitive structures, semiological constructs. When do symbolic configurations change? Why do they not change? Here we have to reintroduce the distinction between change in the messages, the codes, and the armatures of symbolic configurations, a distinction used effectively by Lévi-Strauss, which I feel is of major empirical relevance here.

Asking these questions in the context of Zinacantan, can we answer them? Are such configurations, as Ruth Benedict argued, eternal? If they were, there would be no process of culture change or evolution. Have Zinacantecans preserved intact and whole the symbolic structures of their prehispanic forbears? Clearly they have not done so. Is the Zinacantecan symbol system a totally new configuration, a contemporary structure starting from scratch? Obviously, if I thought this to be so, I would never have delved into history. What then? Is the Zinacantan religious system a thing of threads and patches, made up of survivals? That cannot be the case. The Zinacantecans would then have no sense of cultural coherence, and I have shown that they do. If the forest of symbols were a chaos, all we could see would be individual trees. Is it my position that the symbol structure has changed, but in the fashion of "plus ça change, plus c'est la même chose"? Yes. Do I believe that all symbol systems are of this kind? No.

The relation between symbol systems and social systems that I propose is partially that espoused by Marx and formally accepted by Lévi-Strauss, although he ignores it in practice. Social systems and cultural systems are no more than parts of the larger action system of humanity. One is the basic structure, the other the superstructure. However, I do not insist that one is the cause of the other, because there is no sound evidence either way. Unlike Marx or Durkheim I do not see the social system as the single origin or source of culture, and unlike Parsons I do not see the cultural system as cybernetically dominant. From the perspective of general systems theory, subsystems mutually influence one another, are deeply enmeshed in one another; each is both cause and product of other subsystems. It is clear, as Weber proposed, that culture molds social action, and that, as Marx proposed, societies make up their own culture as they move along the stream of history. Marx's own position on the issue of the role of culture is ambiguous, but clearly in his less dogmatic moments he understood that cultural ideologies and symbol systems have powerful effects on the social process—for example, he realized that revolution (social action) could not take place without class consciousness (cultural belief, commitment at the ideological level).

In the long run—that is, in terms of universal processes of man's history—cultural configurations change more or less simultaneously with social configurations, because of systemic readjustments. (Which subsystem adjusts to which is an empirical question.) In some cases the sequence of change runs one way, in others it reverses its path. Feedback processes are multidirectional. At one level the process of systemic decay may result in culture and society being temporarily disjointed, one lagging behind the other. And at another, the process of systematization may be recreating a temporary congruency, that is, structural compatibility. At any point in time, both processes can be seen going on simultaneously, and at any point in time, the degree of structural compatibility or disjunction can be determined by empirical observation. Man's evolutionary history itself sets the pace of change.

History, in the long run, is evolution. Species evolve from other species, preserving much of their previous character, fundamentally restructuring some features. So do symbol systems. At one level, symbolic configurations constantly change and are always in a process of "becoming," new codes being created in each historic phase of a society's life. The old symbols do not die out, but persist as the echoes of the past in the present. Sometimes they are only scattered and eroded fragments of systems and schemata shredded by history. But, often, the symbols continue to have an ordered structure. They continue to be fitted into equivalent or new armatures. The elements from the past are not so many dead or dying words. They are living designs embedded in the armatures, giving buried meanings to the present by enabling man to utilize the experiences of ordered cognitions from the past.

I am arguing here in the manner of Freud, that just as dream symbol systems reflect the contemporary state of the dreamer, but also include symbols whose meaning comes from previous crucial states of the dreamer's life (his childhood and adolescent traumas), so myth and ritual symbol systems reflect the contemporary state of the society, and also include symbols whose meanings come from crucial states of its history. I will argue further that there must be an interplay between the synchronic analysis of a structure and the discussion of its history. If the interplay is absent, we are either historians, rather than social scientists, or naive sociologists who ignore the historical dimensions crucial to sound interpretation.

In a socio-historical perspective, symbol structures have components which change at different rates for different reasons. Both synchronically and diachronically the messages of symbol systems are rapidly affected by the immediacy of the flow of social process, and by minor changes in social organization (using Firth's [1956] definition). Any event may add to or subtract from the message pool. The codes of the messages change more slowly, and are less affected by social process in the immediate sense. Symbol codes are cumulative, shifting, molded by the imagination of the symbol makers, sometimes with rates of change independent of the socio-structural factors. Language is, of course, a prime example of a code that changes in these ways, as glottochronology maintains. It is at the code level that the ethnographic richness of symbol systems is realized. It is at this level that every culture chooses its own idioms and plays creatively between the multiplicity of levels and depths of meaning which mytho-poetic structures exhibit.

Symbol systems, however, have a still deeper structure, their armature. Armatures appear quite fixed over long periods of time, across geographic, social, and culture boundaries. They may appear not to change at all. In fact they do change, but seldom in radical ways, and it is theoretically important to know this fact, and to understand why they change when they do.

Reading Lévi-Strauss, one may get the impression that armatures are immutable. Every change of message, every change of code, simply restates the same armature in redundant fashion. When is an armature said to have changed? Lévi-Strauss does not provide an answer. He cannot do so, because he does not distinguish between the myths of societies at different evolutionary levels. For it is when societies evolve into new types that armatures change. He does not, I think, believe in evolution. He never says that he does not, simply and boldly, but the inference is obvious when one studies the passages in his writings where he makes major theoretical statements or compares cultures. First, Lévi-Strauss treats as equivalent units the myths of tribal peoples (central Brazil) and those of agrarian states (for example, the Aztec, Classical Greece, and medieval Christian Europe). Second, he views the role of history in the development of mythic configurations or armatures as arbitrary in effect; history, for him, is accidental. His position is very different from Marx's evolutionary view of history and clearly derives from Hegelian metaphysics.

History, for Lévi-Strauss, is "a pattern of development which we see, perhaps arbitrarily, as being the cause of subsequent events— although we cannot be sure of this, since there is not and never will be any term of comparison. . . . [A] historical occurrence . . . can have no meaning beyond its actual happening." Thus, Lévi-Strauss cannot distinguish between history as general evolution, history as specific evolution, and history as accidental sequence. He further claims not to reject history in structural analysis, but he believes that the use of history is ultimately the bending of the analysis "to the powerful inanity of events" (Lévi-Strauss 1973b:474–475).

Hence, history for him is not a structured process, nor is it cross-culturally patterned; rather it is a series of random unique occurrences. This view means that for him man's culture and society are the only phenomena not affected by the general process of evolution which operates on the rest of nature. It also means that there is no specific evolution, but only specific historical events. For him, societies are "hot" or "cold" depending on their historically arbitrary typological transitions.

One has to understand Lévi-Strauss's position in context, because it is derived from his view of "mind," and from his desire to protect primitive societies from accusations of mental inferiority. Since mind is the same for all men (that is, he agrees with the orthodox anthropological view of the psychic unity of mankind), and myth is its universal product, if one agreed that "evolution" is different from nondirectional "change," it "would be too easy to conclude that, wherever such an evolution has not taken place, its absence is to be explained by the inferiority or inadequacy of societies or individuals" (*ibid.*, p. 474).

Evolution : random change : : mind is unequal : mind is equal. But why is it necessary not only to see the patterns of armature development as internally ordered by "mind" but also to deny their external ordering by social structure? Probably because Lévi-Strauss does not conceive of culture (for example, mythic constructs) as the product of the interaction between the material conditions of human life and man's perceptual capacities, but as the simple product of man's mind, self-generated, attached to external reality only by way of the internal dialectic of the myth.

The function of mind is not therefore to process what is observed of what is out there, already produced in reality; mind is the producer of itself. Marx's view of the difference between himself and Hegel (1972:19) would apply with great economy to the difference between himself and Lévi-Strauss:

My dialectic method is not only different from the Hegelian, but is its direct opposite. To Hegel the life-process of the human brain, i.e., the process of thinking, which under the name of "the Idea," he even transforms into an independent subject, is the demiurgos of the real world, and the real world is only the external, phenomenal form of "the Idea." With me, on the contrary, the idea is nothing else than the material world reflected in the human mind, and translated into forms of thought.

Lévi-Strauss clearly argues, in agreement with Hegel, that ideas (which he calls the structure of the mind or the human spirit) rule themselves and cause themselves. One of the most revealing statements, in *The Raw and the Cooked*, reads: "myths signify the mind that evolves them by making use of the world of which it is itself a part. Thus there is simultaneous production of myths themselves, by the mind that generates them, and, by the myths, of an image of the world which is already inherent *in the structure of the mind*" (p. 341; emphasis mine). Definitely, then, not in the structure of the world outside it!

I take a very different position. I agree that there is a psychic unity of mankind. I disagree that this psychic unity implies identity. Rather, I maintain that there is a functional equivalence of societies or cultures. If the differences among societies are caused by the adaptations of the basic structure to the external world, and the symbols (myths and rituals, ideologies) are their systemic cultural counterparts, it is not necessary to imply inferiority or inadequacy in the part of the culture carriers. In fact, every human group has the potential to develop the best possible cultural configuration according to their society's needs in terms of their mode of adaptation. As Turner puts it, "in man, as in other living species, genotypical goals prevail over phenotypical interests, the general good over the individual welfare. . . . Root paradigms are the cultural transliterations of genetic codes" (1974a:67). All men are "equal," potentially, in their creative capacities. All societies are not equal in their adaptive strategies and therefore they are unequal in the type of culture products they create. Unequal does not mean inferior, a fallacy accepted by many. When I say that men and women are physically unequal (for instance, only women bear babies), I don't mean that women are superior to men. Unequal is an objective observation. Only inferior or superior, in this context, are subjective evaluations.

Societies have produced different forms of evolutionary adaptation not because their members were superior or inferior to those of other societies, but because external environmental determinants of the system (for instance, ecological constraints) restricted their general evolutionary development and guided it in certain directions. The most elegant proof of this differential adaptation is that even the most subjective of culture products (for example, mythic symbols) are adjusted to the objective patterns of the social structure, as Durkheim well knew, and the very fact that the religious configurations of different societies vary so radically in code and message, and less so in armatuare.

The type of society is thus the constant factor, and it is to this that the cultural armature, the deep level of symbolism, adapts to achieve correspondence. But if this constant factor changes radically, by revolutionary socio-structural change, or by evolutionary leaps, the symbolism changes by systemic adjustment. Furthermore, revolutionary cultural inventions can have the reverse effect, and themselves induce social change. This is what Turner means when he speaks of the creative power of liminal and liminoid genres.

Taking the standpoint of my own analysis, it is possible to say, quoting Godelier: "thus behind the conscious rationality of the behavior of the members of a society there always lies the more fundamental and unconscious rationality of the hierarchic structure of the social relationships which characterize that society" (1973:357). This is very different from Lévi-Strauss's position.

One could argue (as others have done before me) that Lévi-Strauss is a follower of Plato rather than Hegel. It is at least obvious that his view of the superstructure as "the shadows on the wall of the cave" is a Platonic one. In this view, mankind is a prisoner inside the cave, seeing the outside world only as a shadowy reflection upon its wall, perhaps projected there only by his imagination. Neither the shadow nor the outside world is "real." The external world is an Eternal Idea which exists forever, in Mind. The shadow is an impermanent idea in man's mind.

Marx, on the other hand, views the world as a set of interconnected realities. The first reality (Plato's outside world) is the material existence of the cosmos, nature, and the social order. This reality has a bimodal existence, or two major modalities. One is the visible surface structure (for example, the roughness on the outside of a pebble); the other, the invisible deep structure (the molecular and atomic arrangement inside the same pebble). The second major reality, the superstructure, is man's approximation of an objective description of the first realities, mediated by his observations and the communicative codes of his culture. In simplest terms the first reality set is not "ideal" because it is independent of the observer's thought about it. In fact, the deep level is not even directly observable; some deep structures are hypothetic notions (such as the Greek concept of the atom) and all deep structures require some form of inference. This first reality set is also not eternal, because nature as well as the social order is in a constant state of transformation. The second reality, which is the culturally derived image of the first, is also neither permanent nor ideal, because it is a product of the social collectivity, specific to time and space.

At any point in time, observations may lead man to believe that the outside material reality is eternal (that is, unchanging or static), but this belief is simply the product of imperfect, incomplete, or short-range observation. Similar distortions in observation perhaps explain why some early anthropologists doing short stretches of field work saw societies in homeostatic balance. It seems that in looking at the long-range deep social history of mankind, Marx and the later anthropologists have been able to approximate more closely the social reality "out there in the depths" by improving their observational and inferential armamentarium, their tool kit. In a sense, this process simply repeats the process by which human beings, and particularly theologians and scientists, have been able to create theories, that is, "scientific cultures" or "religious visions" (root paradigms), which better approximate the description of the realities "out there" in other domains of observation. It seems clear that most historians of astronomy, for example, see the advances of the science and its separation from religion and astrology as the product of the constant interplay between theories, faulty observation, improvements in the observational armamentarium, and the constant reality of the galaxies that were being observed and that were, ultimately, the measure of the quality of observation.

In dealing with symbols of religion, however, we have another factor to consider. First, to the scientist or objective observer, much scientific discovery appears independent of ethical, moral, or normative concerns. From this perspective, scientific observations "ought to have" a neutral moral quality, and are or should be value-free. However, from the point of view of social institutions, the mechanisms that sustain the moral order, no scientific observation is totally value-free because all are necessarily rationalizations of the "visible surface reality." We need only to remember that the major astronomical discoveries of Copernicus, Newton, Galileo, and Kepler were considered heretical by both the Roman Catholics and the different Protestant sects, because these discoveries undermined Biblical teachings about a geocentric universe, and thus were seen as undermining the theoretical base of the root paradigm of Christian morality.

Social institutions build into their culture (that is, their maintenance devices) the scientific teachings of a prior historical period which have been incorporated and syncretized as part of the cognitive sacred moral order. In the astronomical example I have just given, we must remember the Church had accepted the Pythagorean-Aristotelian paradigmatic view of the universe as part of its dogma. The Bible, that treasure trove of parables, states this problem well. The Tower of Babel, with which man "attempted to reach the heavens" and for which he was eternally punished with cultural pluralism, was nothing but an astronomical observatory. In the *Popol Vuh*, the gods blinded men for the same reason, because "they have reached for the knowledge of everything there is in the world . . . they saw all hidden things . . . great was their knowledge. . . ." They "completed their knowledge of everything, examined the four corners and the four points of the celestial vault and the face of the earth" (*Popol Vuh*, pp. 177–178, 1947 edition of the Fondo de Cultura, my translation). And thus the parental gods blinded them, "throwing vapor over their eyes, and their eyes were misted (dimmed) as when one blows over the surface of a mirror. . . . Thus was destroyed all their wisdom" (*ibid.*, p. 179). This sort of knowledge = wisdom = seeing is the privilege, today, of Zinacantecan shamans or religious experts, who are called "seers." As in the old days, scientific knowledge in a theocratic society is a priestly privilege.

There is more to the relationship of religion and science, however, for scientific discoveries also include observations of the human social order. But, compared with theories about the heavens, theories about society have a sharpened immediacy, because they cannot at any point be divorced from the moral issues of a society's self-justification and mechanisms of homeostasis, that is, from social ideology. To protect its self-perceived social order, a society tends to deify it in symbols that proclaim it immanent, eternal, and given, as well as "good." This phenomenon is what Durkheim meant when he equated the church with society, and God with the society's own image. It partly explains, I believe, why Marx called religion the opium of the masses, since he thought that the ideologies prevalent in a society were those of the ruling elites and functioned to support their claims to hierarchic superiority. For similar reasons Engels saw in the history of early Christianity, when it was a movement of oppressed minorities, a positive revolutionary ideology with "notable points of resemblance with the modern working-class movement" (1959:168–194).

What we need to observe objectively is what kind of society is likely to produce what kind of religious-scientific moral justification for its own existence. Moreover, it seems to me of immense value to determine the exact relations between scientific or ideological advances, obsolete scientific or religious theories of the social order, the social order itself, and the changes which take place in that order. It is by focusing on the symbolic armatures of different types of societies that we may find answers.

Assuming for the moment (as I think we safely can) that Durkheim was right in holding that religious symbolism incorporates a morally validated social map, an ideology, and a science (a system of classifications), it seems pertinent to ask if different levels of social configurations produce different types of religious cultures. Then we must make a second assumption: that mankind has evolved in terms of a few gross cultural configurations, which we could call general evolutionary types (Steward's levels of socio-cultural integration). If this assumption is correct, it should follow that societies of different evolutionary types must have different sacred symbolic configurations (cultures), and those of the same or a similar type must have the same or similar symbolic armatures.

Much nineteenth-century research on religion was focused on this set of assumptions and questions. Unfortunately, the scientific observations made in the field of study of the history of religions were not supported by coherent, viable theories of the evolution of society, and were handicapped by the confusion of evolution with progress or improvement. To a large extent, the nineteenth century saw the world divided into two evolutionary types: We (the West), the civilized, the superior, and They, the others, the primitive, the inferior. Let us assume, for the sake of argument, that our present evolutionary theories are somewhat more sophisticated. We have at least four major evolutionary stages, and some anthropologists may be even brave enough to argue for five!

If these stages correspond to any true approximation of the reality out there, it must follow that a valid typology of societies in these stages (Steward's levels of socio-cultural integration) should correspond to and clarify the types of religious structures and cultures that belong to each stage. In fact, anthropology has already acquired some quite good general descriptions and theories of the religious culture of the types of societies we call bands and tribes (see Sahlins 1968; Wallace 1966). We do not, however, have anything resembling these objective advances for societies more similar to our own, that is, those that are state-organized. I do not mean we do not have good ethnographic descriptions. These are becoming abundant (for example, Geertz's and Spiro's work in Southeast Asia). What we do not have is an integrated theoretic description of the religion of societies with state systems, either agrarian or industrial, which are distinct types of societies with certain sacred symbolic ideologies over and above their ethnographic particularism. One only needs to look at the disguised ways in which some anthropologists and most sociologists of religion have argued for the superiority of our own religious views, scientific notions, or moral systems.

The paucity of research is not accidental but is deeply bound up with the ethical "dangers" of creating objective typologies of symbol systems which include our own religious traditions. In some circles, such inquiry may be perceived as socially dangerous or subversive, because in the process of objectivization we may discover that the moral bases of our own society are corrupt, or that in fact, our social order is neither perfect nor superior and our ideology or religion is an anachronistic illusion. But scientists have done some work of this kind. Thus we have some tentative theories that deal with the religions of social systems like our own, and these are taught in philosophy, sociology and anthropology departments and even in theology schools.

In the context of the Judeo-Christian religious traditions, the moral dangers of the scientific discovery of the nature of religion are exacerbated, because we live in an industrial age while our religious configurations correspond in gross terms to a type of society historically prior to our own, which some anthropologists and historians have called the complex agrarian state. Zinacantan's religion, again, is the religion of an agrarian society.

What are the characteristics of agrarian states which can be reflected in religious symbolism? Let us look briefly at recent evolutionist thought on the issue.

Agrarian states are characterized by an economic structure based on peasant production of domestic cultigens and animals. This core structure is geared to an annual calendric cycle of production and distribution of man-controlled crops and herds. It has a complex division of labor which includes factors other than sex and age and separates consumers and producers, with a non-food-producing elite.

Second, agrarian states exhibit a political hierarchization of social relations. Kinship as a principle of ordering is no longer basic to other relationships and has low dominance in the overall structure. Territoriality, defined as a subsystem of nested political units in space, has high dominance as an overall organizing principle. That is, territorially defined political units are the building blocks of the society in terms of spatial arrangements.

Third, agrarian states are internally organized in a hierarchy of human groups, more or less amorphous, membership in which is based on different criteria of wealth, power, ethnic origin, language, descent, prestige and so on. In other words, these states are stratified. The type of hierarchization varies from very loose class structures with high social mobility to very tight pluralistic systems, such as castes, with very low social mobility. In between are societies with dual or multiple ranking systems, such as that of Mexico today. Such human aggregates occupy different statuses and roles in the system of production and distribution, in access to life-sustaining resources, in power allocation, and in socially defined moral worth.

Fourth, agrarian states in history exhibited scientific systems dependent on a postneolithic preindustrial technology for the observation, recording, storing, and communication of socially valued information.

This information itself is utilized as a maintenance device of the social hierarchy, by making it the esoteric property of the ruling elites, restricting its diffusion among the masses, and simultaneously making the esoteric knowledge culturally relevant for their life. Thus the development of specialized priesthoods, horoscope-casting systems, schools for the education of the elite which are the necessary stepping stones to positions of power and so on. Some of this knowledge can have a major impact on the development of efficient social planning. For example, in the absence of a solar astronomy, planting schedules are at the mercy of uncertain weather conditions. And without Euclidian geometry or positional or place-value numerals which permit sophisticated arithmetical calculations (such as

Arabic numerals or the Mayan numeration), astronomical observations cannot be recorded or interpreted with any degree of
accuracy or heuristic power.

However, agrarian states also often develop esoteric knowledge
which has no direct social relevance for the masses or for the manage-
ment of the social system, but the possession of which is defined as a
criteria for high rank: for example, the requirement of Confucian
knowledge for those seeking bureaucratic posts in Imperial China,
the Latin requirement in English boys' public schools in the nineteenth century, the privileges of the mantric knowledge of the Brah-
mins of India, and the need for the Aztec elites to inform their
offspring of the celestial wanderings of the morning star. In other
words, agrarian states invented parasitic intellectuals attached to the
elites, theologians, astrologers, philosophers, poets. These people
neither produced food, nor served *directly* to make the social system
run smoothly. Often, history tells us, they worked in their own
devious paths simply to satisfy their own hunger for knowledge for
knowledge's sake. We have seen the impact of this pursuit in the
character of Mesoamerican symbol systems. It is obvious that much
of the complexity of the religious symbol systems of agrarian states
stemmed from the intellectuals' proclivity for making up ideas for
their own pleasure. But an ideological paradigm could become a
powerful social tool and a vehicle for emotion as well as for thought.
Eventually, the unconscious emotion that attached itself to an accepted symbolic paradigm would become part of its function, and
promote its endurance over time among the members of the collectivity. Ultimately, the root paradigm would become a strong focus
of social feeling, whatever its intellectual origin. Such root paradigms are painful to give up.

Following Maine, Fried (1967), and others, we could add other
characteristics of agrarian states. They developed political systems
with tendencies toward centralization, and simultaneously developed lines of internal political fission. Thus, under most conditions,
agrarian states exhibited various degrees of integration and several
foci of political control, also hierarchically arranged. In addition,

they had a system of contracts and markets rather than one of simple reciprocity or redistribution of surpluses. They developed internal sovereignty and an ethic of political legitimacy, coupled with systems of law. Monopoly of force was in the hands of the government, which itself defined justice and the punishable offense. Furthermore, as it seems to hold for all known agrarian states in history, we could add Redfield's (1956) differentiation of such societies into rural (folk) and urban, peasant and nonpeasant, the little and the great tradition. An examination of this last characteristic, that of rural-urban differentiation, will lead us to see how the religion of Zinacantan fits in with the agrarian system and why its armature has not changed.

Count, in his article, deals with the rural-urban issue in deft fashion, working in the ethnographic context of Western European mythology. With sound evidence and great clarity he poses the argument that the mythic systems of prior evolutionary stages become the "back yard" mythology (the little traditions) of new high traditions, which represent the "front yard" mythology (Count 1960:317). It is among the folk, those of the low or little tradition (in Redfield's sense of the term), among the humble, the peasants, the common folk of the countryside, that Vedic hymns, Greek deities, Babylonian schemata, prehispanic Mesoamerican rituals—in other words, the old symbols—live on and are cherished.

It was in the nineteenth century, with the upsurge of nationalism which brought an interest in "folklore," that the beliefs of the peasantry, which first appeared to be superstition without cosmology, to have a truncated mythology or no mythology at all, were suddenly understood as "relics of a common pagan past," with a system behind them of deities, beliefs, and rituals that were still alive and well, although long since repudiated by the elites. The present ideology is "truth." "The repudiated or forgotten is myth; current extra- or anti-canonical beliefs held by the peasantry are folklore" (Count 1960:317). But, are they? In fact, "it might be called a sociological accident that myth and folk tale have traditionally been considered two separate categories of primitive or unsophisticated literature.

The two genres were first set up as distinct from each other; only after a long time was their essential and more basic oneness discovered" (*ibid.*, p. 316). One could add that it is also a socio-historical accident that religious symbolism and ideology were set up as distinctly different, or that ideology today has become identified with false or unproven beliefs, as Geertz argues (1973).

Thus the urban elites are always at opposite poles from the rural masses. The first group is the body of worshippers of new rationalistic religious paradigms, modern ideologies, recent scientific discoveries. The second holds dear the worship of old, partially superseded symbolic forms, old-fashioned ideologies of prior historical periods, and anachronistic scientific notions, that is, the mythology rejected by the urbanites, the folklore that they misunderstood.

In many of the anthropological monographs on Mexico or Guatemala, the chapter on religion or beliefs manages to inform us that the system is incomplete for some reason or other, that it is not very coherent or structured, that it is a sort of conglomeration of beliefs held together only by the fact that they exist in a single locale, and not by some more fundamental logic (see also sections on religion, myth, folklore, and related subjects, in Wauchope, *Handbook of Middle American Indians*, vols. 6, 7, and 8). Anthropologists who have worked in Mesoamerica have behaved much like the nineteenth-century folklorists who looked upon European peasants as carriers of truncated mythologies without any cosmology. Moreover, even many of the monographs dedicated to and focused on religion (I am here excluding those concerning Zinacantan) show a deeply prejudiced point of view. Even in such recent works as the *Handbook of Middle American Indians* the religious beliefs of the Indians are called "superstitions" or "paganism," probably because they did not fit the authors' notions of a proper system of belief in the Christian style (although it can also be argued that the apparent lack of system in the Indians' beliefs reflects the unsystematic style of the research!). In fact, we do not have, for the whole culture area, a single complete systematic account of the religious symbolism as a structure; what we have is a collection of more or less juicy, ethnographic tidbits.

Even Mexican anthropologists, who are often prone to idealize the Indians, have chosen to defend their religious beliefs in cliché-ridden statements about the "beauty of their folkways" or "their impoverished, exploited condition," thus unconsciously asserting that the Indian systems are somehow anachronistic, defective, or retrograde. I maintain instead that the Indian religious systems are old peasant versions of highly sophisticated structures, living and creative symbolisms that carry not just beauty but also fundamental functional visions of their life conditions, and deep emotional commitments. The religion of Zinacantan is not an exceptional case, but it is probably the only one that has been studied in sufficient depth to reveal the structure of the system—where there is a cumulative redundancy of symbolic data. In defense of previous researches, however, I would suggest that the Mesoamerican evidence "did not make sense" because it was not illuminated by modern theories on the nature of this kind of system, such as structuralism offers.

Let us see now how Zinacantan reflects the religion of an agrarian society. First, both the religions from which Zinacantecans developed their present symbolic structures accurately reflected a hierarchical political order as experienced by the peasants. Roman Catholicism in its sixteenth-century folk version was not so very different from prehispanic religion with its hierarchy of gods. The Roman Catholicism of the masses all over the world, even today, little resembles the monotheistic sophistication of a Teilhard de Chardin. Folk Catholicism was stronger before the Industrial Revolution in the postmedieval Spanish areas where Christianity was dominant, and at the time of the major impact of Christian symbolism on the New World. However, even today, in the back yard of the Vatican, in rural Italy, the peasants are not monotheistic in the purest sense. Folk Roman Catholicism is made up of a parade of hierarchically arranged divine personages and saints, as prehispanic religion was. From a top "oneness"—God the Father—through the Trinity of Father, Son and Holy Ghost, one descends in power and rank to the Virgin Mary and her apparitions, to the hierarchy of nine types of immortal supernatural spirits (seraphim, cherubim, thrones, dominions, virtues, powers, principalities, archangels and angels), followed by male and female canonized saints, sanctified souls, and finally by the souls of dead human beings who were neither saintly nor famous but make up the multitude of spirits and ghosts that populate our rural traditions and are said to live in purgatory.

A parallel arrangement for prehispanic Mesoamerica has been demonstrated in this book. Zinacantecans simply merged the two sets of deities into one hierarchy. One major difference, however, is the opposition between the fourfolded "quadrilateral" set comprising a deity in the pre-Columbian religion, which Zinacantecans have so zealously preserved, and the Trinity of Roman Catholicism. The problem of fitting a quincunx or quartet into a trio is not exclusive to Indian Mesoamerica. In the medieval traditions of European Christianity many breakaway sects developed over the issue of incorporating a fourth personage (usually the Virgin Mary, but sometimes even the devil) into the Trinity (see Jung 1969). Others argued for a dual Trinity, consisting of a set of five equally divine persons. Murillo represented one form of this arrangement in a painting called *The Two Trinities*, now in the National Gallery in London, in which the divine figures appear as follows:

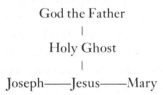

All these differential variations in armature may have something to do with the different nature of the socio-political hierarchies which developed in medieval Europe, in contrast to Mesoamerica, or with other unknown (not sociologically derived) factors. Jung thought they had a psychological archetypal base, but his arguments are not convincing. The European variations do not show major differences of armature but changing fashions of dogma. Zinacantecans in their own situation of change held to the old quadripartite armature, and the Trinity has not served to give a new armature to the system.

The similarities in ritual symbolism between sixteenth-century Catholicism and pre-Columbian religion were extensive, notwithstanding the presence of human sacrifice in the New World. The two had similar baptismal, naming, marriage, and death rituals, solar rituals, water, planting, and hunting rituals, a "communion" ceremony, and so on, controlled by the state church. Both had a specialized class of priests, occupying high positions in the elite. Both theocracies had a monopoly of scientific knowledge and of the dispensation of punishment, including the persecution of witches and imprisonment of deviants. Both societies had a "state" religion (see Wolf 1959 for a discussion of this point). The similarity of some of the symbols and codes was also striking, and was often commented on by the most enlightened Christian priests who came to New Spain (for example, Duran). The picture of the male deity with a halo resembling the sun's rays, or of the Virgin standing on a moon, were and are familiar associations for the native peoples.

Moreover, the basic armature of a quarterly, two-sectioned scheduling of ritual was parallel in the two cultures. The armature was based on the calendar with a space-time frame, which was meaningful for agrarian societies in regions north of the equator. It was geared to solar and seasonal changes that were tied to the cultivation of staple crops (maize in the New World, wheat, barley and other Middle Eastern grains in the Old World). Thus the similarity of belief that the high deity (for example, Huitzilopochtli, Jesus, Krishna) was born of a virgin mother, a neat metaphor of the plant emerging from the seed buried in the earth.

This agrarian paradigm of calendric space-time, around which the symbolism is structured, seems to be a characteristic of many of the religions of agrarian states the world over. Apparently concerns of ecology and of agricultural scheduling, and advances in astronomical observation, led all the early civilizations to use these paradigmatic constructs as basic frames for the building of symbolic edifices. The whole system of geomancy among the Chinese, the Ife divinatory system of the West African kingdoms, the astrological systems of India, the Inca symbolism, all have deeply embedded in them eco-logic-cosmic notions of four-sided space-time continua. Nineteenth-century scholars often wrote about these similarities, explaining them by universal diffusion, while Jung, who was acquainted with the Hindu and Middle Eastern variants, saw in them instead atavistic memory traces of the human species, in fact, the archetype of the mandala. (It does not seem, however, that simpler nonagrar-ian or stateless societies have dominant paradigms of this sort. They focus instead on kinship and descent as organizing root paradigms.)

Since the codes in which the cosmic symbols occur are ethno-graphically specific, it seems more likely that agrarian state societies, faced with the same astronomical realities, building similar models of the universe from solar observations, adjusting them to the indi-vidual problems of their economies (particularly the production of domestic cultigens), ended with parallel symbolic inventions. Since the sun rises in the west for no man, and only four ecliptic points are distinguishable as markers in the solar path, a model of a four-sided sacred universe with a central point is extremely useful in practical science, and very likely to develop into a significant root paradigm. Other peoples who needed an advanced astronomy, although for reasons other than agricultural scheduling, developed similar models. The Norsemen, for example, the prototype of seafaring peoples, had models of the cardinal directions based on the night-time sky, which they utilized both to guide their ships over the northern seas and to build their religious pantheon (Taylor 1957). That these similar root paradigms are independent inventions is shown by the great differences in the symbolic detail with which they have been expressed.

Why then did the Mesoamerican peoples not adopt the codes of Christianity cleanly and purely or completely reject one symbol system or the other? This was not necessary. The marriage of the old and the new was an easy one to arrange. To be converted they had only to reject *one single major ritual parameter*, that is, to change from actual human sacrifice for the maintenance of the social-cosmic order to symbolic human sacrifice, in the most human figure of Christ on the cross. Obviously, the cross itself, so similar in design to the prehispanic quincunx, imbued both the old and new iconographies with the same aura of received sacred truth.

It can be argued that the abandonment of human sacrifice was a fundamental ideological change. I will argue that it was also a societally induced change. European society, with its superior technology and use of force, its well-equipped armies, did not need the threat of human sacrifice as an instrument of political control. Human sacrifice in pre-Columbian society has been well described as a device to maintain social control over reluctantly conquered populations, whatever its other functions. The introduction of the horse, iron, and European forms of warfare did away with the need for it. The major epidemics brought by the Spaniards which swept the New World and produced giant declines of population, eliminated its value as a mechanism for demographic control (see Cook 1946). It was not necessary for the conquerors and conquered to be intellectually or emotionally convinced of the ideological superiority of the bloodless symbolic sacrifice. The question was one of power.

Chiapas Indians, however, still perceive human sacrifice as a live reality. Since all quadrilateral spaces have bearers (Vashakmen), Chiapas Indians believe that any new quadrilateral construction requires that human beings should be sacrificed and buried under it. When I was in Chiapas doing field work, the government was building a new bridge over the Grijalva River to replace an old one that had been washed away by the strong currents of the rainy season. When the Indians heard of it, a rumor swept like fire over the region that the Ladinos were planning to steal Indian children and bury them under the supports of the bridge, so that it would not fall. Unrest in the Indian population was so serious that many Ladino families left San Cristóbal, the seigneurial Mexican city near Zinacantan, because they were afraid of an Indian revolt. The Mexicans still remembered the Wars of the Castes of previous centuries, in which the Indians had crucified their own native Christ and waged

war against the Ladino outsiders (the Christian state) to free themselves from their dominance.

For the Indians, the sacrifice of human dignity and actual life is
still experienced in all their relations with the alien forces of the state
represented by the local Mexicans. Not so long ago, they were
treated as serfs, tied to the land by inheritable debt, used with
contempt. They were not even allowed to walk on the sidewalks of
the preindustrial Ladino city of San Cristóbal, or to sleep there.
Exploited, whipped, undernourished, mistreated in word and deed,
taken away from their homes to die on the coffee plantations—to
them the reality of Christ's suffering is not a symbolic device referring to a unique event. Rather, it is one more example of the cruelty
of the state elite toward its subordinate peoples. And so there is
expressed in Chiapas the opposition of the Christ-sun (the sacrificed)
and the Ladino Earth Lord (the sacrificer). Together they represent
the balance of Indian versus mestizos, peasant versus elite—one the
sun, the other the earth, and without both of them the social order as
the Indians know it cannot be maintained.

The Mexican Indian is a marginal subsistence peasant on the
bottom rung of the class structure of an industrializing nation. But
Mexico is still, fundamentally, an agrarian state. This condition of
course is most visible in the rural areas, particularly in what Aguirre
Beltrán has called the *refuge regions* of the national system (1967).
Fundamentally, the state of Chiapas exhibits local forms of a social
organization that is pseudofeudal in type, as was sixteenth-century
prehispanic society (I am using Sjoberg's [1952] definition of feudal).
Instead of Aztec conquerors, the Chiapas Indians now face Ladinos.
No wonder this characteristic is reflected in their hierarchy of sacred
beings, where the Lord of the World appears as a greedy Ladino.

Like the prehispanic city states and European rural communities,
each town in Chiapas has its roster of local sacred beings. Each saint,
mountain, and waterhole controls health, wealth, crafts, and pun-
ishes behavior, just as the noble lords of the agrarian state did of old,
and the Ladino elites, who run the rural court system, do today.
Both the Mexicans and the Mexican deities as the Indians envisage

them have a monopoly of force. Moreover, just as the state is territorially organized, the sacred beings of Zinacantan control different territories, each one from his mountain home, cave, or sacred precinct in the local churches. The hierarchization of these territorial units becomes apparent in the relative social importance of the mountain peaks and waterholes that mark them. The degree of importance, as Vogt points out, is not related to the actual physical size of the mountains but to their "owners," to the divinities who occupy them as homes or bathing places.

The hierarchization of the pantheon in Zinacantan, however, appears fluid compared with that of other Indian communities. Although in their social life Zinacantecans systematically emphasize hierarchical distinctions between persons and groups, and "the main subject of ritual performed by members of the religious hierarchy is hierarchy itself expressed in the conventional code," the pantheon, at least according to the published literature, appears not to be so ordered in a totally systematic way (Rosaldo 1968). Some autochthonous deities and saints (the Lord of the World, the mother-father gods, Saint Sebastian) are obviously superior to others, but there does not appear to be any overall linear ranking as there is for the shaman's "guild" or the political officerships. Is this an accident of ethnographic reporting or an accurate description of reality? Other comparative evidence suggests that the Zinacantecans may in fact stratify the deities at some level of the structure. Among the Cuicatec Indians, the gods are arranged on the model of the civil-religious hierarchy of the cargo system, the highest god being a "president," followed by senior officers, junior officer gods, and "policeman" gods of small hills and waterholes, and ending with "child" godlings which, like real children, do not occupy cargos (Hunt 1974). This parallel arrangement might be considered a symbolic innovation of the Cuicatec, but in Chiapas, in the community of Pinola, the divine guardian spirits are also organized in this fashion with a "metaphysical elders' council, a president, a secretary, a judge, and various policemen" (Hermitte 1970, my translation).

Perhaps further questioning may reveal an equivalent ranking in

Zinacantan. If none exists, the lack of it may be explained by the partial decentralization of the political apparatus, with its alternative hamlet hierarchies, shaman hierarchies, and cargo hierarchies of the Center (Vogt 1973). That is, as in the social domain, the hierarchies may be partial or only contingent, and the symbolic paradigm equally fluid. Further fieldwork is required before we can decide which is the answer. There is a lesson in humility here for all anthropologists. Even in the best studied of all Mesoamerican ethnographic cases, further work remains to be done. How valuable, in comparison, are the one-man, one-year research schemes on which most anthropological reporting is based?

The scheduling of the yearly agrarian ritual functions followed in both Christianity and prehispanic religion has also continued to operate. Although for the Mexica-Colhua the year started with the spring planting, many other communities and city states in Mesoamerica started the year at other dates around that time. We do not know why there was such variation, but it existed. When the native peoples in Chiapas used to start the year is not clear, but they now do so in the winter quarter. Since the year cycle has four major liminal points, the solstices and equinoxes, any of them could serve to mark its beginning. If the corn cycle is of primary importance, spring makes most symbolic sense for the birth of the deity. As it is now, in spring there is a double rite of passage—sun-Jesus from man to god, and the corn from seed to plant. However, the winter solstice period has some advantages, because the sun is then in an extreme liminal transitional position and because the solstice takes place immediately after the harvest, which means that there is food available for major ritual feasts, money from sold crops, and leisure time. It is not an accident that few Mesoamerican Indian peasants celebrate any major cluster of saints' days during the hardest period of agricultural toil (late July to the end of October).

Again, inasmuch as the contemporary Mexican elites of Chiapas control production and the political apparatus of the state, the old gods serve just as well as the Christian images. One may ask the Lord of the Earth, just as one asks Jesus-the-sun, to bring good rains, to allow one to use the land, to receive the maize seed and make it grow, or to protect one from demons, in the same way that one asks Mexican officials for permission to cut down forests to make new slash-and-burn fields, to provide lands through the Ejido system, and to protect Indian homes from unjust attack by outsiders.

In the eyes of the illiterate Indians of Zinacantan—and indeed all over Mexico—the elites, both native and Mexican, control much esoteric knowledge. The poverty of the school system has mitigated against any major changes in Indian scientific notions. Just as well that Mexicans have powers similar to those of the gods, to control the mysteries of the universe. They provide not only technocrats and politicians, but also priests, practitioners of the sacred arts of a higher rank than the native shamans.

When the colonial Spanish regime forbade Indians to train as Christian priests, it unknowingly insured the survival of native religious experts and with them of non-Christian symbolic structures. Forbidden to exercise religious control over their communities through the Roman Catholic Church, the Indians were forced back upon their own traditional rituals and religious specialists. The undermining of their right of access to positions within the social hierarchy of the new state religion, their lack of serious training in the spiritual intricacies of the new faith, persecution, and the contempt of colonial and present-day priests for the aesthetic and spiritual value of their own symbols, have promoted a defensive, self-preserving religion, hidden in the recesses of the peasant communities, away from the eyes of the conquerers and their contemporary descendants. This religion has become the domain of the Indians' own religious experts, the shamans, who hold the reins of power. Thus the symbols from the overt world of the past have continued to give meaning to the covert world of the present, ordering reality simultaneously in the shape of the root metaphors of the old quincunx and the new cross.

Furthermore, with the post-Reforma separation of church and state in the late nineteenth century, which curtailed the control of

the Christian priests over the religious activities in Indian communities, whatever was left of the native religious system after the
colonial debacle was made even more secure against external interference.

But as Christianity partially lost its historic control over the peasants of Mesoamerica, so did the old religion. Much of the detailed
richness of the pre-Columbian symbol system is dead, never to be
revived—or has changed beyond immediate recognition.

The knowledge of the complexities of astronomical phenomena
and of the esoteric divinatory calendar, which was a monopoly of the
ruling urban priests, has been lost in Zinacantan, as in most other
Indian communities of Mesoamerica. The oral traditions remained
and continued to be enriched by further additions and by the creative processes of readjustment. After all, words are free! But the
traditions of plastic arts, the magnificent massive sculpture and exquisite painted manuscripts, burned by the Spaniards as works of
the devil, died with the prehispanic art specialists. It is only in
marginal media (for example in women's weaving) that some of the
old symbols continue to reappear with new names and interpretations (see Mendez Cifuentes 1967; Turok 1974).

There are other purely cultural reasons why some of the symbolism was preserved with such syncretic absorption. Language is a
conservative medium. Owing to the state's inability to impose Spanish, the native languages were preserved, and incidentally the verbal
aspect of the religious symbolism was preserved with them. Both
vocabulary and speech style have much to do with the structuring of
symbols. Play with homophony, puns, double-entendre, and word
connotation serves as a significant vehicle for the formation, trans-
mission and preservation of symbols. As long as the Indians keep
their own languages, these linguistically based symbol associations
are unlikely to die. Furthermore, because the Indians did not become literate and thus acquire the ability to participate in Western
literary traditions, they have kept alive their own oral tradition,
which has also aided the survival of their symbolic religious struc-

tures—for example, in the double coupling of verse lines and the use of alternate synonyms dealing with cosmic paradigms, which appears in the *Popul Vuh* as well as in contemporary Zinacantecan prayer. (An even better example of the verbal dimension of the space-time continuum, extensively documented and analyzed, appears in Gossen 1974, concerning the nearby Indian town of Chamula.)

In summary, the prehispanic symbols of one agrarian state and the colonial symbols of another have survived in happy conjunction, because the original social and cultural processes that gave them birth and meaning, that created the order that was symbolized, are still alive.

In contrast to the sociological emphasis of these arguments, but also to carry them one step further, I will suggest a reason—valid for *all societies*—why peoples are unwilling to give up their old symbolic armatures.

All definitions of the divinity, however derived, are ultimately images produced by man—his aesthetically coherent visions of the unknown and unknowable. There is no objective test, no final empirical evidence to prove in an ultimate sense that any religious vision or paradigm is better or more accurate than any other. The prehispanic poet sensed this with Shakespearean elegance:

> Perchance, here, do we speak something truthful,
> Giver of Life?
> We are only dreaming,
> We are only lifting ourselves from sleep.
> Thus we speak on Earth.
> But no one, here, speaks truth.

> (Manuscript *Cantares Mexicanos*,
> my translation from the Spanish)

Since there is no test, all societies are ultimately free to believe that their own religious symbols and paradigms are best, just as they believe ethnocentrically that they are the true people and hold to the emotional verity that they are the best example of divine creation on earth. Why, then, should any of them reject their own intimately felt and understood symbol structures, substituting alien ones? If reality is a world of contradictions, "glittering with conflict as with diamonds," both "paradox and mystery," any human explanation of its numinous nature is the best possible within its own time and place, and within the society of those who created it.

Structural Messages of "The Hummingbird"

Transformational Class	Relevant Line of Poem	First symbol	Transformation ("Becomes, Is, Changes into, Has to do with . . .")	Second symbol
Volatile	1,2,25 1,2,5 13,14	hummingbird "	is the same as is just like a	hawk dove
Size	17,18, 23,24	(small bird)	is	big, large (bird)
Color	15,16	(blue-green)	is	white
Element fire, water, season, geographic location	3	hot country, tall fire (dry)	(becomes)	(colder country), (rain), (wet)
Agricultural activity	4,5,9, 10	burning bean pods (preparation of fields for planting)	(is followed by)	(planting)
Kinship of deities	1,26	hummingbird (messenger, child, younger brother incarnation of the gods)	has to do with	father-mother (ancestral) gods
Climate, element, falling water, man-made fire	4,5,6, 7,8,11, 12	burning (time) (end of dry season)	(is followed by)	(planting time) (rain) comes down (season)
Solar position, volatile behavior	6,7,8	hummingbird came out (sun of spring)	(and)	came flying in the sky (sun of summer)
All elements deified in conjunction	27	(equinoctial summer storms)	(are same as)	(hurricanes, cyclones from the Gulf)
Associated images of gods	27	hummingbird (hummingbird = Huitzilopochtli)	we call it	One leg (One-legged god = Tezcatlipoca)

Note: Sections in parentheses are ideas implicit or latent in the poem, derived from structural analysis. Those without parentheses are words in actual lines of the poem.

Prehispanic Transformational Associations of Huitzilopochtli (explained in the text)

Note: This is not a complete list, but a selection of examples of frequent associations occurring in myth, ritual, and primary texts, and those listed by chronicles as most important or significant.

Animal

   1. Volatiles: hummingbird, eagle, hawk (high and fast flying levels, "warrior" birds).
   2. Swimmers and crawlers: blue snake, "sky snake": his tool, "the light of day."
   3. Earth walkers (mammals): rabbit, because rabbit is sign of summer months.

Plant

   4. Domesticated: nopal cactus.
   5. Powerful: morning glory (*ololiuhqui*)?
   6. Trees: willow, palm, silk cotton tree.
   7. Part of plant: thorns.
   8. Flower: rose (not European one, but a native flower with thorns).

   9. Dominant cardinal directions: south, southeast, up and high, above.
   10. Color: blue-green, white, gold stripes.
   11. Season: spring and summer, the rainy season.
   12. Natural phenomena: celestial fire (of the sun), drought at the end of the dry season, first rains of spring, and water and wind storms following the equinox.
   13. Body parts and directions: up and left side of body, the left hand.
   14. Sex: masculine.

15. Age: youth, young maturity.

16. Planet: the triumphant sun aspect (in the northward journey of the ecliptic), associated with the equinoctial solstice period which contains the summer; sun aspect at the top of the sky in the daily journey, and at the beginning of the day to midday.

17. Features of the landscape: islands, thorny deserts, hot country; the Cerro de la Estrella in the Valley of Mexico (southeast of Tenochtitlan), Colhuacan.

18. Ethnic group: Mexica (Aztecs).

19. Historical figure: the leader of the Aztec migration to the valley of Mexico, of the same name.

20. City: Tenochtitlan.

21. Tools and weapons: those of a warrior or king: a white shield with tufts of white feathers, four arrows, blue snake-staff, atlatl darts.

22. Clothing: blue-green mantle, blue sandals, gold bracelets, headdress with hummingbird beak.

23. Furniture: "a blue wooden bench in the fashion of a litter."

24. Face painting: a blue forehead with a blue band over the nose, reaching from ear to ear; gold stripes between the blue ones.

25. Profession: warrior, leader of men—the officer order of Eagle Knights (an Aztec military title), thus, under his protection.

26. Cooked foodstuffs: amaranth, sweet cakes cooked with honey; pulque dyed blue.

Mathematical Calendrical Series

27. Days: 1 Flint: day of birth of Huitzilopochtli, start of Aztec peregrination, and calendrical name of H.

   1 Death: day of the death of H., propitious for rituals to him.

   2 Cane: day propitious for rituals to H. because it is birthday of Tezcatlipoca (see associated gods).

28. Months: Tozcatl, Miccailhuitontli, Pachtontli, and Panquitzalistli, month of holidays of H.

29. Years: 2 Cane, date of the birth of H., also of death of Quetzalcoatl.

30. Calendrical non-annual ceremonies: The New Fire, occurring every 52 years.

Divine Kinship Association Series

Tezcatlipoca: H. was one of his four aspects, corresponding to the blue south, and the Tochtli days. Indirectly he is grandfather of H. because he created Coatlicue who was H.'s mother.

Coyolxauhqui: H.'s older sister, also his enemy.

Coatlicue: Mother of H., by parthenogenetic birth.

Centzon Huitzinahua: the 400 gods, stars of the southern part of the sky, who were H.'s elder half-brothers and enemies.

Paynal: Brother of H.; also one of H.'s aspects, a younger brother or unfolding of the major god, probably signifying the planet Mercury or Venus.

Elder brothers of H: Name of the young men who serviced H.'s temple and feasted for a whole year in his honor.

Quetzalcoatl: Partner of H. in the creation of fire, the half-sun and the first couple; also H.'s negative counterpart (one was born in the same year that the other died). In other myths a half-sibling of H. because Q. was born of Coatlicue too. H. was Q.'s successor by myth, and historically H. replaced Q. in Valley of Mexico.

Mictlantecuhtli: In the Borgia Codex the sky bearer of the south, associated with H. by cardinal direction.

Macuilxochitl: Both H. and M. are gods of summer and spring.

Tlaloc: Partner of H. in the main temple of Tenochtitlan, associated with H. because both arrive in the spring, one as the ascending sun, the other as rain.

Teicauhtzin: The younger brother, epithet; aspect of the H. god complex, representing him as younger brother of the other major gods.

Xochiquetzal: On her holyday, rose garlands were placed in H.'s temple. She was Tezcatlipoca's wife.

Xipe Totec: Brother of H. (HDLMPSP), aspect of Tezcatlipoca.

Camaxtli: Brother of H. (HDLMPSP), aspect of Tezcatlipoca; like H., a god of war.

Bibliography

Acheson, Nicholas H. 1966. Etnozoología Zinacanteca. In E. Vogt, (ed.), *Los Zinacantecos*. Pp. 433–454.

Adams, Richard N., and Arthur Rubel. 1967. Sickness and Social Relations. In R. Wauchope (Gen. ed.), *Handbook of Middle American Indians*. Vol. 6, M. Nash (ed.), pp. 333–356.

Aguirre Beltrán, Gonzalo. 1967. *Regiones de Refugio*. Mexico: Instituto Indigenista Interamericano, Ediciones Especiales, No. 46.

Anales de Cuauhtitlán. 1885. Noticias Históricas de México y sus contornos compiladas por D. José Fernando Ramirez. Mexico: Anales del Museo Nacional.

Anders, Ferdinand. 1963. *Das Pantheon der Maya*. Graz, Austria: Akademische Druck-U. Verlagsanstalt.

Anderson, Arthur T. O., and Charles E. Dibble (trans. and comm.). 1970. *The Florentine Codex: General History of the Things of New Spain*. Monographs of The School of American Research, Santa Fe, New Mexico.

Bacon, Sir Francis. 1883. *The Essays, or Councils, Civil and Moral*. New York: A. L. Burt (First published 1597.)

Bamberger, Joan. 1973. Review of Lévi-Strauss's *From Honey to Ashes*. *New York Times Book Review*, June 3.

Barnes, J. A. 1971. Time Flies Like an Arrow. *Man*, N. S. 6:537–552.

Baroco, John. 1970. Notas sobre el Uso de Nombres Calendáricos durante el Siglo XVI. In N. McQuown and J. Pitt-Rivers (eds.), *Ensayos de Antropología de la Zona Central de Chiapas*. Mexico: Instituto Nacional Indigenista.

Barrera Vasques, A., and S. Rendón (trans. and comm.). 1948. *El Libro de los libros del Chilam Balam*. Mexico: Fondo de Cultura Económica.

———, and S. G. Morley. 1949. The Maya Chronicles. *Contributions to American Anthropology and History*, Vol. 10, No. 48. Carnegie Institution of Washington.

Barthes, Roland. 1957. *Mythologies*. Paris: Editions du Seuil.

———. 1964. *Essais Critiques*. Paris: Editions du Seuil.

Benedict, Ruth. 1934. *Patterns of Culture*. Boston: Houghton Mifflin.

Berlin, Brent. 1970. A Universalist-Evolutionary Approach in Ethnographic Semantics. In Ann Fisher (ed.), *Current Directions in Anthropology*.

The Tzotzil Text of "The Hummingbird," Transcribe By Robert Laughlin

1. 7A li tz'unune, lek la muk',
2 & 3. ja7 yech'o la yech
j7abteletik ta k'ixin 7osil,
4. ta la schik'ik pat chenek' 7un,
5. lek xa nat ti k'ok' ta j-mek xvinaj 7une,
6. tal la li tz'unune,
7. ja7 7o la chlok'
8. chvil tal ta vinajel 7une.
9. Bwéno, 7iyil la li k'ok' 7une,
10. 7it up ssat ta ch'ayil 7un,
11. 7iyal la tal,
12. 7iyal la tal,
13. 7iyal la tal 7un,
yo7 7isk'elik la ti muk' 7une,
14. mu xach'un ti bik'ite, muk' la 7un,
15. 7a li ja7 la yech chak paloma sak la xxik' 7un,
16. sak skotlej,
17. 7a li 7altik ka chalik toj . . .
7a li tz'unun bik'it xiike,
18. k'e, batz'i muk' xiik la ti viniketik 7une,
19. ja7 to te yojtikinik k'u x7elan 7un,
20. porke muk' bu xhiltik jkotoltik,
21. mu jna7tik k'u x7elan,
22. ja7 li "tz'un tz'un" xi la ta 7ah'ubaltike,
23. pero mu jna7tik k'u smuk'ul,
24. 7a taj 7une, 7iyilik ti k'u smuk'ule,
25. 7isk'elik ko7ol schi7uk,
ko7ol smuk'ul schi7uk xik 7un,
26. skwenta la totil me7il,
27. jun yok chkaltik 7une.

Bulletin of the American Anthropological Association, Special Issue 3, No. 3 (Part 2):3–18.

Berlin, B., D. E. Breedlove, and P. H. Raven. 1968. Covert Categories and Folk Taxonomies. *American Anthropologist* 70:290–299.

Beyer, Hermann. 1965. Mito y Simbolismo del México Antiguo. *México Antiguo*, Vol. 10. Primer Tomo de sus Obras Completas. Mexico: Sociedad Alemana Americanista.

Blaffer, Sarah C. 1972. *The Black Man of Zinacantan: A Central American Legend*. Austin: University of Texas Press.

Boon, James A. 1972. *From Symbolism to Structuralism: Lévi-Strauss in a Literary Tradition*. New York: Harper and Row.

Borgia Codex. See Seler 1963.

Bricker, Victoria. 1966. El Hombre, la Carga y el Camino: Antiguos Conceptos Mayas sobre tiempo y espacio y el Sistema Zinacanteco de Cargos. In E. Vogt (ed.), *Los Zinacantecos*. Pp. 355–370.

———. 1973. *Ritual Humor in Highland Chiapas*. Austin: University of Texas Press.

———. 1974. Historical Dramas in Chiapas, Mexico. Paper read at the Special Session on Myth, Ritual and Symbolism in the Chiapas Highlands. International Congress of Americanists. Mexico City, September, 1974.

Burland, Cottie A. 1967. *The Gods of Mexico*. New York: Putnam.

——— (ed.) 1966. *Codex Laud*. Bodleian Library, Oxford. Codices Selecti, No. 11. Graz, Austria: Akademische Druck-U. Verlagsantalt.

Calnek, Edward E. 1962. Highland Chiapas before the Spanish Conquest. Ph.D. diss. University of Chicago.

Cancian, Frank. 1965. *Economics and Prestige in a Maya Community: The Religious Cargo System of Zinacantan*. Palo Alto, Cal.: Stanford University Press.

———. 1972. *Change and Uncertainty in a Peasant Economy: The Maya Corn Farmers of Zinacantan*. Palo Alto, Cal.: Stanford University Press.

———. 1974. *Another Place: Photographs of a Maya Community*. San Francisco: Scrimshaw Press.

Carrasco, Pedro. 1960. *Pagan Rituals and Beliefs among the Chontal Indians of Oaxaca, Mexico*. Anthropological Records, Vol. 20, No. 3. Berkeley and Los Angeles: University of California Press.

Carrasco P., Pedro. 1971a. Social Organization of Ancient Mexico. In R. Wauchope (Gen. ed.), *Handbook of Middle American Indians*. Vol. 10, F. G. Eckholm and I. Bernal (eds.), Part I.

———. 1971b. Los Barrios Antiguos de Cholula. *Estudios y Documentos de la Región Puebla-Tlaxcala*, Vol. 3. Mexico: Instituto Poblano de Antropología.

Caso, Alfonso. 1953. *El Pueblo del Sol*. Mexico: Fondo de Cultura Económica.

——. 1965. Zapotec Writing and Calendar, and Mixtec Writing and Calendar. In R. Wauchope (Gen. ed.), *Handbook of Middle American Indians*. Vol. 3, G. R. Willey (ed.), pp. 931–947, 948–961.

——. 1966. Dioses y Signos Teotihuacanos. In *Teotihuacán: Onceava Mesa Redonda*. Mexico: Sociedad Méxicana de Antropología. Pp. 249–279.

——. 1967. *Los Calendarios Prehispánicos*. Instituto de Investigaciones Históricas. Mexico: Universidad Nacional Autónoma de México.

——. 1968. Simposium: Religiones Mesoamericanas 1: Religión Prehispánica. In *Verhandlungen des XXXVIII Internationalen Amerikanistenkongresses*. Stuttgart-Munich. Vol. 3:189–238.

——. 1971. Calendrical Systems of Central Mexico. In R. Wauchope (Gen. ed.), *Handbook of Middle American Indians*. Vol. 10, F. G. Eckholm and I. Bernal (eds.), Part I:333–348.

Caspar, Max. 1959. *Kepler, 1571–1630*. New York: Collier Books.

Cassirer, Ernst. 1946a. *The Myth of the State*. New York: Doubleday Anchor.

——. 1946b. *Language and Myth*. Trans. by Suzanne Langer. New York: Dover.

Chavero, Alfredo. 1892. *Códice Porfirio Diaz*. Mexico: Junta Colombina, Antigüedades Mexicanas.

Chesley Baity, Elizabeth. 1973. Archaeoastronomy and Ethnoastronomy So Far. *Current Anthropology* 14:389–449.

Clavijero, Abate Francisco Javier. 1917. *Historia Antigua de México*. 2 volumes. Trans. from the Italian by T. T. de Mora. Mexico: Departmento Editorial de la Dirección General de las Bellas Artes.

Codex Borbonicus. 1938. *Manuscrito Pictórico Antiguo Mexicano de la Biblioteca de la Cámara de Diputados de Paris, Palais Bourbon*. Mexico: Librería Anticuaria Echaniz.

Codex Fejervary-Mayer. 1901. *Manuscrit Mexicain pre-columbien du Free Public Museum de Liverpool* (12014/M.). Paris: Loubat Reproduction.

Codex Mendocino. In José Corona Nuñez (ed.), 1964–1967, *Antigüedades de Mexico basadas en la recopilación de Lord Kingsborough*, Vol. 1. Mexico: Secretaría de Hacienda.

Codex Vaticanus (B 3773). 1939. *Pictórico Mexicano*. Mexico: Librería Anticuaria Echaniz.

Coe, Michael D. 1966. *The Maya*. New York: Praeger.

Cohen, Percy S. 1969. Theories of Myth. *Man*, N. S. 4:339–353.

Collier, George A. 1975. *Fields of the Tzotzil: The Ecological Basis of Tradition in Highland Chiapas*. Austin: University of Texas Press.

Collier, Jane F. 1973. *Law and Change in Zinacantan.* Palo Alto, Cal.: Stanford University Press.

Comisión del Papaloapam. 1956. *Atlas Climatológico e Hidrológico de México.* Secretaría de Recursos Hidráulicos. Mexico: Estudios y Proyectos, A.C.

Cook, S. F. 1946. Human Sacrifice and Warfare as Factors in the Demography of Pre-Colonial Mexico. *Human Biology* 18:81–102.

Count, Earl. 1960. Myth as World View. In S. Diamond (ed.), *Essays Presented to Paul Radin.* New York: Columbia University Press. Reprinted in E. Count, *Being and Becoming Human: Essays on the Biogram.* New York: Van Nostrand Reinhold, 1973.

Courant, Richard, and Herbert Robbins. 1941. *What Is Mathematics?* London: Oxford University Press.

Dibble, Charles E. 1971. Writing in Central Mexico. In R. Wauchope (Gen. ed.), *Handbook of Middle American Indians.* Vol. 10, F. G. Eckholm and I. Bernal (eds.), pp. 322–332.

Diccionario Porrúa. 1970. De Historia, Biografía y Geografía de México. Tercera Edición Corregida y Aumentada Con un Apéndice. 2 volumes. Mexico: Editorial Porrúa.

Digby, A. 1972. Evidence in Mexican Glyphs and Sculpture for a Hitherto Unrecognized Astronomical Instrument. In *Atti del XL Congresso Internazionale degli Americanisti.* Rome, Genoa, Vol. 1:433–442.

Duran, Fray Diego. 1971. *Book of the Gods and Rites and the Ancient Calendar.* Trans. and ed. by F. Horcasitas and Doris Heyden. Norman: University of Oklahoma Press.

Durkheim, Emile. 1960. The Dualism of Human Nature and Its Social Conditions. (First published 1914.) In *Essays on Sociology and Philosophy.* Kurt H. Wolff (ed.). New York: Harper and Row.

———. 1961. *The Elementary Forms of Religious Life.* Trans. by J. W. Swain. New York: Collier Books. (First published 1912.)

———. 1966. *The Division of Labor in Society.* Trans. by George Simpson. New York: The Free Press. (First published 1893.)

———, and Marcel Mauss. 1963. *Primitive Classification.* Trans. by Rodney Needham. Chicago: University of Chicago Press, Phoenix Books. (First published 1901.)

Eddy, John A. 1974. Astronomical Alignment of the Big Horn Medicine Wheel. *Science* 184:1035–1043.

Edmonson, Munro S. 1967. Native Folklore. In R. Wauchope (Gen. ed.), *Handbook of Middle American Indians.* Vol. 6, M. Nash (ed.), pp. 357–368.

———. 1973. Review of Lévi-Strauss's *L'homme nu: Mythologiques,* 4. *American Anthropologist* 75:374–377.

Eggan, Fred. 1954. Social Anthropology and the Method of Controlled Comparison. *American Anthropologist* 56:743–763.

Engels, Friedrich. 1959. On the History of Early Christianity. (First published 1895.) In Lewis S. Feuer (ed.), *Marx and Engels: Basic Writings on Politics and Philosophy*. New York: Doubleday Anchor.

Escalona Ramos, Alberto. 1940. *Cronología y Astronomía Maya-Mexica*. Mexico: Editorial Fides.

Fernandez Leal Codex. 1895. Antonio Peñafiel, (ed.). Mexico: Oficina Tipográfica de la Secretaría de Fomento.

Firth, Raymond. 1956. *Elements of Social Organization*. London: Watts.

Foster, George. 1944. Nagualism in Mexico and Guatemala. *Acta Americana* 2:85–103.

Frazer, Sir James. 1911. *The Golden Bough*. 10 volumes. London: Macmillan.

Freud, Sigmund. 1963. The Relation of the Poet to Day-Dreaming. (First published 1908.) In *Character and Culture*. New York: Crowell-Collier.

———. 1965. *The Interpretation of Dreams*. Trans. by James Strachy. New York: Avon. (First published 1900.)

Fried, Morton H. 1967. *The Evolution of Political Society: An Essay in Political Anthropology*. New York: Random House.

Garibay, Angel. 1961. *Llave del Nahuatl*. Mexico: Editorial Porrúa.

Geertz, Clifford. 1957. Ritual and Social Change: A Javanese Example. *American Anthropologist* 59:32–54.

———. 1960. *The Religion of Java*. Glencoe, Ill.: Free Press.

———. 1966. Religion as a Cultural System. In M. Banton (ed.), *Anthropological Approaches to the Study of Religion*. ASA Monograph #3:1–46. London: Tavistock Publications.

———. 1972. Deep Play: Notes on the Balinese Cockfight. *Daedalus* (Winter), 1–37. Reprinted 1973 as Warner Modular Publication #72:1–37.

———. 1973. *The Interpretation of Cultures*. New York: Basic Books.

Godelier, Maurice. 1973. System, Structure and Contradictions in *Das Kapital*. In Michael Lane (ed.), *Introduction to Structuralism*. New York: Basic Books. Pp. 340–358. (First published 1966 in *Le Temps Moderne*.)

Gonzales, Yolotl. 1966–1967. El Dios Huitzilopochtli en la Peregrinación Mexica de Aztlán a Tula. *Anales del Instituto Nacional de Antropología e Historia* (Mexico). Vol. 19, No. 48:191–226.

Gonzales Torres, Yolotl. 1975. *El Culto de los Astros entra los Mexica*. Mexico: Colección Sep-Setenta No. 217, Secretaría de Educación Pública.

Gossen, Gary H. 1974. *Chamulas in the World of the Sun: Time and Space in a Maya Oral Tradition*. Cambridge: Harvard University Press.

Govinda, Lama Anagarika. 1973. *The Foundations of Tibetan Mysticism*. Hackensack, N.J.: Wehman.

Greenewalt, Crawford H. 1960. *Hummingbirds*. New York: Doubleday.

Guiteras-Holmes, Calixta. 1961. *The Perils of the Soul*. Glencoe, Ill.: Free Press.

Gurvitch, Georges. 1958. *La Multiplicité de Temps Sociaux* (Le Cours de Sorbonne). Paris: Centre de Documentation Universitaire.

———. 1964. *The Spectrum of Social Time*. Trans. by Phillip Bosserman. Boston: Reidel.

Hainsworth, F., et al. 1970. Regulation of Oxygen and Body Temperature during Torpor in a Hummingbird: Eulampis jugularis. *Science* 168:368–369.

Hall, A. D., and R. E. Fagen. 1956. Definition of System. In L. von Bertalanffy and A. Rapaport, (eds.), *General Systems—Yearbook for the Society for the Advancement of General Systems Theory*. Vol. 1:18–28.

Hammel, Eugene. 1972. The Myth of Structural Analysis: Lévi-Strauss and the Three Bears. *Addison Wesley Module in Anthropology* No. 25. Reading, Mass.: Addison-Wesley.

Heizer, Robert F., et al. 1971. Observations of the Emergence of Civilization in Mesoamerica, No. 11. *Contributions of the University of California Archeological Research Facility*. Berkeley: University of California.

Hermitte, M. E. 1970. *Poder Sobrenatural y Control Social*. Mexico: Instituto Indigenista Interamericano. Ediciones Especiales, No. 57.

Hesse, Herman. 1949. *Magister Ludi* (The Glass Bead Game). Trans. by Mervyn Savill. New York, Frederick Ungar. (First published 1945.)

Heyden, Doris. 1973. Un Chicomostoc en Teotihuacán: La cueva bajo la Pirámide del Sol. *Boletín del Instituto Nacional de Antropología e Historia*, No. 6, Epoca II.

HDLMPSP. 1941. *Historia de los Mexicanos por sus Pinturas*. Joaquín García Icazbalceta (ed.). In *Relaciones de Texcoco y de la Nueva España: Nueva Colección de Documentos Para la Historia de México*. Mexico: Editorial Chavez Hayhoe.

Holland, William. 1963. *Medicina Maya en Los Altos de Chiapas*. Colección de Antropología Social #2. Mexico.

———. 1964. Conceptos Cosmológicos Tzotziles como una Base para Interpretar la Civilización Maya Prehispánica. *América Indígena* 24:11–28.

Hunt, Eva. 1972. Irrigation and the Socio-Political Organization of Cuicatec Cacicazgos. In F. Johnson and R. MacNeish (eds.), *The Prehisotry of the Tehuacan Valley*, Vol. 4. Austin: University of Texas Press.

———. 1974. Ceremonies of Confrontation and Submission: The Symbolic Dimension of Indian-Mexican Political Interactions. Paper read at the Conference on Secular Rituals. Wenner Gren Foundation, Gloggnitz, Austria, August 1974.

Ingham, John. 1970. On Mexican Folk Medicine. *American Anthropologist* 72:76–87.

——. 1971. Time and Space in Ancient Mexico. The Symbolic Dimensions of Clanship. *Man*, N. S. 6:615–630.

Ixtlixochitl, Don Fernando de Alba. 1891–1892. Obras Históricas, Relaciones e Historia Chichimeca. 2 volumes. With notes of Alfredo Chavero. Mexico: Oficina Tip. de la Secretaría de Fomento.

Jimenez Moreno, Wigberto. 1968. Religión or Religiones Mesoamericanas? Simposium sobre Religiones Mesoamericanas. *Verhandlungen des XXXVIII Internationalen Amerikanisten Kongresses.* Stuttgart-Munich. Vol. 3:201–206.

Joralemon, Peter D. 1971. *A Study of Olmec Iconography.* Studies in Pre-Columbian Art and Archaeology #7. Washington: Dumbarton Oaks.

Jung, C. G. 1969. A Psychological Approach to the Dogma of the Trinity. Part I, Sec. II. In *Psychology and Religion.* 2d. ed. Bollingen Series XX:11. Princeton: Princeton University Press. Pp. 107–200.

Kelley, David H. 1965. The Birth of the Gods at Palenque, Mexico: *Estudios de Cultura Maya* 5:93–134.

Kierkegaard, S. 1941. *The Sickness unto Death.* Trans. by W. Lowrie. Princeton: Princeton University Press.

Kirchhoff, Paul. 1952. Mesoamerica: Its Limits, Ethnic Composition and Cultural Characteristics. In Sol Tax (ed.), *Heritage of Conquest.* Glencoe, Ill.: Free Press.

——. 1968. Las 18 Fiestas Anuales en Mesoamérica: 6 Fiestas Sencillas y 6 Fiestas Dobles. In *Verhandlungen des XXXVIII Internationalen Amerikanisten-Kongresses.* Stuttgart-Munich. Vol. 3:207–222.

Klein, Herbert S. 1970. Rebeliones de las Comunidades Campesinas: la República Tzeltal de 1712. In N. McQuown and J. Pitt-Rivers (eds.), *Ensayos de Antropología de la Zona Central de Chiapas.* Mexico, Instituto Nacional Indigenista.

Knorozov, Yuri V. 1965. Principios para descifrar los escritos Mayas. In *Estudios de Cultura Maya* 5:153–187.

Kroeber, Alfred. 1939. Cultural and Natural Areas in Native North America. *University of California Publications in American Archeology and Ethnology,* Vol. 48:1–242.

Kuhn, Thomas. 1962. *The Structure of Scientific Revolutions.* Chicago: University of Chicago Press.

Laughlin, Robert M. 1962. El Símbolo de la Flor en la Religión de Zinacantan. In *Estudios de Cultura Maya* 2:123–140.

——. 1969. The Tzotzil. In R. Wauchope (Gen. ed.). *Handbook of Middle American Indians.* Vol. 7, E. Vogt (ed.), pp. 152–194.

Leach, Edmund. 1954. *The Political Systems of Highland Burma.* London: Bell.

——. 1961. Lévi-Strauss in the Garden of Eden: An Examination of Some Recent Developments in the Analysis of Myth. *Transactions of the New*

York Academy of Science, Ser. II, Vol. 23.

——. 1964. Anthropological Aspects of Language: Animal Categories and Verbal Abuse. In Eric H. Lenneberg (ed.), *New Directions in the Study of Language*. Cambridge, Mass.:M.I.T. Press.

Lear, John. 1965. *Kepler's Dream:* With Full Text and Notes of Somnium, Sive Astronomia Lunaris Joannis Kepleri. Berkeley: University of California Press.

Leon-Portilla, Miguel. 1971. Philosophy in Ancient Mexico. In R. Wauchope (Gen. ed.), *Handbook of Middle American Indians*. Vol. 10, F. G. Eckholm and I. Bernal (eds.), Part I:447–451.

——. 1973. *Time and Reality in the Thought of the Maya*. Trans. by C. L. Boiles and F. Horcasitas. Boston: Beacon Press. (First published 1968.)

Lévi-Strauss, Claude. 1949. *The Elementary Structures of Kinship*. Trans. by J. H. Bell and R. H. von Sturmer. Boston, Beacon Press.

——. 1955. The Structural Study of Myth. *Journal of American Folklore* 78:428–444.

——. 1963. *Totemism*. Trans. by Rodney Needham. Boston: Beacon Press. (First published 1962.)

——. 1968a. *The Savage Mind*. Chicago: University of Chicago Press. (First published 1962.)

——. 1968b. *L'Origine des Manières de Table: Mythologiques*, Vol. 3. Paris: Plon.

——. 1969. *The Raw and the Cooked: Introduction to a Science of Mythology*, Vol. 1. Trans. by John and Doreen Weightman. New York: Harper and Row. (First published 1964.)

——. 1971. *L'Homme Nu: Mythologiques*, Vol. 4. Paris: Plon.

——. 1973a. *Anthropologie structurale Deux*. Paris: Plon.

——. 1973b. *From Honey to Ashes: Introduction to a Science of Mythology*, Vol. 2. Trans. by John and Doreen Weightman. New York; Harper and Row. (First published 1966.)

Lincoln, Steward J. 1942. The Maya Calendar of the Ixil of Guatemala. *Contributions to American Anthropology and History*, No. 38. Carnegie Institution of Washington.

Lombardo de Ruiz, Sonia. 1973. Mitología y Religión en la Fundación de Tenochtitlan. *Boletín del Instituto Nacional de Antropología e Historia*, No. 5, Epoca II, pp. 49–54.

Lynch, Kevin. 1972. *What Time Is This Place?* Cambridge, Mass: M.I.T. Press.

MacNeish, Richard S., and Douglas S. Byers (eds.) 1967. *The Prehistory of the Tehuacan Valley*, Vol. 1: *Environment and Subsistence*. Austin: University of Texas Press.

——, and F. A. Peterson. 1962. *The Santa Marta Rock Shelter, Ocozocoautla,*

Chiapas, Mexico. Papers of the New World Archeological Foundation, No. 14. Provo, Utah.

Madsen, William. 1967. Religious Syncretism. In R. Wauchope (Gen ed.), *Handbook of Middle American Indians.* Vol. 6, M. Nash (ed.), pp. 369–391.

Malinowski, Bronislaw. 1948. Myth in Primitive Psychology. (First published 1926.) In *Magic, Science and Religion.* Boston: Beacon Press.

Marcus, Joyce. 1973. Territorial Organization of the Lowland Classic Maya. *Science* 180:911–916.

Maritain, Jacques. 1953. *Creative Intuition in Art and Poetry.* New York: Meridian Books.

Marx, Karl. 1972. *Capital.* Preface to the Second Edition. In R. and F. DeGeorge (eds.), *The Structuralists from Marx to Lévi-Strauss.* New York: Doubleday Anchor.

Maybury-Lewis, David. 1968. Science by Association. *Hudson Review* 20:707–711.

Mendelson, E. Michael. 1967. Ritual and Mythology. In R. Wauchope (Gen. ed.), *Handbook of Middle American Indians.* Vol. 6, M. Nash (ed.), pp. 392–415.

Mendes Cifuentes, A. 1967. Nociones de Tejidos Indígenas de Guatemala. Guatemala, Ministerio de Educación. Departmento Editorial José Pineda de Ibarra.

Miles, Susan. 1952. An Analysis of Modern Middle American Calendars In Sol Tax, (ed.), *Acculturation in the Americas.* Proceedings of the 29th Congress of Americanists. Reprinted 1967. New York: Cooper Square.

Miller, Arthur G. 1974. The Iconography of the Painting in the Temple of the Divine God, Tulum, Quintana Roo: The Twisted Cords. In N. Hammond (ed.), *Mesoamerican Archeology: New Approaches.* Austin: University of Texas Press. Pp. 167–186.

Millon, René. 1974. The Study of Urbanism at Teotihuacan, Mexico. In N. Hammond (ed.), *Mesoamerican Archaeology: New Approaches.* Austin: University of Texas Press. Pp. 335–362.

Monterrosa Prado, M. 1968. Cruces de la Colonia. *Boletín del Instituto Nacional de Antropología e Historia,* No. 33.

Motolinia, Fray Toribio de Benavente. 1969. *Historia de los Indios de la Nueva España, con estudio crítico de Edmundo O'Gorman.* Mexico: Editorial Porrúa.

Munn, N. D. 1966. Visual Categories: An Approach to the Study of Representational Systems. *American Anthropologist* 68:936.

Myerhoff, Barbara. 1974. *Peyote Hunt: The Sacred Journey of the Huichol Indians.* Ithaca, N.Y.: Cornell University Press.

Nicholson, H. B. 1968. The Religious Ritual System of Late Prehispanic Central Mexico. In *Verhandlungen des XXXVIII Internationalen Amerikanis-*

ten Kongresses. Stuttgart-Munich. Vol. 3:223–238.

———. 1971. Religion in Prehispanic Central Mexico. In R. Wauchope (Gen. Ed.), *Handbook of Middle American Indians*. Vol. 10, F. G. Eckholm and I. Bernal (eds.), pp. 395–446.

Nicholson, Irene. 1967. *Mexican and Central American Mythology*. London: Hamlyn.

Nowotny, Karl Anton (ed.). 1968. *Codex Cospi*. Calendario Messicano 4093. Biblioteca Universitaria Bologna. Codices Selecti, Vol. 18. Graz, Austria: Akademische Druck-U. Verlagsanstalt.

Nuttal, Z. (ed.). 1902. *Codex Nuttall*. Facsimile of an ancient Mexican Codex belonging to Lord Suche of Harynworth, England. Introduction by Z. Nuttall. Peabody Museum, Harvard University.

———. 1903. *Codex Magliabecchiano: The Book of the Life of the Ancient Mexicans*. Berkeley: University of California Press.

Olivera de Vazquez, Mercedes. 1969. Los "dueños del agua" en Tlaxcalcingo. *Boletín del Instituto Nacional de Antropología e Historia*, No. 35.

Ortiz, Alfonso. 1969. *Tewa World: Space, Time, Being and Becoming in a Pueblo Society*. Chicago: University of Chicago Press.

Ortiz, Fernando. 1947. *El Huracán*. Mexico: Fondo de Cultura Económica.

Paso y Troncoso, Francisco del. 1902. Comedies en langue nauatl. *Compte rendu du 13e Congrès International des Americanistes*. Paris. Pp. 309–316.

Peñafiel, Antonio. 1895. *Códice Fernandez Leal*. Mexico: Secretaría de Fomento.

Piaget, Jean. 1972. *Structuralism*. Trans. by C. Maschler. New York: Harper Torch Books. (First published 1968.)

Pina Chán, Román. 1966. *Mesoamérica*. Mexico: Instituto Nacional de Antropología e Historia.

Pomar, Juan Bautista. 1941. Relación de Texcoco. In *Relaciones de Texcoco y de la Nueva España: Nueva Colleción de Documentos Para la Historia de México*. Ed. with Introduction by J. Garcia Icazbalceta. Mexico: Editorial Chavez Hayhoe. (First published 1891, from a sixteenth century manuscript.)

Pozas, Ricardo. 1959. *Chamula: Un Pueblo Indio de los Altos de Chiapas*. Memorias, Vol. 8. Mexico: Instituto Nacional Indigenista.

Prem, Hanns I. 1971. Calendrics and Writing in Mesoamerica. In R. Heizer and T. Graham (eds.), *Observations on the Emergence of Civilization in Mesoamerica*. Berkeley: University of California, Department of Anthropology. Archaeological Research Facility #11, pp. 112–132.

Radcliffe-Brown, A. R. 1952. *Structure and Function in Primitive Society*. Glencoe, Ill.: Free Press.

Recinos, Adrián (trans. and ed.). 1947. *Popol Vuh: Las Antiguas Historias del Quiché*. Mexico: Fondo de Cultura Económica.

Redfield, Robert, 1956. *Peasant Society and Culture: An Anthropological Approach to Civilization.* Chicago: University of Chicago Press.

Rendón, Juan J., and A. Specha. 1965. Nueva Clasificación "Plástica" de los glifos Mayas. *Estudios De Cultura Maya* 5:189–244.

Robertson, Donald. 1959. *Mexican Manuscript Painting of the Early Colonial Period: The Metropolitan School.* New Haven: Yale University Press.

———. 1964. Los Manuscritos Religiosos Mixtecos. *Actas y memorias del Congreso Internacional de Americanistas*, No. 35. Vol. 1:425–435.

Rosaldo, Renato I. 1968. Metaphors of Hierarchy in a Mayan Ritual. *American Anthropologist* 70. (3):524–536.

Roys, Ralph L. 1949a. Guide to the Codex Perez. *Contributions to American Anthropology and History*, Vol. 10, No. 49. Carnegie Institution of Washington.

———. 1949b. The Prophecies for the Maya Tuns or Years in the Books of Chilam Balam of Tizimin and Mani. *Contributions to American Anthropology and History*, Vol. 10, No. 51. Carnegie Institution of Washington.

Russell, Bertrand. 1950. *Unpopular Essays.* New York: Simon and Schuster.

Sahagun, Fray Bernardino de (ed.). 1907. *Codex Matritense.* Textos en Nahuatl de los indígenas informantes de Sahagún. Printed and edited by F. Paso y Troncoso. 8 volumes. Madrid.

———. 1969. *Historia General de las Cosas de la Nueva España.* 4 volumes. Mexico: Editorial Porrúa. (First published 1956.)

———. 1970. *Florentine Codex.* See Anderson and Dibble, 1970.

Sahlins, Marshall D. 1968. *Tribesmen.* Englewood Cliffs, N.J.: Prentice-Hall.

Saler, Benson. 1964. Nagual, Witch and Sorcerer in a Quiche Village. *Ethnology* 3:305–328.

Sanders, W., and B. Price. 1968. *Mesoamerica: The Evolution of a Civilization.* New York: Random House.

Santillana, Georgio de, and Hertha von Dechend. 1969. *Hamlet's Mill: An Essay on Myth and the Frame of Time.* Boston: Gambit.

Satterthwaite, Linton. 1965. Calendrics of the Maya Lowlands. In R. Wauchope (Gen. ed.), *Handbook of Middle American Indians.* Vol. 3, G. R. Willey (ed.), pp. 603–631.

Scholte, Bob. 1966. Epistemic Paradigms: Some Problems in Cross-Cultural Research on Social Anthropological History and Theory. *American Anthropologist* 68:1192–1201.

Schultes, Richard Evans. 1972. An Overview of Hallucinogens in the Western Hemisphere. In P. T. Furst (ed.), *Flesh of the Gods: The Ritual Use of Hallucinogens.* New York: Praeger.

Séjourné, Laurette. 1957. *Pensamiento y Religión en el México Antiguo.* Mexico: Fondo de Cultura Económica.

Seler, Eduard (ed. and comm.). 1901. *The Tonalamatl of the Aubin Collection.* Berlin and London: Published at the expense of his excellency the Duke of Loubat.

———. 1961. *Gesammelte Abhandlungen zur Amerikanischen Sprach- und Altertumskunde.* Graz, Austria: Akademische Druck-U. Verlagsanstalt, Vol. 4.

———. 1963. *Comentarios al Códice Borgia.* 3 volumes. Mexico: Fondo de Cultura Económica.

Simeon, Remi. 1963. *Dictionnaire de la Langue Nahuatl ou Mexicaine.* Graz, Austria: Akademische Druck-U. Verlagsanstalt. (First published 1885.)

Sjoberg, Gideon. 1952. Folk and Feudal Societies. *American Journal of Sociology* 58:231–239.

Spinden, Herbert Joseph. 1957. *Maya Art and Civilization.* Indian Hills, Colo.: Falcon's Wing Press.

Spiro, M. E. 1952. Ghosts, Ifaluk and Teleological Functionalism. *American Anthropologist* 54:497–503.

———. 1966. Religion: Problem of Definition and Explanation. In M. Banton (ed.), *Anthropological Approaches to the Study of Religion.* ASA Monograph #3:85–126. London: Tavistock Publications.

———. 1967. *Burmese Supernaturalism: A Study in the Explanation and Reduction of Suffering.* Englewood Cliffs, N.J.: Prentice-Hall.

———. 1968. Religion, Personality and Behavior in Burma. *American Anthropologist* 70:359–362.

Spranz, Bodo. 1964. *Göttergestalten in Den Mexikanischen Bilderhandschriften der Codex-Borgia-Gruppe.* Wiesbaden: Franz Steiner Verlag.

Tax, Sol. 1937. The Municipios of Midwestern Highlands of Guatemala. *American Anthropologist* 39:423–444.

Taylor, E. G. R. 1957. *The Haven-Finding Art: A History of Navigation from Odysseus to Captain Cook.* New York: Abelard-Schuman.

Teeple, John E. 1930. Maya Astronomy. *Contributions to American Anthropology and History*, No. 403. Carnegie Institution of Washington.

Thiel, Rudolf. 1957. *And There Was Light: The Discovery of the Universe.* New York: Knopf.

Thompson, J. Eric. 1934. *Sky Bearers, Colors and Directions in Maya and Mexican Religion.* Carnegie Institution of Washington. Publication #436. Reprinted 1970. New York: Johnson Reprint Co.

———. 1937. *Maya Chronology: The Correlation Question.* Carnegie Institution of Washington, No. 14, Publication #459. Reprinted 1970. New York: Johnson Reprint Co.

———. 1959. The Role of Caves in Maya Culture. *Mitterlungen aus dem Museum fur Volkerkunde.* Hamburg: Sonderduuck 25:122–9.

———. 1962. *A Catalogue of Maya Hieroglyphs.* Norman: University of Oklahoma Press.

———. 1965a. Maya Hieroglyphic Writing. In R. Wauchope (Gen. ed.), *Handbook of Middle American Indians.* Vol. 3, G. R. Willey (ed.), pp. 632–658.

———. 1965b. Maya Creation Myths. In *Estudios de Cultura Maya* 5:13–32.

———. 1970. *Maya History and Religion.* Norman: University of Oklahoma Press.

Thomson, Charlotte. 1973. *Cylinder Vase Late Classic Maya, Chama Style.* Boston: Museum of Fine Arts Bulletin, Vol. 70, No. 361–2, pp. 146–148.

Tira de la Peregrinación Azteca. 1944. Complete pictographic text with Anonymous Commentary and Translation into English Text. Mexico: Libreria Anticuaria, G. M. Echaniz.

Turner, Victor. 1967. *The Forest of Symbols: Aspects of Ndembu Ritual.* Ithaca, N.Y.: Cornell University Press.

———. 1968a. *The Drums of Affliction.* Oxford: Clarendon Press.

———. 1968b. Myth and Symbol. *International Encyclopaedia of the Social Sciences,* pp. 576–82.

———. 1969. *The Ritual Process: Structure and Anti-Structure.* Chicago: Aldine.

———. 1973. Symbols in African Ritual. *Science* 179:1100–1105.

———. 1974a. *Dramas, Fields and Metaphors: Symbolic Action in Human Society.* Ithaca, N.Y.: Cornell University Press.

———. 1974b. Liminality, Play, Flow and Ritual: An Essay in Comparative Symbology. *Rice University Studies,* Vol. 60, No. 3, pp. 53–94.

Turok, Marta. 1974. Diseño y Símbolos en el Huipil Ceremonial de Magdalenas, Chiapas. Paper read at the 51st International Congress of Americanists. Section 8: On Myth, Ritual, and Symbol in the Highlands of Chiapas. August 1974.

Tylor, Edward B. 1920. *Primitive Culture: Researches into the Development of Mythology, Philosophy, Religion, Language, Art and Custom.* New York: Putnam.

Van Gennep, Arnold. 1960. *The Rites of Passage.* Trans. by M. B. Visedom and G. L. Caffee. Chicago: University of Chicago Press, Phoenix Books. (First published 1909.)

Vansina, Jan. 1965. *Oral Tradition.* Trans. by H. M. Wright. Chicago: Aldine. (First published 1961.)

Vogt, Evon Z. 1969. *Zinacantan: A Maya Community in the Highlands of Chiapas.* Cambridge: Harvard, Belknap Press.

———. 1970. Human Souls and Animal Spirits in Zinacantan. In Jean Pouillon and P. Maranda (eds.), *Echanges et Communications.* The Hague: Mouton. Vol. 2:1148–1167.

———. 1973. Gods and Politics in Zinacantan and Chamula. *Ethnology* 12:99–114.

——. 1974. Trends in Town (Cabecera) Planning in Highland Chiapas. Paper read at the Annual Meeting of the American Anthropological Association, Mexico City, November 1974.

——. 1976. *Tortillas for the Gods*. Cambridge: Harvard University Press.

——. (ed.) 1966. *Los Zinacantecos: Un Pueblo Tzotzil de los Altos de Chiapas*. Colección de Antropología Social, Vol. 7. Mexico: Instituto Nacional Indigenista.

——, and Catherine C. Vogt. 1970. Lévi-Strauss among the Maya. *Man*, 5:379–392.

Wallace, Anthony F. C. 1961. *Culture and Personality*. New York: Random House.

——. 1966. *Religion: An Anthropological View*. New York: Random House.

Wauchope, Robert (Gen. ed.). 1964–75. *Handbook of Middle American Indians*. 15 volumes. Austin: University of Texas Press.

Wolf, Eric. 1958. The Virgin of Guadalupe: A Mexican National Symbol. *Journal of American Folklore* 71:34–39.

——. 1959. *The Sons of the Shaking Earth*. Chicago: University of Chicago Press.

Yalman, Nur. 1971. *Under the Bo Tree*. Berkeley: University of California Press.

Index

THE TRANSFORMATION
OF THE HUMMINGBIRD

Designed by R. E. Rosenbaum.
Composed by Dix Typesetting Co. Inc.,
in 10 point VIP Janson, 3 points leaded,
with display lines in Helvetica.
Printed offset by Vail-Ballou Press
on Warren's No. 66 text, 50 pound basis,
with the Cornell University Press watermark.
Bound by Vail-Ballou Press
in Columbia book cloth
and stamped in All Purpose foil.

Library of Congress Cataloging in Publication Data

Hunt, Eva, 1934-
  The transformation of the Hummingbird.

  (Symbol, myth, and ritual series)
  Bibliography: p.
  Includes index.
  1. Tzotzil Indians—Religion and mythology. 2. Symbolism. 3. Indians of
Mexico—Religion and mythology. I. Title.
F1221.T9H86   299'.7   76-12909
ISBN 0-8014-1022-3